THE ALLOTMENT GARDENER'S COOKBOOK

The fruit derived from labour is the sweetest of pleasures.

Luc de Clapier de Vauvanargues

READER'S DIGEST

THE ALLOTMENT GARDENER'S COOKBOOK

PUBLISHED BY READER'S DIGEST ASSOCIATION LTD
LONDON • NEW YORK • SYDNEY • MONTREAL

Contents

Let my words, like vegetables,
be tender and sweet.

Anon

These days there are so many good reasons for growing your own produce it is not surprising that those wanting an allotment can sometimes wait years to achieve their little plot. Here are just a few of them: we are all encouraged to eat at least five portions of fruit and vegetables a day; the environmental cost of transporting out of season produce thousands of miles is becoming increasingly unsustainable; it is much cheaper; fresh fruit and vegetables taste infinitely better; it is fun, relaxing and immensely fulfilling.

Introduction

Although this book is called *The Allotment Gardener's Cookbook* it is for anyone who grows some of their own fruit and vegetables, whether you have a serious allotment with carefully planned seasonal beds, a small dedicated plot in your own garden or just the space to grow a few vegetables in pots.

When you grow your own produce, paradoxically success can sometimes be more difficult to deal with than failure. You really can have too much of a good thing. Glorious seasonal fruit and vegetables can go to waste simply because you can't think of anything to do with them. So this book has been conceived to provide a whole range of different options for more than 30 varieties, so that you won't be at a loss even if you have a glut.

The recipes are organised alphabetically by varieties of fruit and vegetables and we have included produce that most gardeners should be able to raise easily, usually without the need for a greenhouse or particularly favourable climatic conditions.

There is a range of recipes for each fruit or vegetable, from soups and snacks to more substantial main meals – and dishes that include meat, desserts where appropriate and finally plenty of jams, preserves, pickles and wines. So whatever you grow, there should be a recipe for cooking it here. And use it fresh. What could be more delicious and satisfying than a meal cooked with produce just hours out of the earth?

Carrots
Carrots can be sown from early spring to late winter to crop from summer through to spring. Cook them in a warming *Carrot and butter bean soup*, (above) with pork, new potatoes and cauliflower for a *Summer casserole*, or preserve them as *Pickled carrots* or as wine.

Leeks
Leeks take care to establish, but are a tasty asset to many dishes and will survive hard winters. They are superb in soups such as *Chicken, leek and sweetcorn chowder*, add sweet flavour to a *French leek flan*, are an excellent accompaniment as *Braised leeks with capers & currants*, and go beautifully with *Duck breasts with ginger sauce* or in a new version of *Turkey likkey pie*.

Brussels sprouts
Brussels sprouts are surprisingly versatile. Try them in a *Brussels sprout soup*, as a baked main dish in *Brussels sprouts with pork*, in a *Winter salad of shredded brussels sprouts* or sautéed with bacon and mustard, or in a *Stir-fried hot slaw* with hazlenuts, apple and celery.

Strawberries
Strawberries are at their best in June and July. Use them in summer desserts such as *Rose-strawberry yoghurt ice*, fresh *ice cream* and *Strawberry trifle*. If you have a bumper crop, make jam (above) and serve with scones and clotted cream for a sumptuous tea.

What will I do when I can no longer dig?

Knute Hamsen

How to use the book

Using the recipes
• Ingredients are given in metric measurements.
• All spoon measures are level unless otherwise stated; 1 level teaspoon equals 5ml and 1 level tablespoon equals 15ml.
• All eggs are medium unless otherwise specified.
• Where recipes use black pepper, use it freshly ground if possible for best flavour.

Nutritional analyses
• These figures are intended only as a guide as results may vary depending on a number of factors including the time of year and method of cooking.
• Figures given for each recipe are for average portions.
• The nutritional figures do not include accompaniments unless they are part of the dish.

The apple is one of the oldest fruits known to man, and also one of the most widely cultivated. Originally, they grew wild in Europe and the Near East, but now thrive inland throughout the British Isles.

Apples do not grow well in coastal areas exposed to salt-laden winds, and in the north there is a greater risk of blossom being destroyed by spring frosts. This applies also in local frost pockets, in gardens in valleys or at the base of slopes where the temperature may be much lower than nearby.

The earliest apples are ready for picking and eating in August; the latest can be stored for eating until as late as the following April/May.

Apples

HARVESTING AND STORING

To test whether an apple is ready for picking, place the palm of your hand beneath it and give a simultaneous lift and gentle twist. It should part easily from the spur. Eat early varieties as soon as possible after picking as they will not keep more than a few weeks. Handle carefully later varieties intended for storing. Keep the apples in a frost-proof garage or spare room where the temperature is stable but cool.

The apples can be wrapped in specially oiled paper, stacked on fibre trays or kept in clear plastic bags with the tops unsealed or the sides perforated.

COOKING WITH APPLES

Both dessert and cooking apples can be used for cooking, although soft dessert apples, especially those that ripen in summer and early autumn, are best eaten fresh, as they tend to lose flavour and texture when cooked. Firm dessert apples are excellent on their own or with cooking apples in pie fillings, in fruit and green salads, in cakes and fruit puddings.

To prevent apples turning brown after peeling, either drop them into a bowl of cold water and lemon juice, or brush apple slices with fresh lemon juice.

chargrilled pork [with little baked apples]

Seared pork fillet is made deliciously sweet with the contrasting flavours of apples, lemon and rosemary.

500g pork fillet
4 dessert apples, such as Cox's
    Orange Pippin
4 sprigs fresh rosemary
4 tsp golden caster sugar, optional
For the marinade:
1 sprig fresh rosemary
1 clove garlic, crushed
Grated zest of 1 lemon
2 tbsp olive oil
Salt and black pepper
A few sprigs of fresh rosemary to garnish

Serves: 4
Prep time: 30 minutes, plus 1 hour or
    overnight marinating
Cooking time: 25 minutes

Nutrients per serving: Calories 247,
Carbohydrate 15g, Protein 25g, Fat 10g
(saturated fat 2g)

1 Trim any fat from the pork, cut the meat into 1cm thick medallions and place them in a mixing bowl.

2 To make the marinade, remove the leaves from the sprig of rosemary, chop them roughly and add them to the pork with the garlic, lemon zest, olive oil and pepper. Cover and chill for at least 1 hour – overnight is best as it allows the flavours to permeate the meat.

3 Heat the oven to 180°C/gas 4. Thirty minutes before you want to serve, core the apples and cut a ring through the skin around their circumference, so they can expand as they cook. Tuck a sprig of rosemary into the centre of each apple, with a teaspoon of caster sugar if using, and bake the apples for 25 minutes, or until just soft.

4 Meanwhile, heat a ridged, iron grill pan or nonstick frying pan over a medium-high heat. Remove the medallions from their marinade, season with salt and sear them for 2-4 minutes on each side until browned. Serve with the baked apples and garnish with sprigs of rosemary. To vary the recipe make a simple gravy by reducing some chicken or pork stock. You could also deglaze the grill pan or frying pan with a little dry cider.

chicken breasts [with apples and cider]

A lovely, creamy sauce for chicken, of sweet apples imbued with the tang of dry cider and Worcestershire sauce.

1 tbsp olive oil
1g butter
2 shallots
2 crisp, red-skinned dessert apples, about 17g each
½ tbsp light muscovado sugar
2 boneless, skinless chicken breasts, about 17g each
150ml dry cider
1-2 tsp Worcestershire sauce
2 tbsp crème fraîche
Salt and black pepper

Serves: 2
Cooking time: 30 minutes

Nutrients per serving: Calories 495, Carbohydrate 28g, Protein 40g, Fat 23g (saturated fat 11g)

1 Put the oil and butter into a frying pan or flameproof casserole and heat gently over a low heat.

2 Peel and finely chop the shallots. Add them to the oil and butter in the pan or casserole, increase the heat to moderate and fry, stirring occasionally, for 3-4 minutes, or until they are soft.

3 While the shallots are cooking, rinse, dry, quarter, core and slice the dessert apples, then add them to the shallots and sprinkle them with the muscovado sugar. Raise the heat fairly high and fry until the mixture starts to turn a golden caramel colour.

4 Lift the shallots and apple slices from the frying pan or casserole with a slotted spoon and set aside.

5 Add a little more oil to the pan, if necessary. Add the chicken breasts and fry them over a fairly high heat for about 6 minutes, turning once, until they are golden.

6 Pour the cider over the chicken. Bring it to the boil and simmer, uncovered, for about 8-10 minutes, stirring occasionally and turning the chicken once more, until it is cooked. The chicken is ready if the juices run clear when it is pierced with the tip of a knife.

7 When the chicken is ready, stir in the Worcestershire sauce and crème fraîche, and season to taste with salt and black pepper. Return the shallots and apple slices to the pan and warm them through for another 1-2 minutes, but do not allow the sauce to boil.

sausages [with spiced wine and apples]

300ml dry white wine
250g good-quality pork or chicken sausages
1 shallot or ½ small onion
2 crisp dessert apples
70g butter, at room temperature
200ml chicken or vegetable stock
2 tbsp light brown sugar
½ tsp ground cinnamon

Serves: 2
Cooking time: 25 minutes

Nutrients per serving: Calories 929, Carbohydrate 42g, Protein 15g, Fat 69g (saturated fat 34g)

1 Bring the wine to the boil in a large frying pan and poach the sausages gently for 10 minutes.

2 Meanwhile, peel and grate the shallot or onion and peel, quarter, core and slice the apples.

3 Gently melt a small knob of the butter in a second frying pan. Remove the sausages from the first pan, reserving the wine. Discard any loose skins and fry the sausages slowly in the butter until they have browned all over.

4 Meanwhile, add the shallot or onion to the white wine in the first pan, with the apples, stock, brown sugar, cinnamon and the remaining butter. Then bring the mixture to the boil, reduce the heat and simmer it until the apples become tender and the liquid is reduced to a thin syrup. Serve the sausages with the apple sauce.

It is better to wear out than to rust out.

Bishop Richard Cumberland

perfect apple pie

For the pastry:
225g plain flour
50g self-raising flour
A pinch of salt
25g caster sugar
175g chilled butter, diced
1 egg, beaten with 2 tbsp cold water
Caster sugar for dredging

For the filling:
25g plain flour
175g-225g caster sugar
1 tsp ground mixed spice
Finely grated rind of 1 lemon
1kg Bramley apples
25g ground almonds
25g butter, diced
6-8 cloves
1 tbsp lemon juice

Serves: 6
Prep time: 45 minutes
Cooking time: 1 hour

Nutrients per serving: Calories 675, Carbohydrate 97g, Protein 7.5g, Fat 32g (saturated fat 18g)

1 To make the pastry, sift the flours, salt and caster sugar into a large mixing bowl then rub in the butter until the mixture resembles fine breadcrumbs. Make a well in the centre, pour in the beaten egg and water and mix with a rounded knife to form a soft, but not sticky dough.

2 Knead the dough on a lightly floured surface for a few seconds until smooth, then wrap and chill while preparing the filling. Put an ungreased baking tray on the centre shelf of the oven and heat the oven to 220°C/gas 7.

3 Put the flour, caster sugar, mixed spice and lemon rind into a mixing bowl and stir together.

4 Core, peel and slice the apples, add them to the bowl and mix.

5 To assemble the pie, roll out half the chilled dough into a neat round about 28cm in diameter. Line a 25cm enamel pie plate with the dough. Roll out the remaining dough into a neat round just a little larger than the first.

6 Sprinkle the ground almonds over the dough on the dish and spread half the spiced apple mix on top. Dot half the butter over the apples and add half the cloves. Cover with the rest of the apple slices and add the remaining cloves. Dot with the remaining butter and sprinkle over the lemon juice. Add any juices left in the apple bowl.

7 Brush in the edge of the dough on the plate with cold water, then cover the pie with the second round of dough. Squeeze the edges firmly together to seal then trim off the excess dough with a knife, holding the knife angled outwards to help to prevent the edge shrinking inwards as the pie bakes.

8 Using the back of the knife blade, tap all round the edge of the dough to give it a flaky appearance. With the tip of the knife, make shallow indents around the edge of the pie at 2.5cm intervals to make a fluted pattern.

9 Roll out the dough trimmings and use them to make apple shapes and leaves to decorate the pie. Brush the shapes with cold water and arrange them on top if the pie. With a small sharp knife, make a small hole in the top of the pastry lid to allow the steam to escape during cooking.

10 Put the pie on the heated baking tray and bake on the centre shelf of the oven for 30 minutes.

11 Lower the temperature to 190°C/gas 5, cover the pie loosely with foil to prevent it over-browning, and continue cooking for another 25-30 minutes, or until the apples are tender. Check that the filling is fully cooked by pushing a skewer through the hole in the top: it should meet no resistance.

12 When cooked, remove the pie from the oven and dredge it with caster sugar while it is hot so the sugar melts slightly and sticks to the pie. For the best flavour, allow the pie to cool for an hour or so to room temperature before serving.

13 Serve with vanilla-flavoured whipped cream or with ice cream.

marzipan apples

4 large, even-size cooking apples
Juice of 1 lemon
50g melted butter
100g marzipan
1 dessertspoon brandy or rum
12 blanched, roughly chopped almonds
150ml whipped cream

Serves: 4
Cooking time: 20-25 minutes
Oven temperature: 200°C/gas 6

Nutrients per serving: Calories 545,
Carbohydrate 38g, Protein 7g, Fat 40g
(saturated fat 17g)

1 Peel the apples and remove the cores. Brush the apples first with lemon juice and then with melted butter – inside and out – and arrange in a buttered, ovenproof dish.

2 Knead the marzipan with the brandy until pliable, stuff most of it into the apple centres and lay the remainder over the top of the apples.

3 Sprinkle with the chopped almonds and bake in the centre of the oven for 20-25 minutes or until the marzipan is golden.

4 Serve warm with a separate bowl of whipped cream.

apple chutney

3kg cooking apples (peeled and finely
    chopped)
1kg onions (peeled)
300ml water
40g salt
40g ground ginger
2 tbsp ground cinnamon
½ tsp cayenne pepper
1l vinegar
1kg brown sugar
500g golden syrup

Nutrients per tablespoon: Calories 29,
Carbohydrate 7g, Protein 0g, Fat 0g
(no saturated fat)

1 Simmer the apples and onions for 20 minutes in the water.

2 Add the salt, spices and half the vinegar.

3 Cook until soft, then add the sugar, syrup and the rest of the vinegar and simmer until smooth and thick.

4 Spoon into glass jars and cover.

apple wine

3.5kg mixed apples (windfalls will do)
250g sultanas
875g sugar
3l water
1 tsp citric acid
1 Campden tablet
1 tsp pectin-destroying enzyme
Hock yeast and nutrient

Nutrients per small glass: Calories 118,
Carbohydrate 7g, Protein 0g, Fat 0g
(no saturated fat)

1 Pour the water into a bin and add the citric acid, the pectin-destroying enzyme and a crushed Campden tablet.

2 Wash the apples, crush them into a mash or cut them up and drop them into the bin. Cover the bin and leave it in a warm place for 24 hours.

3 Activate the yeast in a starter bottle. Add the sultanas, nutrient and yeast to the mash, re-cover the bin and place it in a warm place for four to five days.

4 Press and strain the pulp and then add the sugar, having first dissolved it in warm water.

5 Pour the strained mixture into a fermentation jar, top up with cold water and fit an airlock to the jar. Tie on a label describing the contents and store the jar at room temperature until fermentation is complete.

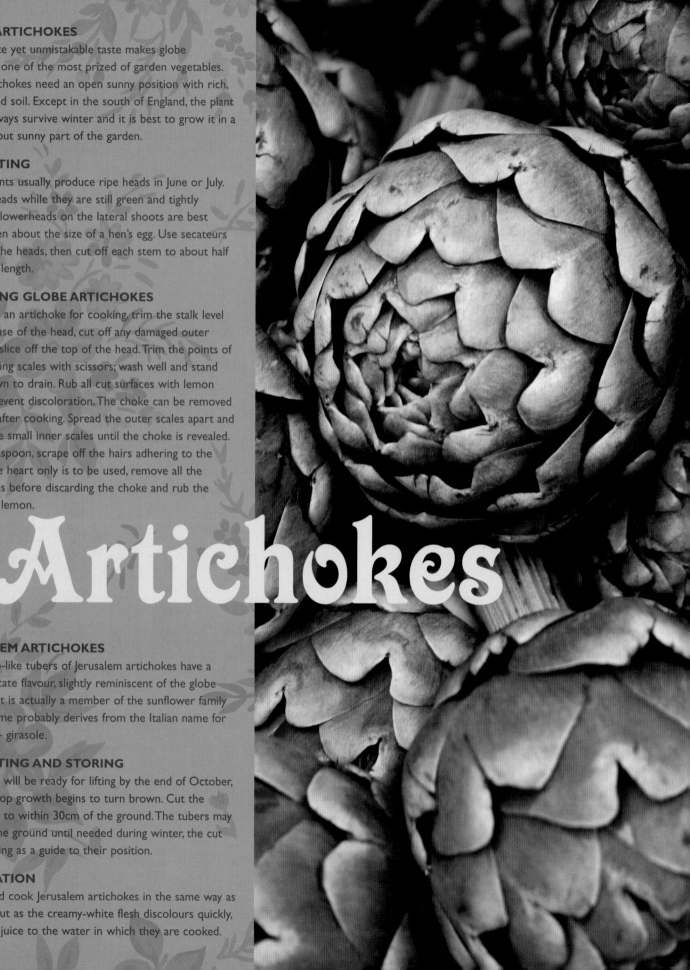

GLOBE ARTICHOKES

The delicate yet unmistakable taste makes globe artichokes one of the most prized of garden vegetables. Globe artichokes need an open sunny position with rich, well-drained soil. Except in the south of England, the plant will not always survive winter and it is best to grow it in a sheltered, but sunny part of the garden.

HARVESTING

Mature plants usually produce ripe heads in June or July. Pick the heads while they are still green and tightly wrapped. Flowerheads on the lateral shoots are best picked when about the size of a hen's egg. Use secateurs to cut off the heads, then cut off each stem to about half its original length.

PREPARING GLOBE ARTICHOKES

To prepare an artichoke for cooking, trim the stalk level with the base of the head, cut off any damaged outer scales and slice off the top of the head. Trim the points of the remaining scales with scissors; wash well and stand upside-down to drain. Rub all cut surfaces with lemon juice to prevent discoloration. The choke can be removed before or after cooking. Spread the outer scales apart and pull out the small inner scales until the choke is revealed. Using a teaspoon, scrape off the hairs adhering to the heart. If the heart only is to be used, remove all the outer scales before discarding the choke and rub the heart with lemon.

Artichokes

JERUSALEM ARTICHOKES

The potato-like tubers of Jerusalem artichokes have a sweet, delicate flavour, slightly reminiscent of the globe artichoke. It is actually a member of the sunflower family and the name probably derives from the Italian name for that plant – girasole.

HARVESTING AND STORING

The tubers will be ready for lifting by the end of October, when the top growth begins to turn brown. Cut the stems back to within 30cm of the ground. The tubers may be left in the ground until needed during winter, the cut stems serving as a guide to their position.

PREPARATION

Prepare and cook Jerusalem artichokes in the same way as potatoes, but as the creamy-white flesh discolours quickly, add lemon juice to the water in which they are cooked.

Jerusalem artichoke

[& smoked haddock chowder]

A chunky chowder of sweet Jerusalem artichokes makes a filling meal. Here the creaminess of milk and mashed potatoes is offset by the smoky flavour of the fish.

3 medium floury potatoes
450g smoked haddock
1 onion, roughly chopped
500g Jerusalem artichokes
Juice of ½ lemon
2 sticks celery, destrung and diced
50g butter
600ml milk
Black pepper
Snipped spring onions to garnish

Serves: 6
Prep time: 30 minutes
Cooking time: 30 minutes

Nutrients per serving: Calories 304, Carbohydrate 32g, Protein 21g, Fat 12g (saturated fat 7g)

1 Peel the potatoes, boil until soft, then drain, mash and set aside.

2 Put the haddock into a pan with the onion and enough cold water to cover. Bring to the boil and skim. Simmer the fish for 5-7 minutes or until it is just beginning to flake.

3 Drain the fish through a sieve, keeping the liquor and making it up to 500ml with fresh cold water. Discard the onion.

4 When the fish is cool, skin, bone and roughly flake it. Stir half of the cooking liquor into the potatoes.

5 Peel the artichokes and slice them thinly into a small bowl of cold water and lemon juice.

6 Fry the celery for 2-3 minutes in butter, then add the milk, drained artichokes and the rest of the fish stock. Bring to simmering point, then partially cover and cook for 10-15 minutes.

7 Mix the mashed potato and flaked fish into the vegetable mixture and grind in some black pepper.

8 Heat the soup again, garnish with the spring onions and serve with hot wholewheat toast and butter.

artichokes vinaigrette

4 globe artichokes
1 tbsp lemon juice
Salt
French dressing

Nutrients per serving: Calories 98, Carbohydrate 0g, Protein 0g, Fat 11g (saturated fat 1.5g)

1 Wash the artichokes thoroughly, trim the stalks level with the base and peel off any ragged scales. Cut off the top 1cm of each artichoke and snip off the points of the other scales with scissors. Brush the cut surfaces with lemon juice.

2 Bring a large pan of lightly salted water to the boil, then add the artichokes, Cover and cook for 40-45 minutes, depending on size, until a scale can easily be pulled off. Drain the artichokes upside down.

3 Pull the scales apart and remove the small inner scales until the central choke of fine hairy filaments is reached; remove this with a teaspoon.

4 Arrange the cooled artichokes on plates and pour the dressing into a jug. The French dressing is poured into and round the artichoke and as each scale is pulled off, the fleshy base is dipped into the dressing and eaten. The heart is eaten with a knife and fork.

artichoke quiche

Artichoke hearts, plenty of onions, a dash of sherry and a little chervil or dill according to your preference, are the basis of this delicious quiche.

6-8 globe artichokes
175g shortcrust pastry
250g finely chopped onions
½ tsp chopped dill or chervil
1 tbsp sherry
2 egg yolks
300ml thick white sauce
Salt and pepper

Serves: 6
Cooking time: 30-40 minutes

Nutrients per serving: Calories 377, Carbohydrate 35g, Protein 10g, Fat 23g (saturated fat 9g)

1 Prepare and cook the artichokes as for artichokes vinaigrette (page 15); drain and cool. Remove and discard all scales and the chokes and cut the hearts into 1cm slices.

2 Heat the oven to 200°C/gas 6. Line a 20cm flan ring with the shortcrust pastry and set it on top of a baking sheet.

3 Arrange the sliced artichokes and onions over the base and sprinkle with dill or chervil.

4 Beat the sherry and egg yolks into the cooled white sauce, season to taste with salt and pepper and spoon over the flan filling.

5 Bake in the oven for about 30 minutes, covering the flan with buttered greaseproof paper if the top browns too quickly.

6 Serve hot, garnished with dill or chervil or with an accompanying green salad.

sautéd Jerusalem artichokes

Gently sautéd in butter until tender and then seasoned with Tabasco, Jerusalem artichokes are a wonderful accompaniment to a variety of dishes.

500g Jerusalem artichokes
1 tbsp lemon juice
50g butter
Salt and pepper
Tabasco sauce
2 tbsp chopped parsley

Serves: 6
Cooking time: 20 minutes

Nutrients per serving: Calories 443, Carbohydrate 13g, Protein 2g, Fat 10g (saturated fat 7g)

1 Peel or scrape the artichokes, dropping them into a bowl of cold water and lemon juice.

2 Cut them into slices and put in a pan of lightly salted boiling water. Cover, cook gently for 10 minutes then drain.

3 Melt the butter in a pan, add the artichokes, and sauté gently until well coated with the butter and lightly browned. Season with salt, pepper and a few drops of Tabasco. Stir in the parsley.

Any garden demands as much of its maker as he has to give.

Elizabeth Lawrence

Jerusalem artichoke [& herb croquettes]

225g floury potatoes, peeled and
  cut into chunks
450g Jerusalem artichokes, peeled and
  cut into chunks
Juice of ½ lemon
85g ricotta cheese
1 tbsp chopped chives
1 tbsp chopped parsley
1 tsp chopped fresh thyme
Salt and black pepper
85g fresh brown breadcrumbs
1 small egg, beaten with 1 tbsp water
1-2 tbsp sunflower oil

Makes: 10-12 croquettes
Prep time: 20 minutes
Cooking time: 30 minutes

Nutrients per croquette when making 12:
Calories 71, Carbohydrate 10g, Protein 3g,
Fat 2.5g (saturated fat 0.5g)

1 Cook the potatoes in lightly salted, boiling water for about 15 minutes, or until tender. Drain well.

2 Put the artichokes into a saucepan of lightly salted water and add the lemon juice. Bring to the boil and simmer for about 10 minutes until tender. Drain well.

3 Put the drained artichokes and potatoes into a bowl with the ricotta and fresh herbs. Add a little salt and pepper to taste and mash well. Set aside until cool enough to handle.

4 Put the breadcrumbs in a shallow bowl and put the beaten egg into another shallow bowl. Using your hands, shape a generous tablespoon of the artichoke mixture into a small sausage about 7.5cm long. Dip briefly in the beaten egg and then roll it in the breadcrumbs. Repeat with the remaining mixture.

5 Heat a little oil in a frying pan and fry the croquettes, a few at a time, for 3-4 minutes, turning frequently, until golden. Serve with turkey, venison, pheasant or sausages.

broad beans, artichokes & spinach
[with pasta]

2 tbsp olive oil
1 medium onion
1 large clove garlic
1 medium red pepper
175g dried pasta shapes (small shells
  or rigatoni)
Salt and black pepper
400g canned chopped tomatoes
A pinch of dried oregano
½ tsp brown sugar
225g frozen broad beans
350g young spinach
300g canned artichoke hearts
50g Parmesan cheese; 1 Italian loaf
  to serve

Serves: 4
Cooking time: 30 minutes

Nutrients per serving: Calories 741,
Carbohydrate 92g, Protein 26g, Fat 30g
(saturated fat 6g)

1 Bring a large saucepan of water to the boil, and heat the oven to its lowest setting. Heat the olive oil in another large saucepan. Peel and roughly chop the onion, then peel and crush the garlic. Add them both to the oil and fry them gently for 5 minutes, until soft.

2 Rinse, halve, deseed and slice the pepper. Add it to the onion and fry for a further 2 minutes.

3 Add the pasta and some salt to the boiling water. Return to the boil and cook for 10-12 minutes, until the pasta is *al dente*.

4 Stir the tomatoes, oregano, sugar and some black pepper into the onion, garlic and red pepper. Bring to the boil, then partially cover and simmer for 10 minutes.

5 Put the bread into the oven to heat through. Add the broad beans to the tomato sauce, return to the boil and simmer for 3 minutes.

6 Rinse and drain the spinach, then remove any tough stalks, add the leaves to the sauce and cook for a further 3 minutes.

7 Drain and quarter the artichoke hearts. Drain the pasta. Add both to the sauce and heat through for a minute or two.

8 Turn the pasta and sauce into a warm serving bowl, grate some Parmesan over and serve with the hot bread.

Asparagus

Prized for the delicate flavour of its young shoots, asparagus is still a luxury if you have to buy it. In some respects, it is even a luxury to grow at home, because it has a cropping season of only six weeks, but being a perennial, requires space all year round. Gardeners who relish its flavour may find this acceptable. Asparagus does best in a fairly open position sheltered from wind. It needs a rich, well-drained soil, so the initial preparation of the bed will set it up for years to come.

HARVESTING AND STORING

Harvest the ripe spears when their tips are about 10cm above the soil. Use either a special asparagus cutter or a serrated knife, cutting the base of the spear up to 10cm below soil level. If not used immediately, stand the spears in iced water for a few hours, then wrap and store in the fridge until needed. In this way it is possible to cut a number of spears daily, saving them until you have enough for a meal.

PREPARATION

Wash the asparagus carefully so as not to damage the tender tips. Trim the woody parts from the bases of the stems. Green stems need only washing but white stems have a bitter and hard skin which must be peeled off from the tip downwards. Trim the spears so that they are of uniform length and tie in small bundles with string. Stand the bundles upright in a deep pan of boiling salted water for 10-12 minutes, depending on their thickness. Keep the asparagus tips above the water level so that they cook in the rising steam.

asparagus soup

Older asparagus stems can sometimes be rather woody. Don't waste them but use them to make a delicately flavoured creamy soup.

Asparagus stems
1l asparagus water
50g butter
1 onion, finely chopped
1 heaped tbsp flour
600ml milk
Salt and pepper
150ml cream
Finely chopped parsley to garnish

Serves: 6
Cooking time: 25-30 minutes

Nutrients per serving: Calories 272, Carbohydrate 9g, Protein 5g, Fat 24g (saturated fat 15g)

1 Measure 1l of water in which the asparagus has been cooked. Melt the butter in a large pan and cook the onion over a gentle heat until soft but not coloured.

2 Stir in the flour and mix thoroughly. Gradually add the asparagus water and the stem sections, discarding the trimmings. Bring to the boil and simmer for 10 minutes, stirring occasionally.

3 Blend the soup in a liquidiser, then strain to get rid of any woody bits. Return to the pan and add milk to give the desired consistency; season with salt and pepper.

4 Stir in the cream, heat through but do not boil.

5 Garnish with parsley.

asparagus salad

Fresh new asparagus is lightly dressed with spice and wine vinegar for a chilled salad that makes an excellent accompaniment to cold chicken or poached salmon.

500g cooked asparagus
75-100g sugar
2 tbsp boiling water
1 tsp pickling spice
125g white wine vinegar
Finely chopped chervil to garnish

Serves: 4
Chilling time: 30 minutes

Nutrients per serving: Calories 112, Carbohydrate 22g, Protein 4g, Fat 1g (no saturated fat)

1 Cut the cooked, drained asparagus spears into 5cm lengths and put in a shallow serving dish.

2 Melt the sugar in the boiling water, add the spice and bring to the boil, stirring until the sugar has dissolved.

3 Stir in the vinegar, and strain this marinade over the asparagus.

4 Chill in the fridge for about 30 minutes. Sprinkle with chervil.

chicken with asparagus
[in a white wine sauce]

Poached chicken served with a light asparagus sauce proves that fine ingredients need only the simplest cooking to make a delicious meal.

4 skinned, boned chicken breasts,
   about 125g each
1 bay leaf
2 shallots, finely chopped
150ml chicken stock
125ml dry white wine
225g asparagus, cut into 7.5cm lengths
2 tbsp cornflour
150ml skimmed milk
Salt and black pepper
Sprigs of fresh flat-leaved parsley
   to garnish

Serves: 4
Prep time: 5 minutes
Cooking time: 25 minutes

Nutrients per serving: Calories 224, Carbohydrate 15g, Protein 33g, Fat 2g (no saturated fat)

1 Place the chicken breasts in a single layer in a large frying pan with the bay leaf and shallots. Pour in the stock and wine and bring to the boil, then reduce the heat, cover and simmer for 20 minutes, turning the chicken over after 10 minutes.

2 Meanwhile, put a kettle on to boil. Cook the asparagus in a pan of lightly salted boiling water for 4-5 minutes until it is just tender when tested with a knife. Drain and refresh under cold running water, then drain again thoroughly and set aside.

3 Remove the chicken breasts from the frying pan and keep them warm. Blend the cornflour and milk together in a large jug. Strain the hot cooking liquid then whisk it into the jug. Return the sauce to the frying pan and boil, stirring continuously, until thickened and smooth. Season with salt and pepper to taste.

4 Stir the cooked asparagus into the sauce and heat it through for 1 minute. Serve the chicken breasts, spoon the sauce and asparagus over them, sprinkle them with pepper and garnish with sprigs of parsley.

Asparagus inspires

gentle thoughts.

Charles Lamb

salmon & asparagus salad

A velvety mango, yoghurt and mustard dressing with a subtle hint of aniseed gives the freshly cooked salmon in this salad a luxurious, tropical taste.

4 salmon fillets, about 675g in total
1 tbsp olive or sunflower oil
200g asparagus spears
1 large stick celery
250g mixed salad leaves
For the dressing:
2 large mangoes
4 chives
100g natural yoghurt
1 tsp wholegrain mustard
1 tbsp Pernod or ouzo
Black pepper

Serves: 4
Cooking time: 25 minutes

Nutrients per serving: Calories 576, Carbohydrate 33g, Protein 48g, Fat 28g (saturated fat 5g)

1 Put a kettle of water on to boil. Skin the salmon, remove any bones, and cut it into large cubes. Heat the oil in a frying pan and stir-fry the salmon for 2-3 minutes until just cooked through and lightly browned. Drain on kitchen paper.

2 Rinse and trim the asparagus spears, cut them into 4cm pieces, cover with the boiling water and blanch for 2 minutes. Rinse in cold water and drain.

3 To make the dressing, peel the mangoes and cut into cubes: you need about 500g. Place in a food processor or bowl. Rinse and dry the chives and snip them into the mango. Add the yoghurt, mustard and Pernod or ouzo and purée. Add black pepper to taste.

4 Rinse, destring and finely slice the celery. Put it into a bowl with the salmon and asparagus. Pour the dressing over the top, holding a little back in case there is more than you need. Toss together gently, taking care not to break up the salmon.

5 Trim, rinse and dry the salad leaves, then arrange them on four serving plates and top with the salmon salad.

warm asparagus [with egg crumble]

A simple topping of fried breadcrumbs and hard-boiled egg adds crunch to tender green stems of fresh asparagus.

1kg asparagus
100g soft white bread, crusts removed
150g butter
2 eggs, hard-boiled
Salt and black pepper

Serves: 6
Prep time: 15 minutes
Cooking time: 10-15 minutes

Nutrients per serving: Calories 293, Carbohydrate 11g, Protein 10g, Fat 24g (saturated fat 12g)

1 Cook the asparagus until tender in an asparagus steamer, a wok or a deep saucepan.

2 Meanwhile, put some plates to warm. Make the breadcrumbs in a food processor, or with a grater.

3 Heat the butter in a heavy-based pan, add the breadcrumbs and fry them until golden brown. Mash the eggs with a fork, mix them into the crumbs and season to taste.

4 When the asparagus is cooked, drain the stems well and arrange them on the warmed plates. Scatter the egg crumble mixture over each helping and serve immediately.

BROAD BEANS

The broad bean is thought to have been brought to Britain by the Romans. The flavour is best when the bean is no larger than a 2p piece and before the pods become tough. Broad beans thrive in fertile, well-drained soil with a dressing of manure. In general, spring-sown beans do best in medium to heavy soil while autumn-sown beans are more likely to thrive in lighter soil.

HARVESTING

The earliest crops are ready in May. Start to pick them when the pods are no more than 5cm long, and cook them whole. In all other cases pick the beans as they are required, feeling the pods to get an idea of the size of the beans inside.

PREPARATION

Young beans no thicker than a finger and 7.5cm long are the most delicious. They are cooked in their pods. Larger broad beans must be shelled before cooking. Mature beans, which tend to be floury, should also be shelled and after boiling, the outer tough skin of the beans should be removed and the inner flesh mashed to a purée with butter and seasoning.

FRENCH BEANS

French beans actually seem to have originated in Peru before being brought to Europe in the 16th century and will thrive in the smallest vegetable plot. Dwarf beans can be grown in tubs or window boxes while climbing beans are grown up poles or netting. French beans thrive in a light well-drained soil in a sunny position, ideally with some shelter from wind.

HARVESTING

Dwarf beans start to crop within eight weeks of sowing and many produce pods for eight weeks after that. Pick over them every day to keep them cropping. To remove pods, hold the stem with one hand and pull the pods downwards with the other. To get dried haricot beans, leave the pods on the plants until they have ripened and turned white. Pull up the plants whole and hang them in a dry airy place. When the pods are crisp and dry, shell the beans and spread them out on trays to dry thoroughly.

PREPARATION

French beans are at their best when young and before the seeds begin to show through the pods. Top and tail and cook whole in their pods in boiling water for about 7 minutes.

RUNNER BEANS

A succulent summer and autumn crop, runner beans are larger, coarser and less flavoursome than french beans. They grow best in a sunny position with plenty of shelter for the insects that pollinate them. They prefer a rich, well-drained soil, well manured to allow maximum root development.

HARVESTING

Pick the beans while they are still young and tender, before the seeds begin to swell in the pods. The more they are picked, the more the plants will produce. When pods cannot be used immediately, stand them in a cool place with the ends of their stems in shallow water.

PREPARATION

To prepare runner beans for cooking, wash them thoroughly, cut off the tops and tails and peel off any stringy edges. Chop the bans into diagonal lengths no shorter than 4-5cm. Cook in a small amount of boiling, lightly salted water for 5-7 minutes.

Beans

gammon & broad bean soup

2 tbsp olive oil

150g gammon steak, chopped into
  1cm pieces

1 onion, chopped

2 large, thick leeks, about 400g in total,
  sliced

4 sprigs of thyme

2 bay leaves

115g pearl barley

1.5 litres vegetable stock

225g podded broad beans

Salt and black pepper

3 tbsp chopped flat-leaved parsley

Serves: 4
Prep time: 5 minutes
Cooking time: 45 minutes

Nutrients per serving: Calories 275,
Carbohydrate 31g, Protein 19g, Fat 9g
(saturated fat 1g)

1 Heat the oil in a large saucepan and fry the gammon, onion and leeks over a medium-low heat, stirring occasionally, for about 10 minutes or until the vegetables are soft and golden. Add the thyme and bay leaves towards the end of cooking.

2 Add the barley and cook for 1-2 minutes, then pour in the stock. Bring to the boil and simmer, uncovered, for about 30-40 minutes until the barley is tender and the stock reduced to a soupy consistency.

3 Remove the bay leaves. Add the broad beans 4-5 minutes before the end of the cooking. Season with salt and pepper and transfer the soup to warmed bowls. Sprinkle with parsley and serve with granary bread.

creamy mixed bean salad

This hearty salad mixes a variety of fresh and canned vegetables into a nutritious dish packed with flavours. Fresh basil infuses a creamy yoghurt and mustard dressing.

250g stringless green beans
440g canned kidney beans
440g canned cannellini beans
440g canned lentils
280g artichoke hearts in oil
150g button mushrooms
75g spring onions
1 soft, round lettuce
For the dressing:
225g natural Greek yoghurt
½ lemon
1-2 tsp Dijon mustard
A large handful of fresh basil
Salt and black pepper

Serves 4
Cooking time 25 minutes

Nutrients per serving: Calories 598, Carbohydrate 64g, Protein 32g, Fat 24g (saturated fat 5g)

1 Bring a saucepan of water to the boil. Rinse, top, tail and halve the green beans. Cook them for 5-6 minutes or until just tender. Rinse under cold water then drain.

2 Rinse the kidney and cannellini beans and lentils, drain and spread them on a tea towel to dry.

3 Drain the artichoke hearts on kitchen paper and cut them into quarters. Clean and slice the mushrooms; trim, rinse and slice the spring onions.

4 To make the dressing, put the yoghurt into a large bowl, squeeze in the lemon juice, add mustard to taste, and stir well.

5 Rinse and dry the basil, reserve a few sprigs for a garnish, tear the rest and add them to the dressing. Season to taste.

6 Rinse and dry the lettuce leaves and arrange them on a serving dish. Mix the vegetables into the yoghurt and mustard dressing. Spoon on top of the leaves and garnish with the reserved basil.

warm salad [of tangled runner beans]

500g runner beans
½ red onion
Salt and black pepper
4 tbsp olive oil
1 tbsp red wine vinegar
150g cherry tomatoes, some halved
50g small black olives
Basil leaves to garnish

Serves: 4
Prep time: 15 minutes
Cooking time: 4-5 minutes

Nutrients per serving: Calories 155, Carbohydrate 6g, Protein 2.5g, Fat 13g (saturated fat 2g)

1 String and thinly slice the beans diagonally. Peel the onion, cut it in half and then slice downwards into thin crescents. Put these slices into an attractive serving bowl.

2 Cook the beans in boiling salted water until just tender; this should take about 4 minutes after the water returns to the boil. Drain and put the beans immediately over the onion slices so the heat slightly wilts them.

3 In a small bowl, stir the oil and vinegar briskly together and toss into the beans, along with the cherry tomatoes, olives and black pepper.

4 Tear a few leaves of basil over the salad just before serving. The dish is best still warm or at room temperature.

I came to love my rows, my beans, though so many more than I wanted.

Henry David Thoreau

broad bean, prawn & feta salad

A pretty salad of broad beans, with fresh mint and juicy prawns, gets an added punch from cubes of salty feta cheese and a strong, refreshing, lemon and garlic dressing.

500g frozen broad beans
2-3 sprigs of fresh mint
200g Greek feta cheese
200g peeled, cooked prawns
For the dressing:
1 large lemon
6 tbsp extra virgin olive oil
1 clove garlic
Salt and black pepper

Serves: 4
Cooking time: 20 minutes

Nutrients per serving: Calories 428, Carbohydrate 16g, Protein 29g, Fat 28g (saturated fat 9g)

1 Put a kettle of water on to boil. Put the beans into a saucepan with a sprig of mint. Cover with boiling water and simmer for 6 minutes. Drain and rinse the beans, then drain them again.

2 Drain and dice the cheese. Put it into a salad bowl; add the prawns.

3 To make the dressing, squeeze half the lemon, mix 2 tablespoons of the juice with the olive oil, then peel the garlic and crush it into the dressing. Rinse, dry and finely chop the remaining mint and whisk thoroughly into the dressing then add salt and pepper to taste.

4 Add the drained beans to the cheese and prawns and stir in the dressing. Serve with wedges cut from the rest of the lemon.

omelette ribbon salad [& french beans]

French beans are threaded with omelette ribbons for this piquant salad. The strips of egg and sun-dried tomatoes add good contrasts in colour and texture.

2 eggs
Salt and black pepper
3 tbsp olive oil
350g French beans
1 large clove garlic, thinly sliced
1 large tsp red wine vinegar
1 tsp chilli vinegar
2 sun-dried tomatoes in oil, chopped
2 tsp capers

Serves: 4
Prep time: 15 minutes
Cooking time: 8-9 minutes

Nutrients per serving: Calories 147, Carbohydrate 3g, Protein 5.5g, Fat 2g (saturated fat 3g)

1 Beat the eggs lightly with a fork, add salt and pepper, then make two thin omelettes and turn onto plates.

2 Top and tail the beans and cook for 3-4 minutes in boiling, salted water. Drain and transfer to a dish.

3 Fry the garlic for 30 seconds in a tablespoon of oil; remove from the heat. Add the remaining oil, vinegars and sun-dried tomatoes, mix together and toss into the beans.

4 Roll each omelette and slice into thin ribbons. Curl the slices loosely over the salad; scatter with capers.

pasta [with broad beans, artichokes & spinach]

Small pasta shapes and a tasty selection of assorted vegetables make a sturdy, healthy meal.

2 tbsp olive oil
1 medium onion
1 large clove garlic
1 medium red pepper
175g dried pasta shapes
Salt and black pepper
400g chopped tomatoes
A pinch of dried oregano
½ tsp brown sugar
225g broad beans, podded
350g young spinach
300g canned artichoke hearts
50g Parmesan cheese; 1 Italian loaf
   to serve

Serves: 4
Cooking time: 30 minutes

Nutrients per serving: Calories 741, Carbohydrate 92g, Protein 26g, Fat 30g (saturated fat 6g)

1 Bring a large saucepan of water to the boil, and heat the oven to its lowest setting. Heat the olive oil in another large saucepan. Peel and roughly chop the onion, then peel and crush the garlic. Add them both to the oil and fry them gently for 5 minutes, until soft.

2 Rinse, halve, deseed and slice the pepper. Add it to the onion and fry for a further 2 minutes. Add the pasta and some salt to the boiling water. Return to the boil and cook for 10-12 minutes, until the pasta is *al dente*.

3 Stir the tomatoes, oregano, sugar and some black pepper into the onion, garlic and red pepper. Bring to the boil, then partially cover and simmer for 10 minutes. Put the bread into the oven to heat through. Add the broad beans to the tomato sauce, return to the boil and simmer for 3 minutes.

4 Rinse and drain the spinach, then remove any tough stalks, add the leaves to the sauce and cook for a further 3 minutes. Drain and quarter the artichoke hearts. Drain the pasta. Add both to the sauce and heat through for a minute or two.

5 Turn the pasta and sauce into a warm serving bowl, grate some Parmesan over and serve with the hot bread.

roast beef [with broad beans & mushrooms]

Juicy fresh vegetables replace Yorkshire pudding as an accompaniment to the Sunday joint, giving a lighter touch.

1 beef topside joint, about 750g
250g shelled broad beans, defrosted if frozen
250g mixed mushrooms, such as chanterelles (girolles), oysters and shiitake
2 tbsp Madeira, sherry or red wine
150-200ml meat stock
Salt and black pepper

Serves: 4
Prep time: 40 minutes
Cooking time: 1 hour 5 minutes-1 hour 40 minutes

Nutrients per serving: Calories 270, Carbohydrate 5g, Protein 48g, Fat 6g (saturated fat 2g)

1 Heat the oven to 180°C/gas 4. Weigh the beef and calculate the cooking time: for rare meat, 35 minutes per kg plus 15 minutes; for medium, 45 minutes per kg plus 20 minutes; for well done, 55 minutes per kg plus 25 minutes. Place the beef in a roasting tin and cook.

2 Meanwhile, bring a large saucepan of water to the boil and cook the broad beans for 5-10 minutes until tender, then drain and refresh them under cold running water. When they are cool enough to handle, peel off their skins to reveal the bright green inner bean. Set aside.

3 Finely slice or tear the mushrooms and set aside.

4 When the joint is done, remove it from the roasting tin and put it to rest in a warm place while you cook the mushrooms and make the sauce.

5 Remove any excess fat from the roasting tin and place the tin over a low heat. Add the mushrooms and fry them for about 10 minutes until they have softened.

6 Raise the heat and add the Madeira, sherry or wine, stirring to take in the cooking juices. When the alcohol has almost evaporated, add the stock and bring it to the boil, stirring frequently. Then lower the heat and simmer for 5-10 minutes to make a syrupy sauce. Season to taste, then stir in the broad beans and heat them through.

7 Spoon the bean and mushroom mixture onto a platter and lay the joint on top. Carve the meat at the table, and serve it with the beans and mushrooms spooned over it.

bean & bacon pot

250g broad beans, shelled
250g potatoes
1 large parsnip
2 carrots
2 medium onions
250g bacon
300ml tomato juice
Salt and pepper
2 tbsp Worcestershire sauce (optional)

Serves: 4
Cooking time: 1½ hours

Nutrients per serving: Calories 246, Carbohydrate 30g, Protein 20g, Fat 6g (saturated fat 2g)

1 Put the beans in a casserole and add the peeled and diced potatoes, parsnip and carrots. Add the peeled and sliced onions.

2 Dice the bacon and fry briskly for 1 or 2 minutes to seal. Add to the casserole with the tomato juice and salt and pepper to taste.

3 Cover and cook at 180°C/gas 4 for 1½ hours. Cool and freeze. When thawed and reheated, add the Worcestershire sauce.

french beans with herbs

500g french beans
3-4 tbsp oil
1 finely chopped onion
1 clove garlic
1 chopped carrot
2 tbsp vegetable stock
1 dsp each of finely chopped parsley,
    tarragon or chives, chervil and
    spring onions
1 tsp chopped marjoram
Salt and sugar

Serves: 4
Cooking time: 20 minutes

Nutrients per serving: Calories 123,
Carbohydrate 8g, Protein 3g, Fat 9g
(saturated fat 1g)

1 Wash, top and tail the beans and cut in half. Heat the oil in a heavy-based pan and cook the onion, crushed garlic and carrot for about 5 minutes or until the onion is golden.

2 Add the beans, stock and all the finely chopped herbs; mix thoroughly, cover with a lid and simmer gently for 15 minutes or until the beans are tender. Stir occasionally, and add a little more stock if the mixture begins to dry out. Season to taste with salt or sugar.

cheesy french beans

500g french beans
2 tbsp olive oil
1 clove garlic
Salt
75g Cheddar or Cheshire cheese
Paprika
2 tomatoes

Serves: 4
Cooking time: 30 minutes

Nutrients per serving: Calories 166,
Carbohydrate 5.5g, Protein 7.5g, Fat 12.5g
(saturated fat 5g)

1 Wash, top and tail the beans. Put in a pan of lightly salted boiling water and cook for 5-7 minutes. Drain, then refresh in cold water.

2 Brush an ovenproof dish with a little olive oil, cut the garlic in half and rub over the dish. Lay the well-drained beans in the dish, brush them liberally with oil and sprinkle with salt. Heat the oven to 190°C/gas 5.

3 Slice the cheese thinly and lay over the beans, sprinkle with paprika and top with tomato slices. Cook near the top of the oven for about 20 minutes, or until the cheese has melted.

4 Serve on its own with hot garlic bread, or as a light supper dish with boiled cold ham or gammon.

sweet & sour beans

500g runner beans
Salt and pepper
4 rashers streaky bacon
1 tbsp white wine vinegar
1 tbsp soft brown sugar

Serves: 4
Cooking time: 15 minutes

Nutrients per serving: Calories 110,
Carbohydrate 8g, Protein 6g, Fat 6g
(saturated fat 2g)

1 Put the prepared beans in a pan of boiling, lightly salted water; cover and simmer for about 7 minutes.

2 Meanwhile, cut the bacon crossways into narrow strips. Fry without any extra fat until the bacon pieces are crisp. Lift them out with a perforated spoon and keep warm.

3 Stir the vinegar and sugar into the bacon fat, add the drained beans and stir to coat them evenly with the sweet-and-sour mixture.

4 Spoon the beans and liquid into a dish and sprinkle with the bacon pieces. Serve with roast pork or boiled ham.

There are two main types of beetroot. Globe varieties are generally grown for eating freshly boiled in summer and autumn; long-rooted kinds are more suitable as a main crop for harvesting in autumn and storing for winter use. Ideally they need an open, sunny site. Although they do best on a light sandy loam, they can be grown on heavier soil if this is suitably prepared.

Beetroot

HARVESTING

Pull globe beetroot out by hand as they are needed. Once out of the ground, hold the base of the leaves with one hand and twist off the remainder with the other. Cutting the leaf stems, or twisting them off too close to the roots results in bleeding. Lift long-rooted beetroot in November by putting a fork alongside the row and easing the soil so that the roots can be pulled out without damage. After twisting off the tops, store the roots in boxes of sand or peat in a frost-proof shed or garage.

PREPARATION

Beetroots are mainly used cold – either freshly cooked or pickled in salads. To cook beetroot, trim the leaf stalks 2.5-5cm above the root and leave the tapering root on. Cutting into the beetroot, or bruising the skin while washing it, will result in 'bleeding'. Boil in salted water for 1-2 hours, depending on size. Refresh in cold water and rub off the skin.

beetroot & horseradish relish

Although vinegar reduces the nutrient content of beetroot, this relish – which is excellent served with cold meats – is still rich in valuable potassium and folate.

450g cooked beetroot, peeled and coarsely grated
115g fresh horseradish, trimmed, peeled and coarsely grated
½ tsp salt
115g granulated sugar
300ml white wine vinegar

Nutrients per 15ml tablespoon:
Calories 11, Carbohydrate 2.5g,
Protein 0.2g, Fat 0g (no saturated fat)

1 Put all the ingredients in a big bowl and stir together until the sugar dissolves.

2 Pack into clean, dry jars and seal with twist-on lids. Label and date, and store in the refrigerator for up to a month.

quick borscht

500g cooked beetroot
1l beef bouillon (or vegetable stock)
1 large onion
2-3 pickled gherkins
2 tbsp lemon juice
150ml sour cream
Salt, pepper and sugar to season
2 hard-boiled eggs to garnish

Serves: 4
Chilling time: 1 hour

Nutrients per serving: Calories 212,
Carbohydrate 21g, Protein 8g, Fat 11g
(saturated fat 6g)

1 Cut the tops and root ends off the cooked beetroot. Peel and grate, on the coarse side of a grater, into a large bowl. Alternatively, chop the roots finely.

2 Peel and finely grate the onion and stir into the beetroot, together with the finely chopped gherkins.

3 Stir the cooked bouillon or stock into the beetroot – at this stage the soup may be blended into a liquidiser or left chunky as it is – followed by the sour cream. Season to taste with lemon juice, salt, pepper and sugar. Chill for at least one hour.

4 Chop the hard-boiled eggs finely and sprinkle on the top of the soup just before serving.

beetroot & sour cream salad

3-4 beetroot (uncooked)
2 large dessert apples
150ml sour cream
Lemon juice
Salt and pepper
75ml whipped cream

Serves: 4
Chilling time: 30 minutes

Nutrients per serving: Calories 190,
Carbohydrate 12g, Protein 2.5g, Fat 15g
(saturated fat 9g)

1 Peel the uncooked beetroot and grate coarsely. Peel and core the apples, grate and mix with the beetroot.

2 Fold in the sour cream and season to taste with lemon juice, salt and pepper.

3 Fold in the whipped cream and chill lightly in the fridge.

Russian salad

3-4 boiled beetroot
4 boiled new potatoes
½ cucumber
1 pickled gherkin
2 hard-boiled eggs
6 tbsp olive oil
2 tbsp white wine vinegar
Salt and pepper
½ tsp dry mustard
1 hard-boiled egg; chopped dill, fennel
    or parsley to garnish

Serves: 4
Chilling time: 1 hour

Nutrients per serving: Calories 277,
Carbohydrate 14g, Protein 8g, Fat 22g
(saturated fat 4g)

1 Dice the beetroot, potatoes, cucumber and gherkin, mix thoroughly and add the roughly chopped eggs.

2 Make a dressing from the oil, vinegar, salt, pepper and mustard; pour the dressing over the diced vegetables, turning well to coat them evenly. Chill for an hour in the fridge.

3 Arrange in a bowl and sprinkle with finely chopped hard-boiled egg and dill.

beetroot chutney

1kg uncooked beetroot
500g onions
750g cooking apples
500g seedless raisins
3 tbsp ground ginger
1kg granulated sugar
1l malt vinegar

Approx yield: 2kg

Nutrients per serving: Calories 47,
Carbohydrate 12g, Protein 0g, Fat 0g
(no saturated fat)

1 Peel and grate the beetroot; peel the onions and chop finely; peel, core and chop the apples.

2 Put in a pan with the raisins, ginger, sugar and vinegar. Bring to the boil. Simmer until thick then pot.

beetroot wine

2.25kg scrubbed, diced beetroot
250g concentrated red grape juice
1kg sugar
15g citric acid
½ tsp grape tannin
4l water
Bordeaux yeast and nutrient

Nutrients per serving: Calories 90,
Carbohydrate 5g, Protein 0g, Fat 0g
(no saturated fat)

1 Simmer the diced beetroot until tender. When cool, strain the liquor into a bin.

2 Activate the yeast and add it to the liquor, together with the concentrated grape juice, the acid, tannin, nutrient and sugar dissolved in warm water.

3 Pour the strained mixture into a fermentation jar, top up with cold water and fit an airlock to the jar. Tie on a label describing the contents and store the jar at room temperature until fermentation is complete.

pickled beetroot

2kg uncooked beetroot
Spiced vinegar

Nutrients per serving: Calories 30,
Carbohydrate 5g, Protein 0g, Fat 0g
(no saturated fat)

1 Wash the beetroot carefully without damaging the skin, then boil in lightly salted water for about 1½ hours until tender. Leave to cool, rub off the skins and then cut into slices ½cm thick.

2 Pack into jars and cover with cold vinegar. If a sweeter pickle is preferred, a little sugar may be added.

3 This pickle must be used within two months. However, a beetroot pickle with a longer storage life can be made by dicing the beetroot instead of slicing it, packing the pieces loosely into jars and covering with boiling, spiced vinegar.

Blackberries

There are few fruits that are more prolific and easier to grow than blackberries. Suitable for any moisture-retaining, well-drained soil, and for growing in all parts of the country, they are ideal for training against a wall or fence where they will yield a worthwhile crop without taking much space from other plants. Blackberries fruit from late July to September, according to the variety. The best fruits are borne on shoots that developed during the previous season. Cultivated varieties produce larger and tastier fruits than wild plants. As blackberries are self-fertile, it is possible to grow just a single plant if that is all you have space for.

HARVESTING

Pick berries when they are large and juicy and come away easily in your hand. Blackberries will deteriorate swiftly after picking unless they are quickly frozen.

PREPARATION

Blackberries are rarely served as a dessert on their own though they are delicious folded into Greek yoghurt. They go well with sharp cooking apples and are often used in this combination as pie fillings, fruit puddings, in jams and jellies. Blackberries bruise easily and should be handled and washed as little as possible.

... if I wanted to have a happy garden, I must ally myself with my soil ...

Marion Cran

duck breasts [with blackberry sauce]

A simple but extravagantly flavoured dish of tender duck breasts coated in exotic spices and served in a fruity wine sauce is perfect for a dinner party or a special celebration.

4 boneless duck breasts with skin, about 175g each
¼ tsp Chinese five-spice powder
Salt and black pepper
5 tbsp crème de mure
5 tbsp red wine
½ small cinnamon stick
1 star anise, optional
1 small orange
300g fresh blackberries
2 level tsp arrowroot

Serves: 4
Cooking time: 25 minutes

Nutrients per serving: Calories 772, Carbohydrate 13g, Protein 24g, Fat 65g (saturated fat 19g)

1 Remove any sinews from the duck and lightly score the fat into a diamond pattern. Mix the five-spice powder with some salt and pepper and rub it over the breasts.

2 Put the crème de mure, wine, cinnamon and star anise, if using, into a small pan. Wash any wax from the orange, grate the rind into the pan, then bring to the boil.

3 Meanwhile, cook the duck, skin sides down, in a dry frying pan over a moderate heat for 4-5 minutes, until the skins have turned a golden brown and enough fat has been released to cook the other sides. Turn and cook for 5-6 minutes more for medium-rare, longer for well-done. Spoon off excess fat.

4 While the duck is cooking, rinse the blackberries and add them to the wine. Squeeze the orange. Add half the juice to the wine, return to the boil, reduce the heat and simmer gently for 5 minutes. Blend the rest of the juice with the arrowroot.

5 Strain the blackberries into a bowl and set them aside. Return the liquid to the pan and stir in the blended arrowroot. Bring back to the boil, stirring, until it thickens, then add the blackberries and heat through. Slice the duck breasts and serve with the blackberry sauce.

blackberry yoghurt shake

250g blackberries
Caster sugar
600ml natural yoghurt

Serves: 4
Chilling time: 30 minutes

Nutrients per serving: Calories 160, Carbohydrate 21g, Protein 9g, Fat 4.5g (saturated fat 2.5g)

1 Pick over the blackberries, hull and rinse them if necessary, and drain thoroughly. Put the blackberries in a liquidiser and blend until quite smooth, then strain the mixture thoroughly to get rid of the pips.

2 Sweeten the blackberry mixture to taste with sugar and gradually blend in the yoghurt to an even mixture. Pour into glasses and chill in the fridge for 30 minutes or serve at once with the addition of a couple of ice cubes.

blackberry fool

375g blackberries
Caster sugar
1-2 tbsp lemon juice
300ml whipping cream

Serves: 4
Cooking time: 5 minutes
Chilling time: 1 hour

Nutrients per serving: Calories 335,
Carbohydrate 13g, Protein 2g, Fat 30g
(saturated fat 19g)

I Hull, rinse and drain the blackberries. Set 12 berries aside and put the remainder in a pan. Simmer over a low heat for about 5 minutes, or until the berries have softened and the juices are running.

2 Rub the blackberries through a sieve to make a purée. Sweeten to taste with sugar and sharpen with lemon juice. Leave to cool.

3 Whip the cream until it holds its shape, then fold it thoroughly into the cooled blackberry purée. Spoon the mixture into tall glasses and chill in the fridge for about 1 hour.

4 Decorate each glass with the reserved blackberries just before serving, accompanied by tiny macaroons if liked.

blackberry & apple crumble

450g cooking apples, such as Bramleys
250g blackberries
40g light brown sugar
For the topping:
100g butter
125g plain flour
25g caster sugar
150g mixture of: chopped hazelnuts,
    sunflower seeds, pumpkin seeds or
    pine nuts
100g oat flakes or rolled oats

Serves: 6
Prep time: 15 minutes
Cooking time: 40-45 minutes

Nutrients per serving: Calories 510,
Carbohydrate 53g, Protein 8g, Fat 31g
(saturated fat 10g)

I Heat the oven to 180°C/gas 4. Cut the apples into quarters and remove the core. Peel each quarter, then cut into slices. Transfer to a large ovenproof dish, about 1.4l capacity. Add the blackberries and sugar and mix.

2 For the topping, rub the butter into the flour, then stir in the sugar, nuts, seeds and oat flakes or rolled oats. Sprinkle the topping evenly over the fruit to cover it in a thick layer.

3 Bake for 40-45 minutes, until the topping is crisp and golden and the fruit is cooked and beginning to bubble up around the edges. Leave to stand for 5 minutes before serving, with custard.

blackberry jam

3kg blackberries
150ml water
Juice of 2 lemons, or 1 tsp citric acid
    or 300ml apple-pectin stick
3kg sugar

Nutrients per teaspoon: Calories 13,
Carbohydrate 4g, Protein 0g, Fat 0g
(no saturated fat)

I Hull and pick over the berries; rinse and drain carefully. Put in a pan with the water, lemon juice or citric acid. If pectin stock is used, add it with the sugar after the preliminary cooking.

2 Simmer until the berries are soft, then add the sugar and stir until dissolved. Boil rapidly to setting point. Test for setting point by dropping a teaspoon of jam onto a cold saucer. If it is not ready, continue boiling and testing every 10 minutes until it is.

3 Pour into pots and seal.

blackberry & apple jelly

Brambles bring a glorious natural bounty to autumn hedgerows. Wild berries taste delicious but home-grown varieties are good too for this jewel-coloured preserve.

1.8kg ripe blackberries, stalks removed
900g Bramley apples, wiped and roughly chopped, with core
1.2l water
Preserving or granulated sugar (see step 3)

Makes: 1.6kg
Prep time: 30 minutes, plus overnight draining
Cooking time: 1½ hours

Nutrients per 5ml teaspoon: Calories 18, Carbohydrate 5g, Protein 0g, Fat 0g (no saturated fat)

1 Put the fruit into a large pan and add the water. Bring to a boil, then simmer, stirring frequently, for 1 hour until soft and pulpy. Mash lightly with a potato masher, then let it cool slightly.

2 Pour into a jelly bag with a bowl set underneath to catch the juice. Leave overnight. Avoid squeezing the bag, as this will make the jelly cloudy.

3 Put two saucers in the refrigerator or freezer to chill. Measure the juice in the bowl, then pour it into a large, clean pan. Warm the juice, but do not boil. Remove from the heat and add 450g sugar for each 600ml juice. Stir over a gentle heat until all the sugar has melted. Increase the heat and boil vigorously for 8 minutes, stirring constantly. Remove from the heat.

4 Test for setting by dropping a teaspoon of jelly mixture onto a chilled saucer. If it is not ready, continue boiling and test every 8 minutes.

5 Pour the jelly into clean, warmed jars. Cover and seal immediately, then label and date each jar. Store in a cool, dark place for up to a year.

The purple or white heads of sprouting broccoli help to fill a lean period in late winter and early spring, when brussels sprouts have almost finished and spring season cabbage has not yet begun. Sprouting broccoli grows spears – many small heads 2.5-5cm across, which are cut with a length of stem and cooked in a bunch. As the spears are cut, more develop over a period of four to six weeks. Calabrese is a less hardy type of sprouting broccoli which produces larger, green heads in autumn. It will not stand winter so do not grow for spring use. Both types of broccoli grow best in fertile, loamy soil in a sunny position. It is helpful to choose a site sheltered from winter winds for sprouting broccoli; otherwise they may require support.

HARVESTING

Cut the heads of calabrese with about 2.5cm of stalk in late summer and early autumn when the flower buds are green and tightly closed. After the main head is cut, sideshoots will grow and further heads will be produced. When harvesting sprouting broccoli, cut about 10-15cm of stem and cook this with the heads. Cut back to a point just above a pair of sideshoots which will then produce fresh spears.

PREPARATION

To prepare broccoli, wash the spears carefully in cold water, strip off the leaves and trim off any tough parts from the base of the stalks. Cook in boiling, lightly salted water for no more than 12 minutes, and drain thoroughly.

Broccoli

broccoli au gratin

500g broccoli spears or a head of calabrese
Salt and pepper
300ml white sauce
50g butter
3 tbsp breadcrumbs

Serves: 4
Cooking time: 15 minutes

Nutrients per serving: Calories 302, Carbohydrate 25g, Protein 10g, Fat 19g (saturated fat 10g)

1 Put the prepared broccoli spears or calabrese in a pan of boiling water. Bring back to the boil and simmer, covered, until the spears are just tender. Drain thoroughly and arrange in a shallow flameproof dish.

2 Spoon the white sauce over the broccoli. Melt most of the butter in a pan, and mix in the breadcrumbs until the butter has been absorbed.

3 Sprinkle the breadcrumbs over the sauce and dot with the remaining butter. Set under a hot grill for a few minutes.

broccoli cheese puffs

16 broccoli spears
250g puff pastry
50g Cheddar cheese
Salt and pepper
1 egg

Makes: 8
Cooking time: 20 minutes

Nutrients per puff: Calories 166, Carbohydrate 12g, Protein 6g, Fat 11g (saturated fat 5g)

1 Carefully wash the broccoli spears and trim the stalks short. Put in a pan of boiling, lightly salted water. Simmer for about 5 minutes or until just tender then drain through a colander.

2 Roll out the pastry thinly and cut into eight equal size squares with 10cm sides. Cut the cheese into four slices and trim them a little narrower than the pastry squares; cut in half. Heat the oven to 220°C/gas 7.

3 Lay a slice of cheese over half of each pastry square, arrange two broccoli spears on top and sprinkle with salt and pepper. Beat the egg and brush over the pastry edges. Fold over the pastry and seal the edges firmly.

4 Set the pastry parcels on a damp baking sheet, make three slits in each and brush the top with egg. Bake in the centre of the oven for about 20 minutes, or until risen and golden.

broccoli with almonds

This dish makes an ideal accompaniment to try with grilled fish such as trout or mackerel, or more delicately flavoured meats such as veal.

500g broccoli spears
Salt
50g butter
50g flaked almonds
Juice of ½ lemon

Serves: 4
Cooking time: 10 minutes

Nutrients per serving: Calories 211, Carbohydrate 53g, Protein 11g, Fat 24g (saturated fat 3g)

1 Trim the stalks of the broccoli spears and remove the leaves. Wash the spears in cold water. Put the broccoli in a pan with a small amount of boiling, lightly salted water. Bring back to the boil and simmer for about 7 minutes or until just tender.

2 Meanwhile melt the butter in a pan, add the flaked almonds, sprinkle them with salt and fry over a low heat until golden brown. Stir in the lemon juice.

3 Drain the broccoli thoroughly through a colander, arrange in a serving dish and pour the browned butter and almonds over them.

There is nothing ... as thrilling, as gathering the vegetables one has grown.

Alice B. Toklas

Calabrian pasta

Dark green calabrese makes a fine contrast to pale spaghetti and goes well with other Italian ingredients such as anchovies, pine nuts and sultanas.

50g sultanas
200g broccoli
150g dried tagliatelle or spaghetti
100ml olive oil
75g fresh white breadcrumbs
2 cloves garlic, finely chopped
25g pine nuts
2 tsp anchovy sauce or anchovy paste
Black pepper
3 tbsp fresh parsley, chopped
Cayenne pepper

Serves: 5-6 as a starter, 3-4 as a main course
Prep time: 15 minutes
Cooking time: 12-15 minutes

Nutrients per serving when serving 4:
Calories 461, Carbohydrate 53g, Protein 11g, Fat 24g (saturated fat 3g)

1 Leave the sultanas to soak in a cup of boiling water

2 Slice the thick stem bases of the broccoli diagonally and divide the heads into small florets, each with a wedge of stem attached. Then blanch them in boiling water, cooking for just 30 seconds after the water has come back to the boil. Drain, refresh under the cold tap and leave to drain.

3 Cook the pasta in a large pan of boiling water until *al dente* for about 12-15 minutes. While it is cooking, put a serving bowl in a low oven to warm.

4 Heat the oil in a frying pan and fry the breadcrumbs on medium heat for about 5 minutes until they start to become crispy, then add the garlic and pine nuts. After a minute or two, when the pine nuts begin to colour, add the broccoli and stir over the heat until everything is hot.

5 Drain the pasta and then set the colander quickly back on top of the saucepan. This will catch the last tablespoon of water and help to keep the pasta warm and moist.

6 Return the pasta to the pan, stir in the anchovy sauce or paste and mix in the drained sultanas.

7 Add the black pepper to taste and half of the chopped parsley, then tip the pasta into the heated serving bowl.

8 Mix the remaining parsley into the fried breadcrumb and broccoli mixture and scatter over the pasta.

9 Sprinkle with cayenne pepper and toss the mixture at the dining table.

purple sprouting broccoli [& leek bake]

225g purple sprouting broccoli, trimmed
   and cut into even-sized lengths or florets
2-3 leeks, thinly sliced and rinsed
675g potatoes, peeled and thinly sliced
25g butter
20g plain flour
About 225ml semi-skimmed milk
Salt and black pepper

Serves: 2, or 4 as a side dish
Prep time: 25 minutes
Cooking time: 30 minutes

Nutrients per serving: Calories 500,
Carbohydrate 78g, Protein 19g, Fat 14g
(saturated fat 8g)

1 Steam the broccoli for 3-4 minutes until just tender. At the same time, cook the leeks in a little boiling water for 3-4 minutes until just tender. Drain, reserving the liquid. Cook the potato slices in lightly salted, boiling water for 5-6 minutes until tender, then drain.

2 Heat the oven to 190°C/gas 5. Melt 20g of the butter in a saucepan, stir in the flour and then gradually add the milk. Gradually add the reserved leek water, stirring, to make a thin, smooth sauce. Add salt and pepper to taste.

3 Put the broccoli in a shallow ovenproof dish and scatter the leeks over the top. Pour over the white sauce and then add the potato slices in a layer. Dot with the remaining butter and bake for 15 minutes until very hot. For a golden top, brown briefly under a hot grill. Serve with a green salad and crusty bread, or as a side dish with meat or fish.

fish parcels [with creamy broccoli]

Fish parcels cook easily in the oven and stay beautifully moist while you make a delicious accompaniment of emerald broccoli dressed with cream and tarragon.

4 thick fresh white fish steaks,
   about 175g each
2 tbsp extra virgin olive oil
Salt and black pepper
1 shallot
350g broccoli florets
10 sprigs of fresh tarragon
225ml double cream

Serves: 4
Cooking time: 30 minutes

Nutrients per serving: Calories 473,
Carbohydrate 3g, Protein 37g, Fat 35g
(saturated fat 18g)

1 Heat the oven to 180°C/gas 4. Dry the fish steaks, then brush them with a tablespoon of oil and season well.

2 Cut four pieces of foil, each large enough to enclose a steak. Put one steak on each piece of foil, fold the edges together to make a roomy parcel and crimp to seal. Lay the four parcels on a baking sheet and cook for 15 minutes.

3 Meanwhile, peel and grate the shallot. Rinse the broccoli and trim it into small florets.

4 Heat the remaining oil in a frying pan and fry the shallot until translucent.

5 Add the broccoli to the pan, stems down, with 150ml of water, and bring to the boil, then cover and simmer for 4-5 minutes until the broccoli is barely tender. Remove the lid, raise the heat, and cook until only 1-2 tablespoons of water remain in the pan. Do not let the broccoli burn.

6 Rinse and dry the tarragon. Reserve four sprigs for a garnish, then strip the leaves off the rest and add them to the broccoli. Stir in the cream, season to taste with salt and pepper and keep warm.

7 Remove the foil parcels from the oven, unwrap them and transfer the fish onto four warmed plates. Spoon the broccoli over the fish, garnish with the reserved tarragon and serve.

grilled chicken, broccoli [& pasta gratin]

Precooked chicken is the basis for this quick and easy supper dish, which can be made in less than 30 minutes.

175g dried pasta shapes, such as spirals (fusilli)
Salt and black pepper
225g broccoli florets
2 sticks celery, thinly sliced
300g canned condensed half-fat tomato soup
200ml skimmed milk
350g skinned, boned cooked chicken
25g fresh white breadcrumbs
½ tsp dried herbes de Provence, or dried mixed herbs

Serves: 4
Prep time: 5 minutes
Cooking time: 20 minutes

Nutrients per serving: Calories 419, Carbohydrate 57g, Protein 38g, Fat 4g (saturated fat 1g)

1 Bring a large saucepan of water to the boil over a high heat, add the pasta and a pinch of salt and cook according to the instructions on the packet. Drain well and set aside.

2 Meanwhile, bring another pan of water to the boil, then add the broccoli, celery and a pinch of salt and boil for 5 minutes, or until the broccoli is just beginning to soften. Drain well, rinse under cold water, drain and set aside.

3 Heat the grill to medium-high. Put the soup and milk into a large pan over a medium heat and bring to a simmer, stirring occasionally.

4 Trim any fat off the chicken and cut it into bite-size pieces. Add them to the tomato soup mixture along with the broccoli, celery and pasta, and reheat at a simmer for 5 minutes. Season to taste.

5 Pour the chicken mixture into four individual gratin dishes, or a single shallow 1.75l flameproof serving dish. Scatter the breadcrumbs and herbs evenly over the top, then grill until the sauce is bubbling and the crumbs are crisp and golden. Serve hot.

Brussels sprouts

Brussels sprouts are one of the most loved and loathed of vegetables. But they have plenty to recommend them. Rich in vitamin C, they will provide a crop in autumn and winter if both early and late varieties are planted. If you have a freezer it may be easier to make a single sowing of either type and freeze the surplus. Brussels sprouts occupy a fair amount of space over a longer period (about eight months) than most crops and so may not be a wise choice for a small plot. Sprouts will grow well only in fertile soil with an adequate lime content.

HARVESTING

The best time to pick sprouts is when they are small and their leaves are tight and firm as they will be crisper to eat. Harvesting after a slight frost also ensures a good flavour. Pick the lower sprouts first. Sprouts at the top of the plant can be encouraged to swell by removing the cabbage-like head which can be cooked as a separate vegetable.

PREPARATION

Pick the sprouts just before cooking, peel off any ragged outer leaves, trim the base and cut an 'X' across it. Wash the prepared sprouts in cold water. Cook in a minimum of boiling water for 8-10 minutes. The cooked sprouts should still be slightly chewy, not watery and squashy.

brussels sprout soup

1kg brussels sprouts
250g sliced potatoes
1 sliced onion
50g butter
850ml vegetable stock
300ml milk
Salt, pepper, ground nutmeg
150ml single cream

Serves: 6
Cooking time: 35-40 minutes

Nutrients per serving: Calories 309,
Carbohydrate 20g, Protein 11g, Fat 21g
(saturated fat 12g). High fibre

I Sauté the potatoes and onion in the butter for 10 minutes over a gentle heat, until they have absorbed the butter. Toss the sprouts with the potatoes and onion and transfer to a large pan with the stock and milk. Bring to the boil, cover with a lid and simmer for 20 minutes. Season to taste with salt and pepper.

2 Blend the soup in a liquidiser. Season with nutmeg, add the cream and reheat the soup without letting it boil.

3 Serve with crispy croutons. Alternatively, serve chilled, stirring in the cream at the last minute.

brussels sprouts & pork

500g brussels sprouts
4 pork steaks or lean chops
50g butter
2 cooking apples
Salt and pepper
Juice of 1 lemon
1 tbsp soft brown sugar

Serves: 4
Cooking time: 1 hour

Nutrients per serving: Calories 368,
Carbohydrate 16g, Protein 36g, Fat 18g
(saturated fat 8g). High fibre

I Clean and prepare the sprouts. Blanch in boiling, lightly salted water for 2 minutes, drain through a colander and leave to cool.

2 Meanwhile, flatten the pork steaks and trim away excess fat if chops are used; brown in butter over a good heat to seal both sides. Lift out the pork steaks and set them aside.

3 Brown the sprouts lightly in the butter, then remove from the pan. Peel and core the apples and cut into slices. Preheat the oven to 160°C/gas 3.

4 Arrange the pork steaks and sprouts in a shallow, buttered, ovenproof dish, sprinkle with salt and pepper and cover with the apple slices. Spoon over the lemon juice and sprinkle with brown sugar.

5 Cover with a lid or foil and cook in the oven for about 45 minutes. Remove the lid for the last 10 minutes. Serve at once.

brussels sprouts [with chestnuts]

375g brussels sprouts
50g butter
175g chestnuts
Pepper

Serves: 4
Cooking time: 15 minutes

Nutrients per serving: Calories 207,
Carbohydrate 20g, Protein 4g, Fat 12g
(saturated fat 6g). High fibre

I Prepare and wash the sprouts; put them in a pan with a little boiling, lightly salted water. Boil for 5-7 minutes, drain thoroughly and keep warm.

2 Melt the butter in a pan and add the cooked, peeled chestnuts. Unsweetened tinned chestnuts may also be used. Sauté for 5 minutes, then add the sprouts and toss with the chestnuts until evenly coated. Sprinkle with freshly ground pepper.

In order to live off a garden, you practically have to live in it.

Frank McKinney Hubbard

brussels sprouts [with mushrooms]

500g brussels sprouts
250g potatoes
1 grated onion
75g butter
Milk
150ml double cream
Salt and pepper
250g button mushrooms

Serves: 4
Cooking time: 30 minutes

Nutrients per serving: Calories 455, Carbohydrate 19g, Protein 8g, Fat 39g (saturated fat 23g). High fibre

1 Peel the sprouts and potatoes; cut up the potatoes and put to boil in a pan of unsalted water. Add the sprouts and grated onion for the last 7 minutes of cooking time. Drain thoroughly and then purée the vegetables in a liquidiser.

2 Reheat the purée, adding 50g of butter, 2 tablespoons of cream and sufficient milk to give the consistency of creamed potatoes. Season to taste with salt and pepper.

3 Meanwhile, sauté the sliced mushrooms in the remaining butter until golden brown, pour the cream over them and continue cooking over a gentle heat until the cream sauce has thickened slightly. Season with salt.

4 Spoon the purée into a dish and pour over the creamed mushrooms.

sautéed brussels sprouts

Golden fried brussels sprouts mingle with crisp morsels of bacon and water chestnuts in this crunchy dish, while wholegrain mustard and orange add an aromatic touch.

1 tbsp corn oil
75g rindless smoked bacon
500g fresh button brussels sprouts
1 orange
50g butter
2 tsp wholegrain mustard
115g canned whole water chestnuts
   in water
Salt and black pepper

Serves: 4
Cooking time: 25 minutes

Nutrients per serving: Calories 224, Carbohydrate 7g, Protein 8g, Fat 19g (saturated fat 9g). High fibre

1 Heat the corn oil in a frying pan, then dice the smoked bacon and fry it for 2-3 minutes until it turns golden brown.

2 Rinse the brussels sprouts, trim them if necessary, and cut in half. Wash any wax off the orange and grate the rind into the frying pan with the bacon and add the butter, mustard and sprouts. Cook over a moderate heat for 5 minutes, stirring, until the sprouts are crisp.

3 Meanwhile, drain and roughly chop the water chestnuts, stir them into the sprouts and cook them for 3-4 minutes until the sprouts are golden and the chestnuts are heated through. Add salt and black pepper to taste and serve.

brussels sprouts [with mustard]

Spice up your sprouts with this quick-and-easy Indian recipe, which will add extra interest to plainly cooked meat and poultry.

500g small brussels sprouts
1 tbsp sunflower oil
½ tsp black mustard seeds
½ tsp cumin seeds
2 large cloves garlic, finely chopped
½ tsp cayenne pepper
Salt and black pepper
1 tbsp gram flour, sifted

Serves: 4
Prep time: 15 minutes
Cooking time: 15-20 minutes

Nutrients per serving: Calories 86, Carbohydrate 7g, Protein 5g, Fat 5g (saturated fat 1g). High fibre

1 Trim the sprouts and cut a cross into each stem end. Bring a pan of water to the boil, add the sprouts and return it to the boil. Cover and simmer for 2-3 minutes. Reserve 150ml of the cooking liquid and drain off the remainder.

2 Heat the oil in a large nonstick saucepan over a medium heat, then throw in the mustard seeds – they will start jumping around so you may need to cover the pan briefly until they have settled down. Then add the cumin, garlic and cayenne pepper in that order. Reduce the heat to low and stir-fry for 1 minute, or until the garlic begins to brown.

3 Add the sprouts to the pan, season to taste, stir well, cover and cook for 2-3 minutes.

4 Pour in the reserved sprout stock, increase the heat to medium and simmer the mixture, uncovered, until the stock has reduced by half.

5 Sprinkle the gram flour evenly over the top, then stir until all the stock has been absorbed and the sprouts are coated with a thin sauce.

stir-fried hot slaw [of brussels sprouts]

400g brussels sprouts
50g hazelnuts
3 tbsp olive oil
2 sticks celery, destrung and finely sliced
2 cloves garlic, crushed or finely chopped
4 fat or 6 slender spring onions, sliced
2 tbsp lemon juice
1 eating apple
2 tbsp hazelnut or walnut oil
Salt and black pepper

Serves: 4
Prep time: 15 minutes
Cooking time: 4-6 minutes

Nutrients per serving: Calories 260, Carbohydrate 8g, Protein 6g, Fat 23g (saturated fat 3g). High fibre

1 Trim the sprouts and slice them thinly across their girth. Toast the hazelnuts on a baking tray under a hot grill, shaking regularly until the skins are flaky. Rub the skins off the nuts when they are cool enough to handle, then leave them to cool.

2 Heat the olive oil in a wok or wide pan and stir-fry the celery for a minute. Add the garlic then, after just 30 seconds, the spring onions, sprouts and lemon juice. Stir-cook until they are all hot through.

3 Grate the unpeeled apple straight into the pan, leaving only the core. Stir to heat through, then stir in the hazelnuts and the hazelnut or walnut oil. Season thoroughly, adding more lemon if desired (it depends on the sweetness of the apple), and serve hot.

winter salad [of shredded brussels sprouts]

Chestnuts and sprouts are a popular combination used here in a different way. This crunchy vegetable salad has a delicious honey and mustard dressing.

8-10 fresh chestnuts
225g brussels sprouts
2 medium carrots, cut into ribbons with
   a potato peeler
2 medium leeks, thinly sliced
1 bunch watercress, trimmed
Small bunch of parsley, finely chopped
Salt and black pepper
1 rounded tsp Dijon mustard
1 tsp runny honey
1 tbsp cider vinegar
4 tbsp olive oil
1 tbsp walnut oil

Serves: 4
Prep time: 20 minutes
Cooking time: 10 minutes

Nutrients per serving: Calories 230, Carbohydrate 18g, Protein 4g, Fat 16g (saturated fat 2.5g). High fibre

1 Roast the chestnuts on a baking tray for 5-10 minutes until the skins crack. Peel them while they are still warm then break into rough pieces.

2 Trim the sprouts and shred thinly across. Mix the prepared vegetables, watercress, parsley and the broken chestnuts in a wide salad bowl. Add salt and black pepper to taste.

3 In a small bowl, mix together the mustard, honey and cider vinegar then beat in both of the oils. Toss the dressing into the salad and serve.

By means of water, we give life to everything.

The Koran

Cabbages are hardy and easy to grow and if different varieties are planted, will provide a succession of crops throughout the year. Spring cabbages have bright green, loose-leaved heads and are in season during April and May. The small varieties can be cut early, in March, before they mature, when they are known as spring greens. Summer cabbages have larger, more compact heads. They are ready during August and September. Autumn and winter cabbages which have solid heads like the summer varieties, are ready for cutting from October to February. Savoy cabbages are round-headed, with crisp, crinkled leaves. They are very hardy and easy to grow, and with successional sowing, will provide a crop of fresh green vegetables from September, right through winter to May.

Cabbage

HARVESTING

Cut cabbages when their heads are firm and fleshy. Savoy cabbages are best after a slight frost, which brings out their flavour.

PREPARATION

Remove the outer coarse leaves and cut into quarters, removing the hard centre core and base. Wash thoroughly and drain, and cook either in wedges or shredded. Use a minimum of boiling, lightly salted water – just enough to prevent sticking. Cook shredded cabbage for 5-7 minutes, wedges for about 12 minutes. Red cabbages require longer cooking.

cabbage, potato & sausage soup

550g floury potatoes
2 cloves garlic
350g green cabbage, curly kale or
    spring greens
1 tsp dried dill weed
85g chorizo sausage
Salt and black pepper
4 tbsp extra virgin olive oil
Crusty bread or toast to serve

Serves: 4
Cooking time: 25 minutes

Nutrients per serving: Calories 469,
Carbohydrate 68g, Protein 14g, Fat 16g
(saturated fat 4g). High fibre

1 Peel and thinly slice the potatoes and put into a large saucepan. Cover with
   1l of cold water and bring to the boil. Peel and slice the garlic and add to
   the pan.

2 When the water reaches boiling point, skim off the white froth and lower
   the heat, then partially cover the pan and gently boil the potatoes for
   7-10 minutes.

3 Meanwhile, trim the greens, removing any coarse stalks, then rinse and
   shred the leaves into strips, about 1cm wide.

4 When the potatoes are nearly cooked, remove the pan from the heat and
   mash the potatoes in the water to break them up as much as possible.

5 Add the greens and dried dill to the potatoes, bring back to the boil then
   reduce the heat and cook for a further 4-7 minutes (depending on the
   variety of greens).

6 While the potatoes and greens are cooking, cut the chorizo sausage into
   wafer thin slices.

7 Take the pan off the heat and mash the potatoes again to reduce them to
   more of a purée and to help to break down the cooked greens into the
   soup, though they should still retain their colour and shape.

8 Season the soup generously with salt and black pepper, then ladle it into the
   soup plates.

9 Garnish with slices of sausage. Trickle olive oil in a zigzag pattern over each
   serving and grind on more black pepper. Serve with crusty bread or toast.

coriander & cabbage slaw

200g cucumber
500g green cabbage, shredded
50g red onion, thinly sliced
2 tbsp chopped fresh coriander
For the dressing:
2 cloves garlic
Salt and black pepper
3 tbsp lime juice
100g low-fat natural yoghurt

Serves: 4
Prep time: 30 minutes, plus 1 hour chilling

Nutrients per serving: Calories 50,
Carbohydrate 6g, Protein 2g, no fat

1 Peel the cucumber, halve it lengthways and remove the seeds with a
   teaspoon. Slice it into matchsticks about 2.5cm long. Put them in a bowl
   and stir in the cabbage, onion and coriander.

2 To make the dressing, crush the garlic into a paste with ½ teaspoon of salt,
   then whisk in the lime juice and yoghurt and season with pepper. Pour the
   dressing over the slaw, mix well and chill for about 1 hour to let the
   flavours develop.

cabbage & carrot salad
[with spiced yoghurt dressing]

Two winter favourites are given a spicy, minted dressing to bring out all their flavours.

125g white cabbage, finely shredded
125g carrots, grated
For the dressing:
125g low-fat natural yoghurt
1 tbsp finely chopped red onion
1 green chilli, deseeded and finely chopped, optional
2 tbsp finely chopped fresh coriander
1 tsp bottled mint sauce, or
1 tsp each chopped fresh mint and white wine vinegar
A pinch of salt
½ tsp sugar
½tsp ground cumin and ½ tsp paprika to garnish

Serves: 4
Prep time: 15 minutes

Nutrients per serving: Calories 38, Carbohydrate 7g, Protein 2g, no fat

I Place the cabbage and carrots in a large bowl.

2 To make the dressing, mix all the ingredients together and beat them with a fork until well blended.

3 Stir the dressing into the cabbage and carrots, sprinkle with cumin and paprika, and serve.

cabbage casserole

1 winter or spring cabbage
500g leg or lamb or lean pork
2 tbsp oil
2 large onions
4 tomatoes
Salt and paprika
450ml bouillon

Serves: 4
Cooking time: 1¼ – 1½ hours

Nutrients per serving: Calories 291, Carbohydrate 15g, Protein 32g, Fat 12g (saturated fat 3g). High fibre

I Remove the outer leaves from the cabbage, cut it into quarters, rinse and drain. Cut out the centre stalk and chop the cabbage roughly, or cut each quarter lengthways in half.

2 Trim the meat of any fat and cut into 2.5cm chunks. Heat the oil in a pan, and fry the meat for a few minutes until it is brown and sealed on all sides. Pour off any excess fat. Heat the oven to 180°C/gas 4.

3 Grease an ovenproof dish lightly and arrange in it layers of cabbage, meat, sliced onions and peeled, sliced tomatoes. Begin and finish with cabbage and season each layer lightly with salt and paprika.

4 Pour bouillon into the dish until it stands just level with the top layer of cabbage. Cover with a lid and bake in the oven for 1¼ hours, or until the meat is tender.

sweet & sour red cabbage [with apple]

Red cabbage has been popular in Britain for many years. It was a favourite among the Victorians and is a classic accompaniment for game.

1 tbsp sunflower oil
1 onion, sliced
1 clove garlic, crushed
1 small red cabbage, about 675g, finely sliced
2 tbsp raspberry or red wine vinegar
4-5 tbsp red wine
2 tbsp soft brown sugar
1 large cooking apple, peeled, cored and sliced
Salt and black pepper

Serves: 4
Prep time: 15 minutes
Cooking time: 2¼ hours

Nutrients per serving: Calories 100, Carbohydrate 16g, Protein 2g, Fat 3g (saturated fat 0.5g)

1 Heat the oven to 160°C/gas 3. Heat the oil in a flameproof casserole and fry the onion and garlic for 2-3 minutes.

2 Add the cabbage, stir-fry for a few minutes, then add the vinegar, wine and sugar. Bring to the boil, then remove from the heat and stir in the apple, with salt and pepper to taste.

3 Fold a large piece of foil into four. Place over the top of the casserole and secure with a lid. Put the casserole in the oven and cook for 2 hours, stirring halfway through cooking. The cabbage should be sticky and almost caramelised when ready to eat. Serve with roast or grilled meats, sausages, or with baked potatoes and cottage cheese.

cabbage with cream & Stilton

Savoy, the king of cabbages, richly dressed with cream and hot Stilton, makes a great partner for roast lamb.

1 tbsp olive oil
1 large onion
1 small savoy cabbage, about 450g
Salt and black pepper
115g Stilton cheese
200ml single cream

Serves: 4
Cooking time: 20 minutes

Nutrients per serving: Calories 284, Carbohydrate 10g, Protein 10g, Fat 23g (saturated fat 13g)

1 Heat the olive oil in a saucepan. Peel and finely chop the onion. Add it to the oil and cook gently.

2 Meanwhile, trim off and discard any tough or bruised outer leaves from the cabbage. Cut it in half, then remove the core and finely shred the leaves. Rinse the leaves well and drain them.

3 Add the cabbage to the saucepan and stir, then cover and cook over a moderate heat for 6-8 minutes, shaking the pan frequently. You may prefer not to add salt as the Stilton will give a salty flavour.

4 While the cabbage is cooking, cut the Stilton into small cubes. Remove the pan from the heat, add the cream, Stilton and some black pepper, then return to the heat and stir until the cheese has melted, but do not allow it to boil. The melted cheese will thicken the cream.

cabbage dolmas

1 large green or white cabbage
Salt and pepper
4-6 tbsp oil
1 large onion
250g minced cooked lamb
125g boiled long-grain rice
1 tbsp finely chopped mint
1 tbsp finely chopped parsley or dill
1 egg
3 tbsp tomato paste
450ml bouillon or white wine

Serves: 6
Cooking time: 2 hours (approx)

Nutrients per serving: Calories 290,
Carbohydrate 15g, Protein 16g, Fat 19g
(saturated fat 5g)

I Remove any damaged leaves from the cabbage and trim the stalk. Put the cabbage in a large pan of lightly salted boiling water, bring back to the boil, cover with a lid and remove the pan from the heat.

2 Let the cabbage stand in the hot water for 10 minutes, then drain it carefully and peel off the large outer leaves, leaving them whole. The cabbage should yield at least eight, and preferably 12, whole leaves. Set these aside, remove the stalk from the rest of the cabbage and chop the leaves finely.

3 Heat the oil in a pan and lightly fry the finely chopped onion until soft. Add the minced lamb and fry until it is light brown.

4 Stir in the rice, mint and parsley or dill, season to taste with salt and pepper and remove the pan from the heat. Blend this stuffing with the lightly beaten egg and lay a spoonful or two in the centre of each of the large reserved cabbage leaves. Heat the oven to 160°C/gas 3.

5 Fold the sides of the leaves over the stuffing, roll them up and hold in place with fine string.

6 Butter a large ovenproof dish and line with half the chopped cabbage, lay the cabbage rolls on top and cover with the remaining chopped cabbage. Blend the tomato paste with the bouillon or wine and pour the mixture over the cabbage. Cover with a lid and bake for about 1½ hours.

partridge with port [& red cabbage]

Partridge, seen by many as the king of game birds, has sweet, succulent meat that is also low in cholesterol.

1 onion
1 cooking apple, such as Bramley,
 peeled and cored
4 young partridge, about 275g each
1 tbsp sunflower oil
450g red cabbage, finely shredded
1 bay leaf
3 tbsp red wine vinegar
150ml apple juice
100ml ruby port
8 pickled walnuts, halved
Salt and black pepper

Serves: 4
Prep time: 15 minutes
Cooking time: 45-50 minutes

Nutrients per serving: Calories 500,
Carbohydrate 16g, Protein 45g, Fat 27g
(saturated fat 5g)

I Heat the oven to 180°C/gas mark 4. Cut half the onion and apple into four wedges, and tuck a wedge of each into the cavity of each bird. Dice the remaining onion and apple.

2 Heat the oil in a heavy, nonstick frying pan, add the birds, breast side down, and cook quickly, until browned all over. Remove to a plate. Put the red cabbage in a flameproof casserole with the diced apple and onion, bay leaf, vinegar, apple juice, port and walnuts. Add salt and pepper to taste, bring to the boil and stir well.

3 Place the birds on top, breast sides up, sprinkle with salt and pepper and cover tightly. Cook in the oven for 30 minutes, then remove the lid and cook for a further 10 minutes to crisp the skin. Remove bay leaf.

4 Serve each partridge on a bed of cabbage, with the juices spooned over, with baked or mashed potatoes.

plum-glazed pork [with spicy cabbage]

Plum jam, soy sauce, warm spice and hot cayenne pepper go well with pork chops, while the crisp cabbage served alongside gets its own spicy boost from chilli and garlic.

700g crisp green cabbage, such as savoy
1 large, fresh red chilli
2 cloves garlic
3 tbsp good plum jam
1½ tbsp soy sauce
½ tsp ground allspice
½ tsp cayenne pepper
4 pork loin chops, about 175g each
2 tbsp cider vinegar
Salt and black pepper
3 tbsp olive oil

Serves: 4
Cooking time: 30 minutes

Nutrients per serving: Calories 568, Carbohydrate 19g, Protein 32g, Fat 41g (saturated fat 13g)

I Heat the grill to high. Halve the cabbage and discard the woody centre. Coarsely chop the leaves, rinse them well, then drain them in a colander.

2 Rinse, halve and deseed the chilli, and slice it finely. Peel and roughly chop the garlic. Set them both aside.

3 Gently warm the plum jam and soy sauce in a small pan, season with the allspice and cayenne, then sieve, if necessary.

4 Arrange the chops on the grill rack and cook for 5-7 minutes on each side, brushing the warm plum glaze over them halfway through cooking each side.

5 Meanwhile, mix the cider vinegar with 3 tablespoons of water and some salt and pepper.

6 Heat the oil in a large saucepan, add the chilli and garlic and fry them for 30-40 seconds. Add the cabbage and toss it in the oil. Stir in the diluted vinegar, cover and cook for 4 minutes.

7 Uncover the pan, raise the heat and continue to cook the cabbage until all the liquid has evaporated. Serve the spicy cabbage with the plum-glazed chops.

savoy cabbage in gin

A splash of gin and some juniper berries and garlic turn baby savoy cabbage into an aromatic dish that goes well with strongly flavoured meat.

1 savoy cabbage approx 500-700g
6 juniper berries
2 cloves garlic
Salt
50g butter, softened
3 tbsp gin
Black pepper

Serves: 4 as an accompaniment
Prep time: 15 minutes
Cooking time: 5 minutes

Nutrients per serving: Calories 160, Carbohydrate 6g, Protein 3g, Fat 11g (saturated fat 6g)

1 Trim away any tired or damaged leaves from the cabbage, cut it into quarters and shred it finely, cutting out and discarding the stem. Wash thoroughly and drain well.

2 With a pestle and mortar, crush the juniper berries, garlic and salt together to produce a rough paste. Or chop finely, sprinkle on the salt and mix thoroughly. Mix the paste into the softened butter.

3 Cook the flavoured butter in a large saucepan over a low heat until it starts to sizzle, but do not let it begin to brown. Put a serving dish on to warm.

4 Toss the drained cabbage in the flavoured butter, turn up the heat to coat it in the butter. Stir in the gin, cover the pan tightly and cook on a medium heat for 4 minutes, shaking the pan vigorously once or twice.

5 Remove from the heat, grind on black pepper to taste, stir and serve immediately in the warmed dish.

pickled cabbage

1 large, firm red or white cabbage
Spiced vinegar
Coarse salt

Nutrients per tablespoon: Calories 30, Carbohydrate 7g, Protein 0g, Fat 0g (no saturated fat)

1 Remove the outer leaves of the cabbage, wash, cut into quarters and discard the tough inner cores. Shred finely, layer with coarse salt and leave to stand for 24 hours.

2 Drain and rinse thoroughly, pack into bottles and cover with cold vinegar. Seal at once.

3 Both red and white cabbage pickles are ready for use after a week. Red cabbage with store for two or three months; white cabbage for two months only.

Although carrots were grown for centuries in south-eastern Europe and western Asia, it was not until the 16th century that the British learned to cultivate and grow them. Carrots can be enjoyed throughout the year. Spring sowings of stump-rooted types make a delicious second vegetable from late June onwards. Intermediate and large-rooted types can be grown in later sowings. You will need to use cloches or a frame to protect the earliest spring sowings and late crops of 'new' carrots in autumn. Carrots do best in light well-drained soil in a sunny position or one with minimal shade. Early crops do best in full sun.

HARVESTING

Pull up early, short-rooted varieties in June and July, easing them with a fork if the ground is hard. Harvest maincrop carrots in early October, using damaged carrots immediately and storing the rest for use in winter. Always use a fork to loosen intermediate and long-rooted varieties. Before storing, remove the soil and cut off the foliage close to the crown. Store the carrots in boxes, between layers of sand, and keep the boxes in an airy, dry, frost-proof shed.

PREPARATION

Trim off the tapering root end and the leaves as well as woody or discoloured parts. Scrape young carrots but peel older carrots thinly. Before cooking, cut older carrots into quarters, slices or chunks. Leave young, small carrots whole or cut them in half. Cook in boiling water for 10-30 minutes depending on their age and method of preparation.

Carrots

Turkish carrot salad

4 large carrots
2 cloves garlic
150ml olive oil
300ml natural yoghurt
Salt and pepper
Chopped mint to garnish

Serves: 6
Cooking time: 10 minutes
Chilling time: 1 hour

Nutrients per serving: Calories 234,
Carbohydrate 11g, Protein 3g, Fat 20g
(saturated fat 4g)

1 Peel and wash the carrots and grate them on the coarse side of a grater; peel and crush the garlic.

2 Heat the oil in a heavy-based pan, add the grated carrots and garlic and cook for about 10 minutes over a gentle heat, stirring frequently. Drain the carrots through a sieve until all the oil has strained off and the carrots have cooled.

3 Spoon into a bowl and mix with the yoghurt; season to taste with salt and pepper and chill for at least an hour.

4 Sprinkle with finely chopped mint to serve.

Moroccan carrot dip

Hot, sweet spices bring a taste of North African sun
to this dip that goes beautifully with hummous.

500g carrots, thickly sliced
1 tsp ground cinnamon
1 tsp ground cumin
2 cloves garlic, crushed
½ tsp ground ginger
1 tbsp clear honey
1 tbsp olive oil
1 tsp paprika
3 tbsp vinegar or lemon juice
Salt and black pepper

Serves: 4-6
Prep time: 10 minutes
Cooking time: 25 minutes

Nutrients per serving, when serving 4:
Calories 79, Carbohydrate 12g, Protein 1g,
Fat 3g (saturated fat 1g)

1 Place the carrots in a large saucepan, cover with water, bring to the boil and simmer for 20-25 minutes until they are very soft. Rinse under cold running water, then drain thoroughly.

2 Put them in a bowl and mash with a potato masher. Stir in the cinnamon, cumin, garlic, ginger, honey, oil, paprika and vinegar or lemon juice. Blend well and season to taste.

Sowe Carrets in your Gardens, and humbly praise God for them as for a singular and great blessing.

Richard Gardiner

carrot soup [with butter beans]

The flavours of fresh and ground coriander give this filling soup extra bite.

15g butter
150g onions, finely chopped
450g carrots, finely chopped
100g leeks, chopped
300g potatoes, chopped
1 tsp ground coriander
1 clove garlic, crushed
225g canned butter beans, rinsed and
    drained or use fresh if you have them
300ml skimmed milk
2 tbsp chopped fresh coriander
Salt and black pepper
To garnish: sprigs of fresh coriander

Serves: 4-6
Prep time: 10 minutes
Cooking time: 30 minutes

Nutrients per serving when serving 4:
Calories 185, Carbohydrate 31g,
Protein 8g, Fat 4g (saturated fat 2g)

1 Melt the butter in a large saucepan, add the onions, cover and cook over a low to medium heat for 5-8 minutes until softened.

2 Stir in the carrots, leeks, potatoes, ground coriander and garlic, cover and cook for a further 5 minutes.

3 Add the butter beans and 900ml of water and bring to the boil. Then reduce the heat and simmer, covered, for 20 minutes, or until the vegetables are tender.

4 Remove the soup from the heat and purée it with a hand-held mixer or in a food processor. Stir in the milk and chopped coriander and season to taste. Gently reheat the soup to warm through the added milk then serve it, garnished with sprigs of coriander.

moist carrot cake [with nuts]

A delicious, moist carrot cake packed with fruit and nuts. It can also be topped with light cream cheese and a scattering of nuts for extra health and flavour.

125ml sunflower oil, plus extra for greasing
3 eggs
1 tsp vanilla extract
100g unsweetened desiccated coconut
100g raisins
100g walnuts or hazelnuts, roughly chopped
About 400g carrots, peeled and coarsely grated
225g self-raising wholemeal flour
150g light muscovado sugar
1 tsp ground cinnamon

Serves: 8
Prep time: 25 minutes
Cooking time: 50 minutes

1 Heat the oven to 180°C/gas 4. Lightly oil a 900g loaf tin and line it with baking parchment. Put the oil, eggs and vanilla extract into a small bowl and beat well.

2 Put the coconut, raisins and nuts in another large bowl. Add the oil and egg mixture. Stir in the grated carrot, flour, sugar and cinnamon and mix well.

3 Tip the mixture into the prepared tin and smooth down the top. Bake for about 50 minutes or until a skewer inserted into the middle comes out clean.

4 For the light cream cheese topping: beat 200g low-fat cream cheese with 2 tablespoons runny honey. Spread on top of the cake once it has cooled completely.

Nutrients per serving: Calories 500, Carbohydrate 51g, Protein 10g, Fat 29g (saturated fat 9g)

summer casserole

500g young carrots
500g new potatoes
500g belly pork
50g butter
450ml stock
Salt and pepper
2 sprigs of thyme
1 small cauliflower
250g young green peas
Chopped parsley to garnish

Serves: 6
Cooking time: 1 hour

Nutrients per serving: Calories 431, Carbohydrate 27g, Protein 25g, Fat 26g (saturated fat 11g)

1 Trim the carrots, scrape and wash them and chop into rough slices. Scrape the potatoes, leaving small ones whole but cutting larger ones into slices. Remove the rind, bone and gristle from the belly pork and cut into cubes.

2 Melt the butter in a heavy-based pan and fry the meat until golden brown; add the carrots and potatoes and toss well. Stir in the stock, season with salt and pepper and add the fresh thyme. Cover with a lid and simmer over a gentle heat for 35 minutes.

3 Add the cauliflower, broken into small florets, and the peas. Continue simmering until the ingredients are tender. Check the seasoning. Remove the thyme and if necessary, thicken with a little kneaded butter and flour.

4 Serve sprinkled liberally with finely chopped parsley.

honey-glazed carrots

500g young carrots
Salt
25g butter
1 tbsp honey
½ tsp ground cinnamon

Serves: 4
Cooking time: 30 minutes

Nutrients per serving: Calories 100,
Carbohydrate 13g, Protein 0.8g, Fat 6g
(saturated fat 3.5g)

1 Trim off the roots and top ends before scraping and washing the carrots. Leave very small carrots whole; cut larger ones into halves. Put them in a pan of boiling, lightly salted water, cover with a lid and simmer for about 15 minutes or until just tender. Drain thoroughly.

2 Melt the butter in a pan, add the honey and stir until melted. Toss the drained carrots in this mixture over a gentle heat until they are evenly coated and light brown. Sprinkle with cinnamon.

pickled carrots

1kg small carrots
725ml white vinegar
250g sugar
50g pickling spice
150ml water

Serves: 4
Cooking time: 30 minutes

Nutrients per serving: Calories 125,
Carbohydrate 29g, Protein 0g, Fat 0g
(no saturated fat)

1 Trim and scrape the carrots, simmer for 15-20 minutes in slightly salted water until tender, then drain.

2 Boil the vinegar and water, together with the pickling spices in a muslin bag, for 10 minutes.

3 Remove the spices, add the sugar and the carrots and boil until tender. Pack into hot jars and cover with the vinegar. Seal at once.

carrot wine

2.25kg diced carrots
250g concentrated white grape juice
1kg sugar
20g citric acid
4l water
Sauternes yeast and nutrient
Saccharin

Nutrients per serving: Calories 90,
Carbohydrate 5g, Protein 0g, Fat 0g
(no saturated fat)

1 Simmer the diced carrot until tender. When cool, strain the liquor into a bin.

2 Activate the yeast and add it to the liquor, together with the concentrated grape juice, the acid, water, nutrient and sugar.

3 Press and strain the pulp and add the sugar, dissolving this first in warm water.

4 Pour the strained mixture into a fermentation jar, top up with cold water and fit an airlock to the jar. Tie on a label describing the contents and store the jar at room temperature until fermentation is complete.

5 Add saccharin to taste as soon as fermentation is complete.

Cauliflower

Cauliflowers are the most difficult of the brassica family to grow successfully. They need an open position and rich soil and must be kept growing quickly. Given the right conditions, cauliflowers can be harvested all year round by growing varieties that mature at different times. They also freeze satisfactorily, so surplus heads can be stored before they run to seed.

HARVESTING

Cut the heads when they are firm. If left too long, the curds break up as the plant begins to flower. If a number mature at the same time, pull up the plants and hang them upside-down in a cool shed. They will keep for up to three weeks.

PREPARATION

One of the most delicate and versatile vegetables, cauliflowers are frequently overcooked. They should be tender, yet crisp and must be thoroughly drained before serving. Cut off the outer coarse leaves but leave the inner tender leaves and pale green base leaves. Trim the end of the stalk flush with the base of the cauliflower and cut a cross in it with a sharp knife to help make the stalk tender. Depending on the recipe, cook the cauliflower whole, in boiling water for 12-15 minutes; or for 8-10 minutes if divided into florets. A little lemon juice in the water helps to preserve the white colour.

cauliflower soup

A luxurious soup is given extra flavour with leek and thickened with cream and eggs. Serve topped with a garnish of just-fried crispy bacon.

1 cauliflower
1 large carrot
1 leek
2 sticks celery
4 parsley stalks
1 bouquet garni
1l white stock
Salt and pepper
40g butter
25g flour
2 egg yolks
150ml cream or crème fraîche
Bacon to garnish

Serves: 4
Cooking time: 30 minutes

Nutrients per serving: Calories 300, Carbohydrate 13g, Protein 18g, Fat 22g (saturated fat 11g)

1 Clean the cauliflower and divide it into florets. Scrape or peel the carrot, clean the leek and celery sticks and chop them all roughly. Put all the vegetables in a pan with the parsley stalks, bouquet garni and stock. Add salt and pepper and bring to the boil. Simmer, covered for about 15 minutes.

2 Strain the soup, remove the cauliflower florets, discard the various flavourings and set the liquid aside. Melt the butter and stir in the flour; gradually add the reserved liquid, stirring all the time to give a smooth soup. Add the cauliflower florets and heat through. Season to taste with salt and pepper.

3 Beat the egg yolks with the cream or crème fraîche, add a little of the hot soup, then blend the egg and cream mixture into the soup. Stir until the soup thickens, but do not let it reach boiling point.

4 Serve topped with pieces of crisp, fried bacon.

vegetable macaroni cheese

Broccoli and cauliflower add extra nutrients to a family favourite, while a fat-free sauce keeps it light.

600ml skimmed milk
55g plain flour
Salt and black pepper
Pinch of dried mustard powder
Pinch of freshly grated nutmeg
280g cauliflower, cut into florets
280g broccoli, cut into florets
140g small macaroni
115g mature Cheddar cheese, grated
3 tbsp fresh white breadcrumbs
2 tbsp grated Parmesan cheese

Serves: 6
Prep time: 20 minutes
Cooking time: 35 minutes

Nutrients per serving: Calories 300, Carbohydrate 36g, Protein 18g, Fat 10g (saturated fat 5g)

1 Put the milk in a small saucepan, add the flour and cook over a medium heat, whisking vigorously until the sauce has thickened and is smooth. Add salt and pepper, the mustard powder and nutmeg and reduce the heat to very low. Cook for 5-6 minutes, then remove from the heat and set aside. Heat the oven to 200°C/gas 6.

2 Cook the cauliflower and broccoli in boiling, salted water for 3-4 minutes until just tender, then drain.

3 Meanwhile, cook the macaroni in plenty of boiling, salted water for 4-6 minutes until tender. Drain well, then return it to the pan.

4 Add the white sauce and Cheddar, then stir in the cauliflower and broccoli. Pour the mixture into a large ovenproof dish. Sprinkle over the breadcrumbs and Parmesan.

5 Cook in the oven for 10-15 minutes or until the top is puffy and lightly browned. Serve at once with a green salad.

cauliflower cheese [& bacon gratin]

500g cauliflower
250ml milk
Salt
25g butter plus extra for greasing dish
1 clove garlic, finely chopped
75g rindless bacon, diced
25g plain flour
100ml double cream
50g grated Gruyère cheese
Pepper and grated nutmeg
2 tbsp finely grated Parmesan cheese

Serves: 4
Prep time: 20 minutes
Cooking time: 35 minutes

Nutrients per serving: Calories 408,
Carbohydrate 12g, Protein 17g, Fat 33g
(saturated fat 19g)

1 Break up the cauliflower into florets and cut the stalk diagonally into 5mm slices.

2 Bring a large pan of water to the boil and cook both the florets and sliced stalk for 7-8 minutes. Take 75ml of the cooking liquid and mix it with the milk and then drain the florets thoroughly.

3 Heat the oven to 200°C/gas 6. Butter a gratin dish and scatter chopped garlic over the base.

4 Melt the butter in a frying pan and fry the bacon for 5 minutes or until it releases its fat. While it is cooking, heat the milk mixture.

5 Sprinkle the flour into the bacon pan and stir over a gentle heat for about 2-3 minutes without letting it brown. Remove the pan from the heat and gradually stir in enough milk mixture to make a thick sauce.

6 Add more milk mixture and as the sauce thins, return it to the heat and add the rest of the milk mixture; stir constantly until the sauce begins to bubble. Reduce the heat and simmer for about 5 minutes. Stir in the cream slowly and return to boiling point.

7 Remove from the heat and add half the Gruyère cheese. Stir until the cheese has melted, then season with salt, pepper and grated nutmeg.

8 Spread the cauliflower florets in the prepared gratin dish and slowly pour the sauce over, allowing it to permeate the florets.

9 Mix the remaining Gruyère cheese and the Parmesan and scatter over the sauce. Bake for about 20 minutes, until the top is bubbling nicely and has become well browned.

spiced cauliflower

1 large cauliflower, washed and divided
    into florets
2 onions, peeled and finely chopped
4-6 tbsp oil
½ tsp mustard seeds
1 tsp each of ground ginger and salt
½ tbsp turmeric
2 large tomatoes
½ tsp cumin (optional)
2 tbsp finely chopped parsley
Sugar

Serves: 4
Cooking time: 25 minutes

Nutrients per serving: Calories 216,
Carbohydrate 12g, Protein 7g, Fat 16g
(saturated fat 2g)

1 Heat the oil in a heavy-based pan and cook the onions for a few minutes until they are soft and transparent. Add the mustard seeds, ginger, salt and turmeric; cook, stirring all the time, for about 5 minutes.

2 Add the cauliflower florets to the pan, turning them until thoroughly coated with the spice mixture. Skin and finely chop the tomatoes, stir into the cauliflower mixture with the cumin, if used, and the parsley. Add sugar to taste. Cover the pan with a lid and continue cooking over a gentle heat for 10-15 minutes. Stir occasionally to prevent burning.

old-English piccalilli

Piccalilli was created in the 18th century, by mixing Eastern spices with home-grown vegetables. It is excellent served with a ploughman's lunch, or cold spiced pork.

2.7kg mixture of: cucumber, marrow, cauliflower florets, green beans, and pickling onions peeled and cut, where appropriate, into 1cm pieces
450g salt
1.7l white malt vinegar
250g granulated sugar
1½ tsp ground ginger
20g mustard powder
40g plain white flour
3 tsp turmeric powder

Makes: 4.5kg
Prep time: 2 hours, plus overnight salting
Cooking time: 10-15 minutes

Nutrients per 15ml tablespoon: Calories 6, Carbohydrate 1g, Protein 0.2g, Fat 0g, (no saturated fat)

1 Put the prepared vegetables in a large bowl. Sprinkle in the salt and mix with your hands to coat evenly. Cover with a cloth and leave overnight. The next day, drain, then rinse the vegetables well in cold water.

2 Pour all but 300ml of the vinegar into a large pan. Whisk in the sugar, ginger and mustard, then add the vegetables. Simmer over a low heat until cooked but still crisp and holding their shape. Using a slotted spoon, remove the vegetables to a tray.

3 Blend the flour and turmeric powder with the reserved vinegar to form a smooth paste. Stir in some of the hot vinegar to loosen the mixture, then add to the pan. Cook, stirring, for 2-3 minutes until thick. Return the vegetables to the pan. Bring to the boil, then remove from the heat.

4 Spoon into clean, warmed jars. Knock each jar gently to remove any air bubbles and leave to cool completely. Seal the jars with lids. Label, date and store in a cool, dry cupboard away from light for up to three months.

Cares melt when
you kneel in your garden.

Celeriac has a flavour like that of celery, to which it is closely related; it is in fact a turnip-rooted form of celery. The swollen roots make a good winter substitute for celery in soups, stews and salads. As celeriac needs a long growing season, germinate the seeds in a warm place in March and plant outdoors in late May or June. It is essential to keep the plants growing steadily throughout the year or they will not form roots of an adequate size. Grow celeriac in well-drained soil enriched with rotted manure or compost and choose a position that gets plenty of sun.

Celeriac

HARVESTING

Use the roots as you need them during late October and November. Leave them as long as possible so that they grow to their maximum size. There is no advantage in using them while they are immature. At about the end of November, lift the roots that remain, remove the foliage and store in damp sand or peat in a cool shed or cellar.

PREPARATION

The sweet celery flavour is most pronounced in young roots weighing up to about 500g. Older roots tend to become woody and hollow. Trim off the upper leafy part. Do not discard the leaves; they are excellent for flavouring soups and sauces. Slice off the root and scrub thoroughly. Peel fairly thickly and as the celeriac is prepared, drop it in a bowl of cold water with 1-2 teaspoons of lemon juice to prevent discoloration. Cut the celeriac into slices, chunks or narrow strips and cook in boiling water for 10-120 minutes, depending on the size of the pieces.

celeriac soup

500g celeriac
2 leeks
2 carrots
1 small onion
50g butter
1l white stock or bouillon
4 sprigs parsley
2 sprigs thyme
Salt, pepper and paprika
Milk
Chopped chives to garnish

Serves: 4
Cooking time: 40 minutes

Nutrients per serving: Calories 200, Carbohydrate 10g, Protein 12g, Fat 14g (saturated fat 7g)

1 Pick off a few of the best celeriac leaves, rinse and set aside. Scrub the celeriac, trim off the foliage and roots, peel and cut into small chunks. Clean the leeks, set aside a few of the green tops and chop the stems finely. Peel and chop the carrots and onion.

2 Melt the butter in a heavy-based pan and sauté the chopped vegetables for 5 minutes over a gentle heat. Add the stock or bouillon. Wrap the reserved celeriac leaves, the parsley and the thyme sprigs in the leek tops to make a fresh bouquet garni. Tie with string.

3 Add the herbs to the pan; season with salt, freshly ground pepper and paprika. Bring to the boil, cover with a lid and simmer until the vegetables are tender. Remove the herbs and let the soup cool slightly.

4 Blend the soup in a liquidiser and reheat, adding milk to give the required consistency. Check the seasoning.

5 Serve garnished with chopped chives and hot crusty bread.

celeriac salad

1 celeriac
Salt
Lemon juice
3 tbsp mayonnaise
French mustard

Serves: 4
Chilling time: 1 hour

Nutrients per serving: Calories 105, Carbohydrate 3g, Protein 2g, Fat 9g (saturated fat 1g)

1 Peel the celeriac, cut it into thin slices and then cut it crossways into match-like strips. Put in a pan of boiling, lightly salted water with a little lemon juice to preserve the colour; simmer for 2-3 minutes. Drain thoroughly in a colander and leave to cool.

2 Season the mayonnaise to taste with mustard and toss the celeriac in the dressing. Chill in the fridge for about an hour.

celeriac rémoulade

525g celeriac
250ml rémoulade sauce
1 tsp lemon juice or wine vinegar
2 tbsp single cream
Salt and black pepper
1 tbsp chopped parsley

Serves: 4-6
Prep time: 35 minutes
Cooking time: 30 seconds

Nutrients per serving when serving 4: Calories 427, Carbohydrate 3.5g, Protein 2g, Fat 30g (saturated fat 5g)

Rémoulade sauce: Mash a hard-boiled egg yolk thoroughly, add a tsp of boiling water and stir it to a smooth paste. Gradually add 225ml of olive oil, beating the mixture continuously. When the mayonnaise has thickened, add 2 tablespoons each of finely chopped gherkins and parsley, a tbsp of drained capers and a dash of anchovy essence.

1 Peel the celeriac and cut into thin, julienne sticks, dropping them into water with some added lemon juice to prevent browning.

2 Blanch the julienne of celeriac in boiling salted water for 30 seconds, then drain and leave the sticks to cool in a sieve or colander.

3 Stir in the lemon juice or vinegar and cream into the rémoulade sauce.

4 Place the celeriac in a bowl and toss in the mayonnaise until the celeriac is well coated. Season to taste and serve it sprinkled with the chopped parsley.

celeriac cakes [with ham & apple]

The tart taste of Bramley apples complements celeriac's milder flavour, with ham as a savoury touch.

550g celeriac, peeled and quartered
2 tsp wholegrain mustard
1 large egg, beaten
Salt and black pepper
Vegetable oil for brushing
400g Bramley cooking apples, peeled, cored and chopped
225g thick-cut ham

Serves: 4
Prep time: 10 minutes
Cooking time: 20 minutes

Nutrients per serving: Calories 240, Carbohydrate 13g, Protein 12g, Fat 15g (saturated fat 11g)

I Cook the celeriac in lightly salted, boiling water for about 10 minutes until just tender. Drain, leave until cool, then grate coarsely with a grater or in a food processor. Mix with the mustard, egg and salt and pepper to taste.

2 Lightly brush a nonstick frying pan with oil and heat. When hot, put 2-3 tablespoons of the celeriac mixture at a time in the pan and press each down to a cake about 7.5cm in diameter. Cook for about 3 minutes until set and browned underneath. Turn the cakes over and cook on the other side for 2-3 minutes.

3 Meanwhile, put the apple into a saucepan with 2 tablespoons water, cover and cook gently, shaking the pan occasionally, until beginning to collapse but not disintegrate.

4 Put the ham onto serving plates, top with the celeriac cakes and serve with the apple.

green beans & celeriac [in a stir-fry]

Lightly steamed beans and strips of celeriac in a sweet and sour sauce make a pretty starter or party dish.

250g celeriac, cut into matchsticks
300g green beans
For the dressing:
1 tbsp groundnut or olive oil
1 tsp sesame oil
1-2 fresh red chillies, deseeded and finely sliced
4 cloves garlic, coarsely chopped
1 tbsp grated ginger
1-2 tbsp clear honey
2 tbsp soy sauce
5 tbsp cider, or wine, vinegar
Sprigs of fresh coriander to garnish

Serves: 4
Prep time: 15 minutes, plus 1-2 hours standing
Cooking time: 10-15 minutes

I Steam the celeriac for 1 minute, add the beans and steam for another 4 minutes, or until they are tender but still crisp. Then transfer them to a heatproof bowl.

2 To make the dressing, heat the oils in a wok or a heavy-based frying pan, add the chillies, garlic and ginger and stir-fry over a high heat until they start to brown – do not let them burn. Add the honey, soy sauce and vinegar and boil for 1-2 minutes until thickened.

3 Stir the dressing into the vegetables and leave to stand for 1-2 hours. Serve at room temperature, garnished with sprigs of coriander.

Nutrients per serving: Calories 83, Carbohydrate 9g, Protein 2g, Fat 4g (saturated fat 1g)

chestnut & celeriac purée

275ml vegetable stock
1 bouquet garni
500g celeriac
500g whole cooked unsweetened
    chestnuts, canned or vacuum packed
A small bunch of chives
25g butter
2 tbsp crème fraîche or natural
    fromage frais, optional
Salt and black pepper

Serves: 4
Cooking time: 30 minutes

Nutrients per serving: Calories 240,
Carbohydrate 13g, Protein 12g, Fat 15g
(saturated fat 11g)

1 Pour the vegetable stock into a large saucepan, add the bouquet garni and bring to the boil. Then reduce the heat, cover the pan and leave the stock to simmer while preparing the celeriac.

2 Peel the celeriac, cut it into 1cm dice and add them to the simmering stock. Cover and cook for 10 minutes or until softened.

3 Drain the chestnuts, if necessary, add them to the celeriac and simmer for 3-4 minutes more.

4 Meanwhile, rinse, dry and chop or snip the chives.

5 When the chestnuts and celeriac are cooked, strain them well and reserve the stock. Remove the bouquet garni and purée or blend the celeriac and chestnuts. Then return the purée to the saucepan, add the butter and place over a low heat until the butter has melted.

6 Stir in the crème fraîche or fromage frais, if using, a tablespoon at a time so the purée does not become too thin. If it is still too thick, add a little of the reserved stock, or more crème fraîche or fromage frais, to thin it slightly.

7 Taste, season with salt and black pepper, then turn the purée into a serving dish and sprinkle with the chives.

crab & celeriac salad

1 celeriac, about 450g, peeled and grated
Juice of 1 lemon
200g fresh or frozen white crab meat,
    or drained canned crab meat (from
    two 170g cans)
2-3 tbsp cider vinegar
2 tbsp runny honey
4 tsp Dijon mustard
1 tablespoon low-fat fromage frais
    (optional)
3 tbsp finely chopped fresh parsley
    or chervil
Salt and black pepper

Serves: 4-6 as a starter
Prep time: 15 minutes

1 Put the celeriac in a mixing bowl, add the lemon juice and toss briefly.

2 Pick over the crab meat to ensure there are no traces of shell or cartilage. Add to the celeriac and toss.

3 In a small bowl, whisk together the vinegar, honey, mustard, fromage frais, if using, and parsley or chervil. Add salt and pepper to taste, then add to the salad and toss. Serve at once with brown bread and green salad leaves.

Nutrients per serving, when serving 6:
Calories 80, Carbohydrate 7.5g,
Protein 7.5g, Fat 2.5g (saturated fat 0.5g)

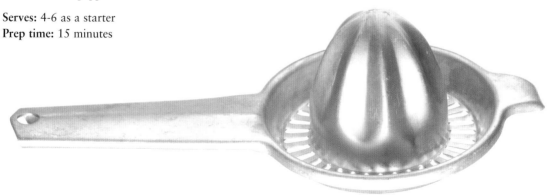

Celery is grown for its thick, crisp, juicy stalks which may be eaten raw in salads, cooked as a vegetable or used to add flavour to soups or stews. There is a hard way and an easy way to grow celery. The hard way is to grow it in trenches and the plants then have to be earthed up or wrapped individually in black polythene to blanch (whiten) the stems. The easy way is to grow self-blanching varieties which are grown at ground level and need no earthing up. Self-blanching varieties are planted in a close block so that they shield each other from the light. Only the outside plants require shading. The disadvantages of self-blanching varieties are that they are not fully hardy and their season is limited to late summer and autumn. Trench-grown celery can be left in the ground for lifting from October until February.

Celery

HARVESTING

At the end of August, start lifting self-blanching celery with a fork, piling up straw against newly exposed plants. All must be cleared before severe frosts set in. Lift celery grown in trenches from late September – about eight weeks after the first earthing up.

PREPARATION

Trim off the lower end and remove the rough outer stems completely. For cooking, cut each head in half lengthways, trim off the leaves and rinse. To cook celery, cut into 5-10cm lengths and cook in a small amount of boiling water for 15-20 minutes or steam for 20-30 minutes. Celery to be used fresh should not be left in water longer than absolutely necessary or the stems will lose their characteristic crispness.

cream of celery soup

Cooking softens the characteristic sharp flavour of celery, to make a favourite soup, sweetened a touch with sugar and nutmet. Serve with tiny croutons, nicely crisped.

2 heads of celery, approx 275g in weight
25g butter
25g flour
850ml vegetable stock
Sugar, grated nutmeg
150ml milk
150ml cream
Salt and pepper
Croutons to garnish

Serves: 4
Cooking time: 35 minutes

Nutrients per serving: Calories 216, Carbohydrate 10g, Protein 12g, Fat 14g (saturated fat 9g)

1 Trim the root ends off the celery, discard the outer stems and scrub. Peel off any tough fibres and cut off the leaves. Chop roughly, blanch in lightly salted boiling water for 7 minutes, then drain.

2 Melt the butter in a heavy-based pan. Add the celery and cook over a low heat, stirring all the time, until the celery pieces are thoroughly coated. Stir in the flour and gradually add the hot stock, stirring until it boils.

3 Season with sugar, pepper and nutmeg, cover with a lid and simmer for about 20 minutes or until the celery is tender.

4 Blend the soup in a liquidiser until smooth. Reheat the soup with the milk and blend in the cream but do not allow to boil. Season to taste.

5 Garnish with crisp croutons, sprinkled with a little nutmeg.

celery with ham & cheese

Celery packed in ham parcels is baked in a creamy cheese sauce, until the top is deliciously brown and bubbling. Serve with small new potatoes.

2 heads of celery, cleaned, trimmed and cut in half lengthways
4 slices of cooked ham
300ml white sauce
Grated nutmeg
50g grated Cheddar cheese
Salt and pepper

Serves: 4
Cooking time 35 minutes

Nutrients per serving: Calories 190, Carbohydrate 2g, Protein 14g, Fat 14g (saturated fat 8g)

1 Boil the celery in lightly salted water, including the cleaned leaves for extra flavour or to retain for later use as a garnish. Simmer for 10-15 minutes, then drain.

2 Wrap each of the celery halves in a slice of ham and arrange in a buttered ovenproof dish.

3 Make up a fairly thick white sauce, using half celery water and half single cream. Season with salt, pepper and nutmeg to taste.

4 Fold in two-thirds of the grated cheese and spoon the sauce over the celery and ham rolls. Sprinkle with the remaining cheese and bake near the top of the oven for 15-20 minutes or until brown and bubbling on top.

5 Garnish with the reserved celery leaves, if using.

pot-roasted pheasant [with celery and barley]

A bird ideal for juicy pot-roasting, pheasant is in season from the end of September to the end of January, but it is available frozen all year.

1 head of celery
70g walnuts, chopped
100g fresh white breadcrumbs
2 pheasant or chicken livers, chopped
Finely grated zest and juice of 1 unwaxed lemon
Salt and black pepper
1 egg white
2 pheasants, about 675g each
2 tbsp sunflower oil
15g butter
55g pearl barley
1 bay leaf
2 slices of streaky bacon, halved
250ml chicken stock

Serves: 4
Prep time: 20 minutes
Cooking time: 1 hour

Nutrients per serving: Calories 580, Carbohydrate 25g, Protein 41g, Fat 37g (saturated fat 9g)

1 Heat the oven to 180°C/gas 4. Finely chop one large celery stick and mix with half the walnuts, the breadcrumbs, livers and lemon zest, with salt and pepper to taste. Add enough egg white to bind the mixture, then use to stuff each pheasant cavity.

2 Heat the oil and butter in a large, flameproof casserole, add the pheasants and cook over a medium heat until lightly browned. Remove the casserole from the heat and remove the pheasants to a plate.

3 Cut the remaining celery into thick slices and add to the casserole with the pearl barley, remaining walnuts and bay leaf. Place the pheasants on top and lay the bacon slices across the breasts.

4 Add the lemon juice and stock with salt and pepper to taste. Bring to the boil, cover, then transfer to the oven for 50-60 minutes, until the pearl barley is tender and the pheasant is cooked through. Discard the bayleaf and serve at once.

celery & leek casserole

2 large heads of celery
8 leeks
250g chopped bacon
125g butter
50g flour
1l white stock
Salt and pepper

Serves: 6
Cooking time: 50 minutes

Nutrients per serving: Calories 346,
Carbohydrate 13g, Protein 17g, Fat 26g
(saturated fat 14g)

1 Prepare the celery and leeks and cut into 2.5cm pieces.

2 Fry the leeks and bacon in the butter until golden, stir in the flour and cook for about 5-10 minutes. Gradually add the stock, bring to the boil and simmer until smooth.

3 Blend in the celery and season with salt and pepper. Cook in a foil-lined casserole for 45 minutes in the oven at 180°C/gas 4.

4 Serve or cool and freeze.

celery & cucumber pickle

2 cucumbers, peeled and cubed
1 large onion, peeled and finely chopped
4 long sticks of celery, scrubbed and diced.
40g coarse salt
1 tsp turmeric
75g plain flour
50g dry mustard
125g sugar
300ml cider vinegar

Nutrients per tablespoon: Calories 35,
Carbohydrate 7g, Protein 0g, Fat 0g
(no saturated fat)

1 Mix the cucumber, onion and celery together and add the salt, leave for 30 minutes, then drain. Add the turmeric, flour, mustard and sugar to the vinegar and simmer for 2-3 minutes.

2 Add the vegetables and cook over a gentle heat for 30 minutes, stirring occasionally. Pack in hot bottling jars, seal and sterilise. The pickle should be used within three to four weeks.

celery relish

5 celery sticks, diced
2 green peppers, deseeded and finely chopped
2 red peppers, deseeded and finely chopped
500g onions, finely chopped
3 tbsp salt
625g sugar
4 tbsp mustard seeds
Large pinch turmeric
300ml distilled vinegar
5 tbsp water

Nutrients per tablespoon: Calories 30,
Carbohydrate 6g, Protein 0g, Fat 0g
(no saturated fat)

1 Mix the dry ingredients and blend into the vinegar and water.

2 Bring to the boil and add the celery, peppers and onion.

3 Simmer in a covered pan for 3 minutes and pot in hot jars, covering the vegetables with hot liquid. Seal in air-tight bottles.

A hardy perennial, native to Europe, chicory is first grown outdoors then forced and blanched inside to produce a conical head of crisp, white, faintly bitter leaves known as chicons. It is easy to grow and is a valuable winter vegetable for eating raw in salads or cooking.

HARVESTING

The plants are ready for use when the chicons are about 15cm high, which usually takes about four weeks. Cut off the chicons just before using them. If you continue to water the plants, you can grow a second, but usually inferior, crop of chicons.

Chicory

PREPARATION

Use chicory while the blanched chicons are still young and firm, before the leaves begin to turn yellow and the tops show pale green. The central hard core of chicory is slightly bitter and this becomes more pronounced with age. The bitterness can be reduced – and this is advisable for chicory to be used fresh in salads by blanching the vegetable for 2 minutes in boiling water. A little lemon juice in the water preserves the white colour. To prepare chicory, remove the outer leaves, trim the root and scoop out any core with a sharp knife. Boil for 15-20 minutes if serving cooked.

To the attentive eye, each
movement of the year
has its own beauty.

Ralph Waldo Emerson

pear, chicory & Roquefort salad

A pale and pretty salad with a great balance of flavours.

25g walnut halves
2 pears
3 heads chicory, or 1 large head radicchio
80g Roquefort cheese
For the dressing:
1 teaspoon clear honey
1 teaspoon Dijon mustard
2 tbsp white wine vinegar or cider vinegar

Serves: 4
Prep time: 15 minutes
Cooking time: 2 minutes

Nutrients per serving: Calories 165, l
Carbohydrate 11g, Protein 6g, Fat 12g
(saturated fat 5g)

1 In a heavy-based frying pan, dry-fry the walnuts for 1-2 minutes until they brown slightly. Be careful not to over-brown them or they will taste bitter. Tip the toasted nuts into a small dish and set aside to cool.

2 Core and dice the pears and place them in a salad bowl. Discard the outer leaves of the chicory or radicchio, then toss the remaining leaves in the salad bowl with the pears. Roughly chop the toasted walnuts and set them aside.

3 To make the dressing, combine the honey, mustard and vinegar in a small bowl, then pour it over the pears and leaves and toss to coat.

4 Use your fingers to crumble the cheese over the salad, then sprinkle it with the chopped walnuts and serve.

grilled chicory & beetroot

A colourful combination of grilled chicory in an orange juice and mustard dressing, mixed with sliced beetroot, that can be served warm or cold with roast or cold meat.

4 large heads of white chicory, each about
   150-175g
4 tbsp olive oil
250g cooked beetroot
1 orange
3 tbsp good-quality mayonnaise
2 tsp wholegrain mustard

Serves: 4
Cooking time: 25 minutes

Nutrients per serving: Calories 223,
Carbohydrate 10g, Protein 2g, Fat 21g
(saturated fat 3g)

1 Heat the grill. Rinse and dry the chicory, then trim the heads and remove any damaged outer leaves. Cut the heads of chicory in half, lengthways.

2 Put the halves on the grill rack, cut sides down, brush with some of the olive oil and grill for 5 minutes, about 10cm away from the heat. Turn them over, brush with the remaining olive oil and grill for 3 minutes more until the edges begin to char.

3 Meanwhile, slice the beetroot into thin discs and set them aside.

4 To make the orange and mustard dressing, squeeze 1 tablespoon of juice from the orange and stir it into the mayonnaise, then stir in the wholegrain mustard.

5 Remove the chicory from the grill. Arrange it, cut sides up, round a serving dish, like the spokes of a wheel. Spoon the orange and mustard dressing on top and lay the sliced beetroot in between.

chicory in ham cases

4 heads of chicory, cleaned, trimmed
   and cored
Salt, pepper and ground ginger
4 slices of ham or gammon
2 tsp French mustard
300ml white sauce
75g strongly flavoured grated cheese
25g butter

Serves: 4
Cooking time: 30 minutes

Nutrients per serving: Calories 266,
Carbohydrate 4g, Protein 16g, Fat 21g
(saturated fat 12g)

1 Put the chicory in a pan of lightly salted boiling water, bring back to the boil, cover and simmer gently for 10-15 minutes, or until tender. Drain thoroughly in a colander. Heat the oven to 190°C/gas 5.

2 Sprinkle the slices of ham with a little freshly ground pepper and ginger and spread lightly with mustard. Lay a head of chicory on each slice, roll up and place, seam down, in a buttered ovenproof dish.

3 Make the whitet sauce. Fold half the cheese into the warm sauce and pour over the ham and chicory. Sprinkle with the remaining cheese and dot with a little butter. Bake near the top of the oven for about 15 minutes, or until the cheese is golden-brown and bubbly.

chicory & egg salad

2-3 heads of chicory, cleaned, trimmed
   and cored
6 tbsp olive oil
2 tbsp lemon juice
Salt and pepper
3 hard-boiled eggs
3 tomatoes

Serves: 4
Chilling time: 30 minutes

Nutrients per serving: Calories 233,
Carbohydrate 4g, Protein 6g, Fat 22g
(saturated fat 4g)

1 Blanch the chicory for 2 minutes in boiling water with a little lemon juice added. Drain and refresh in cold water. Dry thoroughly.

2 Cut the chicory into thin slices, crossways. Make a dressing from the oil and lemon juice, seasoning to taste with salt and pepper. Pour the dressing over the chicory and toss well. Chill for 30 minutes.

3 Arrange the chicory on a shallow serving dish and garnish with quartered eggs and tomato wedges.

Marrows and courgettes, which are simply baby marrows, provide a considerable yield from a modest area. These days courgettes tend to be more popular than marrows and as so many come to maturity at the same time, they are ideal for freezing. Marrows and courgettes both require a sunny position and deep, rich soil. They can even be planted on an old heap of thoroughly rotted manure or compost, if this will remain undisturbed until autumn.

HARVESTING

Marrows and courgettes are best eaten in summer when the fruits are 10-14cm long (courgettes) and 23-30cm long (marrows), and when the skins yield to gentle pressure from the fingers. A few later marrows may be left on the stalk to ripen until early October and harvested just before the first frosts. They can then be hung in nets in an airy frost-free place where they will last for several weeks.

PREPARATION

Marrows and courgettes are best cooked in a minimum of water or steamed; this will retain the taste but allow excess water to evaporate. Boil marrows in a small amount of water for 10 minutes or steam for 20 minutes. Cooked marrow should be firm but not squashy. Courgettes can be cooked while or in slices. Boil for 10-15 minutes or steam sliced courgettes for about 10 minutes; they are particularly delicious in butter. If using courgettes in salads it is a good idea to blanch them for 2-3 minutes to remove any bitterness from the skin.

Courgettes & marrows

grated courgette & potato soup

Colourful courgettes, grated into potato, make a fast and healthy vegetable soup. Plenty of garlic adds flavour and may help to prevent colds and flu.

600g floury potatoes, peeled and cut into 1cm slices
2 large cloves garlic, peeled and chopped
Salt and black pepper
1 yellow and 2 green courgettes, each about 140g, coarsely grated
Extra virgin olive oil for splashing
4 large mint or basil leaves, torn
Cayenne pepper

Serves: 4
Prep time: 10 minutes
Cooking time: 20 minutes

Nutrients per serving: Calories 160, Carbohydrate 27g, Protein 5g, Fat 3g (saturated fat 1g)

1 Put the potatoes in a saucepan and cover with a litre of water. Bring to the boil, skimming off the white foam that rises to the surface. Add the garlic and cook at a fast simmer for 10-12 minutes until the potatoes are soft enough to mash.

2 Remove the pan from the heat and mash the potatoes and garlic in their cooking water, adding salt and pepper to taste.

3 Add the grated courgettes and return the soup to the heat. Cook at a low boil for a further 5 minutes until the courgettes are just soft.

4 Ladle the soup into soup plates or bowls and top each with a splash of olive oil. Sprinkle with the torn mint or basil leaves and a little cayenne pepper. Serve at once, with bread.

courgette & pea fritters

Fritters are pieces of batter containing vegetables, fruit, meat or fish. These are made with nutritious peas and courgettes, plus a little Stilton to add a rich, tangy taste.

280g frozen peas
2 large eggs, beaten
3 tbsp plain flour
25g Stilton cheese, crumbled
½ tsp chopped fresh thyme
Salt and black pepper
3 small or 2 large courgettes, about 350g in total, trimmed and coarsely grated
15g butter
½ tbsp olive oil or sunflower oil
Lemon wedges to serve

Makes about: 20 fritters
Prep time: 15 minutes
Cooking time: 15 minutes

Nutrients per fritter: Calories 44, Carbohydrate 4g, Protein 2g, Fat 2g (saturated fat 1g)

1 Cook the peas in boiling, salted water until tender. Drain thoroughly, then transfer them to a blender or food processor and purée until smooth.

2 Put the eggs in a large bowl and beat in the flour, cheese and thyme. Add salt and pepper to taste. Add the puréed peas and beat to mix, then stir in the grated courgettes.

3 Heat about half of the butter and oil in a nonstick frying pan. Add tablespoons of the courgette and pea mixture to the pan to make fritters about 6cm in diameter. Fry for about 2 minutes until golden underneath. Turn and cook for a further 2-3 minutes. Keep them warm while you cook the rest of the mixture in the remaining butter and oil.

4 Serve hot with lemon wedges as a starter or a snack.

courgette salad

4 courgettes, cleaned and trimmed
Bunch of watercress, trimmed and divided
  into small sprigs
1 small head of celery, separated and cut
  into bite sized pieces
1 green pepper, deseeded and roughly
  chopped
1 shallot, finely chopped
½ tsp each of salt and pepper
4 tbsp olive oil
2 tbsp tarragon vinegar
2 tbsp dry white wine
1 tbsp chopped parsley or 1 dsp
  chopped tarragon
Black olives to garnish

Serves: 4
Chilling time: 1 hour

Nutrients per serving: Calories 144,
Carbohydrate 5g, Protein 3g, Fat 12g
(saturated fat 2g)

1 Blanch the courgettes in lightly salted boiling water for 3 minutes. Drain and refresh in cold water then leave to cool.

2 Cut the cooled courgettes crossways into thin slices. Put in a salad bowl with the watercress, celery, green pepper and shallot and blend well.

3 Stir the salt and pepper with the oil, then add the vinegar, white wine and parsley or tarragon. Blend the dressing well, pour over the salad ingredients and toss to give them an even gloss. Chill in the fridge for an hour.

4 Garnish the salad with whole black olives.

Sicilian caponata

Courgettes, peppers, tomatoes and aubergine are cooked together with a little white wine and then chilled to make a delicious salad, typical of southern Italy.

500g courgettes, cleaned, trimmed and
  cut into thin slices
1 green pepper, deseeded and diced
2 onions, peeled and finely chopped
1 aubergine, cut crossways into
  narrow slices
6 large tomatoes, skinned and roughly
  chopped
100ml olive oil
150ml dry white wine
Sugar
Salt and pepper

Serves: 4
Cooking time: 1 hour

Nutrients per serving: Calories 282,
Carbohydrate 16g, Protein 5g, Fat 20g
(saturated fat 3g)

1 Heat the oil in a heavy-based pan and fry the onions for 3-5 minutes, until soft and golden. Add the courgettes, green pepper and aubergine slices. Stir continuously for about 3 minutes until the vegetables are softening, then add the tomatoes, olive oil and half the wine.

2 Cook the vegetable mixture over a very gentle heat until thoroughly combined, stirring frequently to prevent burning and gradually adding the rest of the wine. Season to taste with sugar, salt and pepper.

3 Serve as a first course hot or cold, with crusty bread.

Gardening is something you learn by doing — and by making mistakes.

Carol Stocker

courgettes, apples & persillade

Persillade, a wonderfully scented combination of chopped parsley and garlic, contributes a classic French flavouring to this fruity dish of fried courgette, tomato, onion and apple.

1 red or regular onion
4 tbsp olive oil
1 medium apple
1 medium tomato
500g small courgettes
Salt and black pepper
A medium bunch of parsley
1 clove garlic

Serves: 4
Cooking time: 25 minutes

Nutrients per serving: Calories 150, Carbohydrate 9g, Protein 3g, Fat 12g (saturated fat 2g)

1 Peel and thinly slice the onion. Heat 2 tablespoons of the oil in a frying pan, add the onion and cook over a low heat for 7-8 minutes, until it has softened.

2 Rinse and core the apple, chop it into cubes, then rinse and cube the tomato. When the onion is soft, stir in the apple and tomato and cook them over a low heat for 5 minutes, stirring them occasionally.

3 Trim and rinse the courgettes, slice them lengthways into thin strips, then cut the strips into 5cm batons. Sprinkle them with salt and toss with your hands. Heat the remaining oil in another frying pan and fry the courgettes over a moderate heat until they release their moisture. Increase the heat and continue cooking until all of the liquid has evaporated, shaking the pan to make sure the courgettes do not burn.

4 Reduce the heat, then add the apple, tomato and onion mixture to the courgettes and leave to simmer for 5-6 minutes.

5 While the mixture is simmering, rinse, dry and chop enough parsley to give 4 tablespoons, then peel and crush the garlic and mix it with the parsley to make the persillade. Stir the persillade into the frying pan with the vegetables. Simmer for a few minutes to cook the garlic, then grind in some black pepper and add some more salt if necessary. Serve immediately.

stuffed marrow rings

1 marrow, cut crossways into 5cm thick slices, peeled and deseeded
Salt and pepper
75g butter
1 large onion, finely chopped
250g minced beef
4 large tomatoes, skinned and roughly chopped
1 dsp chopped marjoram
50g boiled rice

Serves: 4
Cooking time: 1 hour

Nutrients per serving: Calories 328, Carbohydrate 22g, Protein 22g, Fat 18g (saturated fat 4g)

1 Heat the oven to 190°C/gas 5. Arrange the marrow rings in a single layer in a buttered ovenproof dish and sprinkle them with salt and pepper

2 Melt two-thirds of the butter in a pan and fry the onion over moderate heat until soft. Crumble in the minced beef and continue frying until the mixture is brown and separated into grains.

3 Add the tomatoes to the pan, together with the marjoram. Continue cooking until all the ingredients are well blended.

4 Bind this stuffing with as much of the boiled rice as it will absorb without becoming too solid. Season to taste with salt and pepper.

5 Spoon the stuffing into the marrow rings and dot with flakes of the remaining butter. Cover the dish tightly with a lid or foil and bake for 45 minutes.

6 Serve with a hot tomato sauce.

twice-baked courgette [& goat's cheese puffs]

These little courgette soufflé puffs are twice-baked, so you can cook them in advance, then simply reheat them when you need them.

25g unsalted butter, plus extra for greasing
2 tbsp olive oil
2 courgettes, roughly chopped
35g plain flour
300ml semi-skimmed milk, warmed
200g fresh goat's cheese, crumbled
1 tbsp chopped fresh thyme
3 eggs, separated
Black pepper
6 tbsp half-fat crème fraîche
6 thin slices of dry-cured ham

Serves: 6
Prep time: 20 minutes
Cooking time: 40 minutes

Nutrients per serving: Calories 284, Carbohydrate 8g, Protein 17g, Fat 20g (saturated fat 10g)

1 Heat the oven to 180°C/gas 4. Lightly butter six ramekin dishes. Heat the oil in a frying pan over a medium heat. Add the courgettes and cook, covered, for 5 minutes or until just tender. Transfer to a sieve and set aside for a few minutes to drain. Transfer to a blender or food processor and work until finely chopped.

2 Melt the butter in a large saucepan, add the flour and cook, stirring, for 1 minute. Whisk in the milk, then stir until the mixture has boiled and thickened. Remove from the heat and mix in 175g of the goat's cheese, the thyme, courgettes, egg yolks and some pepper.

3 In a separate, clean bowl, beat the egg whites until soft peaks form. Using a large metal spoon, lightly fold the egg whites into the cheese mixture until well combined, then spoon into the prepared ramekins.

4 Place the filled ramekins in a baking dish and add enough hot water to come halfway up the sides of the ramekins.

5 Bake for 20 minutes or until puffed and set. Remove from the oven and set aside to cool, until needed.

6 When nearly ready to serve, run a sharp knife around the sides of the soufflés and invert onto a deep serving dish. Spoon a tablespoon of crème fraîche over each soufflé. Top with a slice of ham and the remaining goat's cheese.

7 Return to the oven and bake for a further 15 minutes or until puffed and golden. Serve at once with a lightly dressed rocket salad.

Let my words, like vegetables, be tender and sweet.

Anon

pork with courgettes, [Spanish-style]

4 lean pork steaks, trimmed of excess fat
Salt, pepper and paprika
1 onion, peeled and finely chopped
2 tbsp oil
375g tomatoes, skinned and roughly chopped
375g courgettes, thinly sliced
1 tbsp tomato paste
1 tsp sugar
150ml chicken stock
25g butter
Chopped chives to garnish

Serves: 4
Cooking time: 65 minutes

Nutrients per serving: Calories 335,
Carbohydrate 8g, Protein 36g, Fat 18g
(saturated fat 6g)

I Heat the oven to 160°C/gas 3. Season the pork steaks with salt, pepper and paprika.

2 Heat the oil in a pan and seal the pork steaks until they are brown on both sides – about 2 minutes on each side. Lift into a lightly buttered ovenproof dish. Fry the onion in the oil until golden, then spoon it over the steaks.

3 Lay the tomatoes over the onion. Arrange the slices of courgette over the tomatoes. Blend the tomato paste and sugar with the chicken stock; pour over the contents of the casserole until it comes just below the courgettes.

4 Cover the dish with a lid and bake in the oven for 50 minutes. Remove the lid from the dish, brush the courgettes with melted butter and return to the oven for a further 15 minutes or until the courgettes have browned.

5 Garnish with finely chopped chives and serve with noodles or rice.

marrow stuffed [with apricots & bacon]

1 medium to small marrow, about 1.5kg
6-8 rashers thinly cut streaky bacon
1 tbsp sunflower oil
1 onion, chopped
70g fresh brown breadcrumbs
85g flaked almonds, lightly toasted
55g ready-to-eat dried apricots, chopped
1 sprig of parsley, chopped
1 tsp chopped fresh thyme
225ml vegetable stock
Salt and black pepper
For the sauce:
1 tsp English mustard
2 tsp chopped fresh herbs
3 tbsp low-fat fromage frais
Brown rice, to serve

Serves: 4
Prep time: 20 minutes
Cooking time: about 1 hour

Nutrients per serving: Calories 434,
Carbohydrate 25g, Protein 16g, Fat 30g
(saturated fat 7g)

I Heat the oven to 200°C/gas 6. Trim the marrow, cutting off about 1cm from the top to remove the stalk. Lay the marrow on its side and slice off the top 2.5cm to make a lid. Using a spoon, scoop out the seeds and pith, leaving a lining of flesh.

2 Grill the bacon for 3-4 minutes until very crisp. Cool slightly and crumble or finely chop into a bowl. Heat the oil in a small frying pan, add the onion and fry until soft. Add to the bacon.

3 Add the breadcrumbs, almonds, chopped apricots and herbs to the bacon and onion. Stir in about 85ml of the stock so that the breadcrumbs are moist but not soggy. Add salt and pepper to taste.

4 Spoon the stuffing loosely into the cavity of the marrow and replace the lid. Place in a shallow baking dish and add the remaining stock to the dish. Cover tightly with foil and bake in the oven for 45-50 minutes until tender. (Pierce the flesh with a knife to check.)

5 Remove the foil and marrow lid and pour the cooking juices into a small pan. Place the marrow, uncovered, under a hot grill for 3-4 minutes until the crumbs are lightly golden.

6 Meanwhile, gently heat the stock with the mustard and herbs. When hot, remove from the heat and stir in the fromage frais.

7 To serve, cut the marrow into thick slices. Arrange on warmed plates and serve with the mustard sauce and brown rice.

There are two main categories of cucumbers, generally described as ridge or frame. Ridge cucumbers are so-called because it was for many years the practice to grow these outdoor varieties on ridges of loam and compost. Frame cucumbers must be grown under glass, either in a greenhouse or a coldframe. The advantage to growing cucumbers under glass is that you can obtain ripe cucumbers in May or June, many weeks before the outdoor varieties are available.

Cucumbers

HARVESTING

Although it is tempting to see how large your cucumbers will grow, they will taste much better if harvested before they reach their maximum size. It is equally important not to cut the fruits too early. As a rough guide, a mature cucumber should have parallel sides. One whose sides dwindle to a point is not developing properly and may have a bitter flavour. Depending on the variety, outdoor cucumbers can be harvested from the end of July to at least the middle of September. Frame plants have a longer season, from early July to the end of September. All cucumbers are at their best immediately after cutting.

PREPARATION

Cucumbers are usually used fresh in salads or in dressings. It can however, be cooked as a separate vegetable dish and is an excellent base for chilled summer soups. For use in salads, wash and dry the cucumber and trim of both flower and stalk end. Don't peel unless the skin is very rough or bruised. Cut crossways into narrow slices or lengthways into 2.5cm chunks. Cook sliced or diced cucumber in boiling water for 10 minutes, steam for about 15 minutes or bake peeled thickly sliced cucumber with butter and fresh herbs in the oven for 30 minutes at 190˚C/gas 5.

cucumber casserole

This dish is reminiscent of moussaka and can be served with a green salad and a chilled sour-cream sauce.

2 cucumbers, peeled and sliced crossways
    into thin slices
6 tbsp olive oil
1 large onion, finely chopped
500g minced veal, lamb or beef
1 dsp tomato paste
150ml water
Salt and pepper
300ml white sauce
Paprika

Serves: 4
Cooking time: 1 hour

Nutrients per serving: Calories 500,
Carbohydrate 7g, Protein 35g, Fat 37g
(saturated fat 13g)

1 Heat the oil in a pan and fry the cucumber slices quickly for a few minutes. Lift them out and drain on kitchen paper.

2 Add the onion to the oil and fry over a gentle heat for about 5 minutes or until soft but not coloured. Stir in the minced meat and continue frying until it is brown and sealed. Add the tomato paste and water, and season to taste with salt and pepper.

3 Cover with a lid and simmer for about 20 minutes or until most of the liquid has been absorbed. Butter an ovenproof dish, and line the base with cucumber slices. Cover with a layer of meat and continue with these layers, finishing with cucumber. Heat the oven to 180°C/gas 4.

4 Make up a fairly thick white sauce and season with paprika. Spoon this into the dish and bake in the oven for about 35 minutes or until it is bubbling and brown.

chilled cucumber soup

1 large cucumber, peeled and diced into
    tiny cubes
Salt and pepper
300ml natural yoghurt
150ml single cream
1 garlic clove, crushed
2 tbsp olive oil
2 tbsp white wine vinegar
40g chopped walnuts

Serves: 4
Chilling time: 1-2 hours

Nutrients per serving: Calories 220,
Carbohydrate 5g, Protein 5g, Fat 21g
(saturated fat 6g)

1 Put the cumber cubes on a flat dish, sprinkle lightly with salt and leave for
30 minutes. Rinse the cubes and drain thoroughly.

2 In a bowl, blend the yoghurt with the cream, garlic, oil and vinegar and
season to taste with salt and pepper. Fold in the cucumber and just over half
the chopped walnuts; blend thoroughly, then chill in the fridge for about
2 hours.

3 Serve sprinkled with the remaining chopped walnuts.

cucumber in dill dressing

1 cucumber
Salt and pepper
75ml soured cream
75ml natural yoghurt
1 heaped tbsp dill, finely chopped

Serves: 4
Chilling time 30 minutes

Nutrients per serving: Calories 63,
Carbohydrate 4g, Protein 2g, Fat 4g
(saturated fat 3g)

1 Wash the cucumber but do not peel it unless the skin is bruised or rough.
Cut it crossways into paper-thin slices, arrange these on a flat dish and
sprinkle with a tablespoon of salt. Chill in the fridge for 30 minutes to let
the water drain out of the cucumber.

2 Rinse and dry the cucumber slices. Blend the soured cream and yoghurt, stir
in the dill and fold in the cucumber slices. Season to taste.

cucumber & pepper salad

1 cucumber, peeled and coarsely grated
1 tbsp tarragon vinegar
1 tsp salt
1 green pepper, trimmed, deseeded and
    roughly chopped
1 small onion, finely chopped
150ml natural yoghurt
Pepper and dry mustard
1 tbsp coriander seeds to garnish

Serves: 4

Nutrients per serving: Calories 61,
Carbohydrate 8g, Protein 3g, Fat 1.5g
(saturated fat 1g)

1 Sprinkle the grated cucumber with salt and leave for 30 minutes to draw
out the water, then drain.

2 Mix the pepper and onion with the drained cucumber. Season the yoghurt
to taste with pepper and mustard, spoon over the cucumber, pepper and
onion mixture and blend thoroughly.

3 Sprinkle with coriander seeds before serving.

pickled cucumber

3 cucumbers, total weight approx 1kg
Coarse salt
Spiced vinegar

Nutrients per tablespoon: Calories 25,
Carbohydrate 5g, Protein 0g, Fat 0g
(no saturated fat)

1 Wash the cucumbers, wipe them dry, but do not peel. Cut in half lengthways and chop into slices 1cm thick. Layer with the salt in a deep dish and leave for 24 hours.

2 Drain off the liquid, rinse the cucumbers in cold water and drain thoroughly again. Pack the cucumbers into clean jars, cover with hot, spiced vinegar and seal at once. The pickle will be ready to eat in a week.

cucumber, radish & melon salad

A wonderful combination of fruit, vegetables and crunchy almonds mixed with a honey and walnut oil dressing, this salad is an ideal accompaniment to cold meat and poultry.

500g piece of watermelon or honeydew
   melon
100g cucumber
Salt
Olive oil for frying
25g flaked almonds
100g fresh bean sprouts
150g radishes
4 spring onions
A small bunch of watercress
For the dressing:
1½ tsp clear honey
3 tbsp walnut oil
1 tbsp cider vinegar
Black pepper

Serves: 4
Cooking time: 20 minutes

Nutrients per serving: Calories 231,
Carbohydrate 15g, Protein 4g, Fat 18g
(saturated fat 2g)

1 Deseed and dice the melon, then rinse, dry and dice the cucumber. Put both into a colander, add a little salt and toss them together. Place a saucer on top and leave to drain.

2 Heat a little oil in a frying pan and fry the almonds until golden, then drain on kitchen paper.

3 Rinse the bean sprouts and drain them well, then rinse, dry and trim the radishes and spring onions. Quarter the radishes, slice the onions and mix all three together in a salad bowl.

4 Whisk the dressing ingredients together and pour over the salad.

5 Trim the watercress, rinse and dry it and arrange it in a shallow serving dish. Add the melon and cucumber to the salad bowl, toss the salad gently, then spoon it onto the watercress. Scatter the almonds over the top to serve.

Currants

BLACKCURRANTS

These hardy shrubs do well in any part of the country. They are easy to grow and long-lived. Blackcurrants thrive in full sunshine but will also do well if planted in slightly shaded positions in well-drained soils.

HARVESTING

Pick blackcurrants only when they are properly ripe, a week or so after they have turned black. The fruits at the top of each cluster usually ripen first.

REDCURRANTS & WHITE CURRANTS

These delicious fruits are related to blackcurrants but do not have the same growing habit and so are cultivated in a different way. They can be grown as bushes or as cordons, the latter being ideal for the small garden as they occupy much less space and can be grown as an ornamental edge or divider. For the space they occupy, red and white currants produce a large amount of fruit from mid June to late July and like blackcurrants are long-lived plants.

HARVESTING

Pick the fruits as soon as they are ripe and use immediately as they do not keep for long.

PREPARATION

Always use the fruits as soon as possible after harvesting as they tend to deteriorate quite rapidly. Like all soft fruits they should be handled carefully to avoid bruising. The blossom and stalk ends are usually snipped off with scissors. The berries are easily stripped from the stalks with a fork. Wash the currants by placing them in a colander and dipping this in lots of cold water. Drain thoroughly before using the fruit.

American blackcurrant tart

500-750g blackcurrants, rinsed and
    drained
1½ tbsp cornflour
175g sugar
Shortcrust pastry made with 250g flour
    2 tbsp lemon juice
25g butter
1 egg

Serves: 6
Cooking time: 45 minutes

Nutrients per serving: Calories 556,
Carbohydrate 63g, Protein 5g, Fat 34g
(saturated fat 17g)

1 Place the blackcurrants in a bowl. Blend the cornflour and sugar with 75ml water until smooth and stir this thickening into the blackcurrants. Leave to stand for 15 minutes. Heat the oven to 190°C/gas 5.

2 Line a 20cm pie dish with the prepared pastry, spoon the blackcurrant mixture over it, sprinkle with lemon juice and dot with butter. Use the pastry trimmings to make a lattice pattern over the top, brush with the lightly beaten egg and dust with a little sugar.

3 Bake the tart at the centre of the oven for about 45 minutes or until the pastry is golden brown.

4 Serve lukewarm or cold, with either a bowl of whipped cream or a jug of fresh cream.

blackcurrant pudding

500g blackcurrants, rinsed and drained
250g self-raising flour
175g caster sugar
100-125g shredded suet [veg alternative]
150ml milk

Serves: 4
Cooking time: 2 hours

Nutrients per serving: Calories 600,
Carbohydrate 93g, Protein 8g, Fat 25g
(saturated fat 13g)

1 Sift the flour into a bowl, blend in half the sugar and all the suet, and mix to a stiff dough with the milk. Knead the dough on a floured surface until smooth and elastic. Leave to rest for 15 minutes under an inverted bowl.

2 Grease a 1l pudding basin. Roll out three-quarters of the suet pastry to ½cm thick, and line the basin with this. Arrange half the currants over the pastry, add the remaining sugar and top with the rest of the currants.

3 Roll out the reserved suet pastry to form a lid to fit the basin and seal the edges. Cover the basin with buttered, greaseproof paper, or foil or a cloth and tie securely in place with string, leaving room for expansion.

4 Place the basin in a pan of boiling water and steam for 2 hours, topping up with hot water as necessary.

5 Turn out the pudding and serve warm with custard.

currant mousse

500g mixed red and blackcurrants,
725ml water
4 tbsp cornflour
250g sugar
Vanilla sugar
Single cream to serve

Serves: 4
Cooking time: 20-25 minutes
Chilling time: 1 hour

Nutrients per serving: Calories 330,
Carbohydrate 86g, Protein 1.5g, Fat 0g
(no saturated fat)

1 Drain and rinse the currants. Put them in a pan with the water and bring them to the boil over a gentle heat. Simmer gently for about 10 minutes or until the currants burst and the juices flow freely. Strain through a sieve lined with muslin and leave the juices to drip through for 30 minutes.

2 Measure the juice and if necessary make up to 1l with cold water. Blend the cornflour with a little of the juice and put the remainder in a pan. Stir in the blended cornflour and bring the mixture to the boil, stirring continuously until it thickens.

3 Remove from the heat; add the sugar, and also about 1 teaspoon of vanilla sugar to taste. Pour into a serving dish and sprinkle the top with a little sugar to prevent a skin forming.

4 Serve lukewarm or chilled with cream.

summer pudding

The glorious deep red colour of a summer pudding celebrates the success of a soft fruit harvest. Use your favourite berries – or whatever is lavishly in season.

6-8 slices stale, crustless white bread, approx 1cm thick
750g mixed red and black currants, trimmed, rinsed and drained. You may also add other soft fruits including blackberries, raspberries and blueberries
100g sugar

Serves: 4
Cooking time: 10 minutes
Chilling time: 8 hours

Nutrients per serving: Calories 230, Carbohydrate 55g, Protein 4.5g, Fat 0.5g (no saturated fat). High fibre

1 Line and base and sides of a 1l pudding basin with the bread slices cut to shape so as to fit together closely. Set some of the bread aside for the top.

2 Put the currants in a pan with the sugar and bring to the boil over a very gentle heat. Simmer for a few minutes only, until the sugar has dissolved and the juices begin to run.

3 Remove the pan from the heat, reserve 2 tablespoons of the juices and spoon the remainder, with the fruit, into the prepared basin. Cover the top closely with bread.

4 Fix a saucer or plate over the pudding inside the basin and place a heavy weight on top. Chill in the fridge for 8 hours.

5 Turn the pudding out, upside-down, onto a serving dish and pour the reserved fruit juice over any parts of the bread not soaked through and coloured. Serve with a bowl of lightly whipped cream.

Wisdom is oftentimes nearer when we stoop than when we soar.

William Wordsworth

redcurrant compôte

500g redcurrants, rinsed and drained
200g caster sugar
1-2 tbsp brandy
150ml single cream

Serves: 4
Chilling time: 1 hour

Nutrients per serving: Calories 312,
Carbohydrate 59g, Protein 2.5g, Fat 7g
(saturated fat 4.5g)

1 Put alternate layers of currants and sugar in a bowl. Leave in a warm room for several hours until the sugar has dissolved then stir in the brandy.

2 Spoon the redcurrants, with their juice, into serving glasses, and chill the compôte in the fridge for about 1 hour.

blackcurrant vinegar

2kg blackcurrants, rinsed and dried
2l good-quality wine vinegar

Nutrients per tablespoon: Calories 10,
Carbohydrate 2g, Protein 0g, Fat 0g
(no saturated fat)

1 Put the blackcurrants in a bowl, bruise them with a wooden spoon and add the wine vinegar.

2 Cover the bowl with a cloth and leave it to stand for three or four days, stirring twice a day.

3 Strain the juice through clean muslin, put it into a pan and boil for 10 minutes.

4 Pour the fruit vinegar into warmed bottles and seal.

5 For a sweet vinegar, add 1kg granulated sugar to each 1l strained liquid just before boiling.

6 Use the vinegars, diluted, as a summer drink, or undiluted, as a flavouring for puddings.

blackcurrant wine

1kg blackcurrants
250g raisins
1kg sugar
1 Campden tablet
1 tsp pectin-destroying enzyme
4l water
Burgundy yeast and nutrient
Saccharin

Nutrients per small glass: Calories 113,
Carbohydrate 6.5g, Protein 0g, Fat 0g
(no saturated fat)

1 Pour the water into a bin and add the pectin-destroying enzyme and a crushed Campden tablet.

2 Wash the blackcurrants, crush them into a mash or cut them up and drop them into the bin. Cover the bin and leave it in a warm place for 24 hours.

3 Activate the yeast in a starter bottle. Add the raisins, nutrient and yeast to the mash, re-cover the bin and place it in a warm place for 4-5 days.

4 Press and strain the pulp and add the sugar, dissolving this first in warm water.

5 Pour the strained mixture into a fermentation jar, top up with cold water and fit an airlock to the jar. Tie on a label describing the contents and store the jar at room temperature until fermentation is complete.

6 Add saccharin to taste when fermentation is complete and the wine has been siphoned into a storage jar.

There are two distinct varieties of fennel: the tall perennial herb cultivated for the flavour of its leaves, seeds and stems and the usually smaller Florence fennel, a biennial, grown mainly for its swollen stem root and used as a vegetable. It has a delicate aniseed flavour with tightly compressed fleshy leaves, like an onion. The stem base of Florence fennel and finocchio, may be chopped raw into salads, but is more usually simmered in a stock. The ferny leaves make an attractive backdrop in a herb or vegetable bed and look pretty as a garnish. Plant in a sunny position in well-drained soil that has been improved with well-rotted manure and a dressing of general fertiliser.

HARVESTING

Gather the swollen stem bases for cooking in late summer or early autumn.

PREPARATION

To prepare Florence fennel, trim away the leafy top stems close to the root. Do not discard the leaves which can be added to the cooking liquid for extra flavour or used, finely chopped, as a garnish. Trim the root base and wash the fennel roots in cold water. For salads, cut the fennel roots in half lengthways and then across into thin slices. For cooking, leave fennel roots in halves and cook in a small amount of boiling water for 15-20 minutes, depending on size.

Fennel, Florence

mussel & fennel broth

The delicate aniseed flavour of fennel complements mineral-rich mussels in this tasty broth.

4 tbsp olive oil
1 fennel bulb, chopped
2 leeks, about 200g, finely sliced
1 large clove garlic, crushed
300ml medium-dry white wine
300ml fish stock
1kg live mussels
150ml low-fat crème fraîche
Black pepper
2 tbsp chopped parsley to serve

Serves: 4
Prep time: 15 minutes
Cooking time: 10 minutes

Nutrients per serving: Calories 290,
Carbohydrate 4g, Protein 15g, Fat 18g
(saturated fat 5g)

1 Heat the oil in a large saucepan, add the fennel, leeks and garlic and cook over a low heat for 5 minutes until the leeks wilt. Add the wine and stock, remove from the heat and set aside.

2 Meanwhile, scrub the mussels if necessary, scraping off any barnacles and pulling away the beards. Discard any with damaged shells, and any that do not close when tapped sharply on the edge of the sink.

3 Bring the wine and vegetable mixture to the boil, then add the mussels. Cook, covered, over a high heat for 3-4 minutes, shaking the pan from time to time, until the shells open.

4 Using a slotted spoon, remove the opened mussels to a bowl, discarding any that have not opened.

5 Pick the mussels from the shells, leaving some in for decoration, if desired, and return them to the broth. Heat gently, whisk in the crème fraîche and add black pepper to taste. Transfer to warmed bowls, sprinkle with parsley and serve with homemade soda bread.

fennel with barley & leek

A risotto with a twist combines the faintly liquorice-like crunch of fennel with braised barley and for extra colour, finely sliced leek and tomatoes.

1 large head of fennel
Juice of 1 lemon
125g pearl barley
Salt and black pepper
3 tbsp olive oil
2 slim leeks, sliced
2 cloves garlic, crushed or finely chopped
3 tomatoes, skinned and chopped
1 tbsp chopped parsley

Serves: 4
Prep time: 20 minutes
Cooking time: 40 minutes

Nutrients per serving: Calories 216,
Carbohydrate 30g, Protein 4g, Fat 9g
(saturated fat 1.5g)

1 Roughly chop the head of fennel and put it into a bowl of cold water with half of the lemon juice.

2 Wash the barley in a sieve under a cold tap, put it into a saucepan and cover generously with cold water. Bring it to the boil, then drain the barley and discard the water.

3 Rinse the barley and return it to the pan with a litre of cold water. Return to the boil, add salt and simmer for 30-35 minutes until the barley is tender. Drain, mix in the remaining lemon juice and keep warm in a serving bowl.

4 Drain the fennel and pat it dry. Heat the oil in a wok or large frying pan and stir-fry the fennel for a few minutes before adding the leeks and garlic. Continue stir-frying them for a further 2 minutes then add the tomatoes and cook for 3-4 minutes.

5 Mix the hot vegetable mixture into the barley, season to taste and scatter the chopped parsley all over.

braised fennel

The distinctive aniseed flavour of fennel makes it a pleasing partner to most fish or chicken main courses.

900g fennel
1 tbsp butter
150ml dry white wine
2 bay leaves, optional
1 clove garlic, crushed
4 sprigs fresh thyme
300ml vegetable stock
Salt and black pepper
2 tbsp chopped fresh dill and 1 tbsp
   chopped fresh thyme to garnish

Serves: 4
Prep time: 15 minutes
Cooking time: 30-40 minutes

Nutrients per serving: Calories 79,
Carbohydrate 4g, Protein 2g, Fat 4g
(saturated fat 2g)

1 Discard the tough outer layer of the fennel, then cut it lengthways into 1cm thick slices. Melt 1 teaspoon of the butter in a deep heavy-based frying pan over a medium-low heat and fry the fennel, in batches if necessary, for 3 minutes on each side, or until it is golden, adding a little butter with each batch.

2 Return all the fennel to the pan, add the wine and boil for 5 minutes, or until only a small amount of the liquid remains.

3 Add the bay leaves, if using, garlic, thyme and stock and bring to the boil. Reduce the heat to low, cover and simmer for 15-20 minutes until the fennel is tender.

4 Season to taste, scatter with the chopped dill and thyme and serve.

Gooseberries

Ever since Tudor times, gooseberry fools, tarts, crumbles, jellies and pies have been a feature of the British menu. They are easy to grow, do well in any part of Britain and may be grown as bushes or cordons. If different varieties are planted, a succession of berries may be obtained from May to August. The different varieties may be sweet or acid, white, yellow, green or pink. The sweet fruits may be eaten for dessert, while the acid ones are more suitable for cooking, and for jam and wine. Gooseberries do well in full sun or partial shade but need a site protected from cold winds and late frosts. Although any well-drained soil is suitable, best results come from planting in a deep, well-manured loam.

HARVESTING

Thin heavy cropping plants from late May onwards, removing some berries from each branch so that ideally there are 75mm intervals between those remaining, which will then grow larger. The unripe picked fruit can be used for cooking or preserving.

PREPARATION

Sweet red or yellow gooseberries are usually served fresh as a dessert fruit. Smaller and harder acid gooseberries are suitable only for cooking. They can be used as fillings for pies and puddings, for creamed desserts such as fools and for sweet and savoury sauces. To prepare gooseberries, snip off flower and stalk ends with scissors. Wash them carefully in a colander, dipping this into several times in cold water. Allow the fruit to dry on absorbent kitchen paper.

huffed pheasant [with gooseberries]

1 small leek, thinly sliced
125g gooseberries
25g breadcrumbs
1 tbsp chopped thyme
Salt and black pepper
4 pheasant breasts, about 125g each
4 slices of lean back bacon
250g self-raising flour
125g light vegetable suet
1 egg, beaten, plus extra for brushing
2 tbsp lemon juice

Serves: 4
Prep time: 30 minutes
Cooking time: 30-35 minutes

Nutrients per serving: Calories 500,
Carbohydrate 54g, Protein 35g, Fat 37g
(saturated fat 18g)

1 Heat the oven to 200°C/gas 6. Put the leek, gooseberries, breadcrumbs, thyme and a pinch of salt and pepper in a bowl and mix.

2 Remove the skin from each pheasant breast and cut a deep pocket in the side. Spoon the stuffing mixture in, packing it firmly. Wrap a slice of bacon around each.

3 Sift the flour into a bowl and stir in the suet and some salt and pepper. Make a well in the centre and add the egg, lemon juice and enough cold water to mix to a soft, but not sticky, dough.

4 Divide into four and roll out each to about a 15cm round, depending on the size of the pheasant breasts. Place a pheasant breast on each, brush the edges with egg and fold over to enclose. Pinch the edges to seal, place on a baking sheet and brush with egg to glaze.

5 Bake for 20 minutes, until the pastry is firm and golden brown, then reduce to 180°C/gas 4 and cook for a further 10-15 minutes. Serve warm or cold, with a crisp salad and pickles.

foil-baked salmon trout
[with gooseberry & elderflower sauce]

1 salmon trout, about 1.3kg, cleaned
   with head on
Salt and black pepper
2 sprigs of fresh dill
Vegetable oil for brushing
4 tbsp dry white wine
4 courgettes, trimmed
For the sauce:
5 tbsp low-fat mayonnaise
5 tbsp set low-fat yoghurt
5 tbsp lightly sweetened, cooked
   gooseberries
2-4 tsp elderflower cordial
1 tbsp chopped fresh dill

Serves: 6-8
Prep time: 30 minutes
Cooking time: 40 minutes, plus
   1½ hours cooling

Nutrients per serving, when serving 8:
Calories 275, Carbohydrate 5g,
Protein 40g, Fat 10g (saturated fat 1.5g)

1 Heat the oven to 180°C/gas 4. Rinse the fish, flushing out any blood left inside it, then pat dry with kitchen paper. Season inside and out with salt and pepper and put the sprigs of dill inside the fish.

2 Spread a large sheet of foil on a baking sheet or inside a roasting tin and brush with oil. Put the fish in the middle, splash over the wine and parcel the fish loosely, folding the foil into a tight seam and twisting the ends. Bake in the middle of the oven for 40 minutes, then remove and leave to cool in its foil.

3 Using a vegetable peeler, shave the courgettes lengthways into ribbons, discarding the outer slices. Bring a saucepan of salted water to the boil and add the courgette ribbons. As soon as the water returns to the boil, drain into a colander and run under the cold tap for 2 minutes to cool. Set aside in a bowl of cold water.

4 For the sauce, put the mayonnaise, yoghurt and gooseberries in a bowl and mix, adding elderflower cordial to taste. Season with salt and pepper, and more sugar if needed.

5 To serve, remove the head and skin from the fish, if preferred. Remove the dill sprigs from inside and place the fish on a long, oval platter.

6 Drain the courgette ribbons and pat them dry gently but thoroughly on several changes of kitchen paper. Arrange them around the fish. Add the chopped dill to the sauce and serve separately in a bowl, with the fish, new potatoes and salad.

curd tart [with glazed gooseberries & grapes]

A traditional recipe, curd tart is creamy and rich, but made with low-fat curd cheese.

150g plain flour
75g butter
400g curd cheese
Grated zest and juice of 1 unwaxed lemon
75g caster sugar
2 tbsp self-raising flour
55g currants
2 eggs
4 tbsp semi-skimmed milk
For the glazed gooseberries and grapes:
450g dessert gooseberries
300ml unsweetened apple juice
350g seedless green grapes

Serves: 8
Prep time: 25 minutes, plus 30 minutes
  chilling
Cooking time: 1¼ hours

Nutrients per serving: Calories 367,
Carbohydrate 47g, Protein 7g, Fat 18g
(saturated fat 10g)

1 Put the plain flour in a bowl and rub in the butter until the mixture resembles fine breadcrumbs. Stir in 3 tablespoons cold water until the mixture clumps together, then bring the pastry together by hand.

2 Roll out the pastry on a lightly floured surface and use to line a 23cm round dish, 3cm deep. Chill for 30 minutes. Heat the oven to 200°C/gas 6.

3 Line the chilled pastry case with greaseproof paper and baking beans and bake for 10 minutes. Remove from the oven and set aside. Reduce the oven temperature to 160°C/gas 3.

4 Beat the curd cheese with the lemon zest and juice, and the sugar. Sift the flour over the mixture, then beat it in. Add the currants, eggs and milk, and beat until combined. Pour the mixture into the pastry case, then bake for 40-45 minutes until set and lightly browned. Set aside until warm.

5 To glaze the fruit, put the gooseberries in a saucepan and add the apple juice. Bring slowly to a simmer and poach the fruit for about 1 minute to soften it very slightly. Transfer the gooseberries to a bowl.

6 Boil the apple juice until reduced to about 50ml of dark golden syrup. Add the grapes to the gooseberries and pour over the apple syrup. Mix well. Serve the curd tart in slices with spoonfuls of the glazed fruit arranged on top.

gooseberry granita

This delicately tart water ice, with a crystalline texture, makes an elegant dessert.

450g gooseberries, topped and tailed
150g caster sugar
200ml Muscat dessert wine
1 tbsp lemon juice

Serves: 4
Prep time: 10 minutes, plus 5 hours
  freezing
Cooking time: 25 minutes

Nutrients per serving: Calories 215,
Carbohydrate 46g, Protein 1g, No fat

1 Place the gooseberries in a saucepan with the sugar and 300ml of water. Bring to the boil, then cover and simmer for 25 minutes, or until the fruit has softened to a pulp.

2 Purée the gooseberry pulp in a food processor or with a hand-held mixer, then strain it through a fine sieve, discarding the pips. Stir in the wine and lemon juice and leave it to cool.

3 Transfer the cooled mixture to a shallow, freezerproof plastic container, cover and freeze for 1 hour.

4 Use a fork to mash into the liquid any ice crystals that have formed around the rim and base, then cover and return to the freezer for a further 4 hours, beating in any ice crystals every hour. Serve the granita in glasses as soon as it is ready.

gooseberry sauce

A refreshing, pale green sauce of ripe gooseberries makes a pleasantly sharp contrast to creamy deep-fried cheese such as Camembert or oily fish like mackerel.

250g green gooseberries, topped and tailed
15g butter
15g sugar
1 tbsp chopped fennel leaves (optional)

Serves: 4
Prep time: 10 minutes
Cooking time: 15 minutes

Nutrients per serving: Calories 55, Carbohydrate 6g, Protein 1g, Fat 3g (saturated fat 2g)

1 Place the gooseberries in a saucepan with a tablespoon of water and add the butter, sugar and fennel. Cover and cook them gently, stirring occasionally with a wooden spoon, for about 15 minutes until the gooseberries are soft. Add another tablespoon of water if it seems dry.

2 Beat well with a wooden spoon to a pulpy consistency and add a little more sugar, if wanted. Serve warm.

gooseberry jam

2.25kg gooseberries, topped and tailed, washed and drained.
850ml water
3kg sugar

Nutrients per teaspoon: Calories 15, Carbohydrate 5g, Protein 0g, Fat 0g (no saturated fat)

1 Put the gooseberries in a pan with the water and simmer gently until the skins burst and the fruit has reduced to a pulp.

2 Add the sugar, stirring until dissolved, then boil to setting point. Test for setting point by dropping a teaspoon of jam onto a cold saucer. If it is not ready, continue boiling and testing every 10 minutes until it is.

gooseberry wine

1.75kg gooseberries
250g sultanas
900g sugar
1 tsp tartaric acid
1 Campden tablet
1 tsp pectin-destroying enzyme
3.5l water
Hock yeast and nutriet

Nutrients per serving: Calories 120, Carbohydrate 9g, Protein 0g, Fat 0g (saturated fat 0g)

1 Pour the water into a bin and add the tartaric acid, the pectin-destroying enzyme and a crushed Campden tablet

2 Wash the gooseberries, crush them into a mash and drop them into the bin. Cover the bin and leave it in a warm place for 24 hours.

3 Activate the yeast in a starter bottle. Add the sultanas, nutrient and yeast to the mash, re-cover the bin and place it in a warm place for 4-5 days.

4 Press and strain the pulp and add the sugar, dissolving this first in warm water.

5 Pour the strained mixture into a fermentation jar, top up with cold water and fit an airlock to the jar. Tie on a label describing the contents and store the jar at room temperature until fermentation is complete.

The national symbol of Wales since the 7th century, when Welsh forces defeated an invading Saxon army, in England the leek was used to make soups and stews during Lent at a time when other vegetables were scarce. Hardy and easy to grow, leeks are able to survive the toughest winters. They will thrive in any well-drained soil, even in the coldest areas, providing it is well-manured during the winter before planting.

Leeks

HARVESTING

To extend the harvesting period, start lifting leeks when they are about 2cm thick. Ease them out of the soil with a fork, otherwise they may break. Continue lifting the leeks during winter as and when they are needed. They will keep on growing during winter, though only slowly during the coldest months.

PREPARATION

To clean leeks for cooking, slice off the root base, cut off the upper green leaves and remove any tough or damaged outer leaves. If the leeks are to be cooked whole, as for braising, make a downward slit into the white part, long enough so as not to prise the leaves apart but not so deep that the stem splits in two. Rinse thoroughly, washing away all traces of soil and grit. Or cut crossways into 3-5cm pieces or even thinner slices. Boil leeks in a minimum of boiling water. Whole and halved leeks need about 15-20 minutes; rings and slices about 10 minutes. Drain thoroughly, return the leeks to the pan and heat for a few minutes to steam off any remaining water.

smoked haddock, bean & leek soup

Creamy butter beans sharpened with onion and leek have their flavour lifted by the salty, smoky taste of the fish to make a richly flavoured family soup.

600ml fish, chicken or vegetable stock
1 medium onion, peeled and finely
    chopped
800g leeks, rinsed, trimmed and cut into
    thin slices
2 tbsp extra virgin olive oil
850g canned butter beans
500g undyed smoked haddock, skinned
    and diced
Small handful of parsley, chopped
Black pepper
4-6 tbsp double cream to garnish
    (optional)

Serves: 4-6
Cooking time: 30 minutes

Nutritional information: Calories 361, carbohydrate 34g, protein 38g, fat 8g (saturated fat 1g)

1 Put the stock on to heat in a saucepan.

2 Heat the oil in a medium-sized saucepan and cook the onion and leeks gently for 5 minutes, stirring occasionally. Add the stock, bring to the boil, reduce the heat, cover and simmer for 5 minutes.

3 Add the butter beans and their liquid to the pan and mash roughly. Return to the boil, reduce the heat, cover and let them simmer.

4 Add the haddock to the soup and simmer until the flesh becomes opaque.

5 Season the soup to taste with the pepper (the smoked fish should be salty enough without adding extra). Sprinkle the chopped parsley over the soup and serve. If you like, swirl a spoonful of double cream into each bowl.

French leek flan

750g leeks
175g shortcrust pastry, made from
    175g flour
100-125g butter
50g flour
150ml milk
Salt, pepper and nutmeg
75g grated mature Cheddar cheese

Serves: 6
Cooking time: 1 hour

Nutrients per serving: Calories 518, Carbohydrate 25g, Protein 9g, Fat 43g (saturated fat 24g)

1 Roll out the pastry and use it to line a 20cm flan ring set on a baking sheet. Set aside to chill. Heat the oven to 190°C/gas 5.

2 Trim the root bases and all the leafy tops from the leeks, wash thoroughly and cut them crossways into thin slices. Melt the butter in a pan, add the leeks and simmer, covered with a lid, for about 20 minutes or until they are soft and tender.

3 Stir occasionally to prevent the leeks browning. Stir the flour into the leeks and gradually add the milk, stirring until the mixture is smooth and has a purée-like texture.

4 Season to taste with salt, pepper and grated nutmeg. Remove from the heat and stir in the grated cheese.

5 Spoon the leek mixture into the pastry shell and bake in the centre of the oven for about 30 minutes or until the filling is golden brown.

6 Serve hot or cold.

chicken, leek & sweetcorn chowder

Sweetcorn is added to the traditional pairing of chicken and leek, to make a heartier, chunky soup. Serve with crusty wholemeal bread.

350g chicken breasts
1 bay leaf
6 black peppercorns
350g sweetcorn, canned, or defrosted
  if frozen
250g leeks, thinly sliced
Salt and black pepper

Serves: 4
Prep time: 15 minutes, plus 5 minutes
  cooling
Cooking time: 35 minutes

Nutrients per serving: Calories 183, Carbohydrate 16g, Protein 25g, Fat 3g (no saturated fat)

1 Remove the skin and any fat from the chicken breasts and place them in a large saucepan. Add 800ml of water, the bay leaf and the peppercorns. Bring to the boil and skim off any foam that comes to the top, then cover the pan and let the chicken simmer for 20 minutes, or until the meat comes off the bones easily. Leave it to cool for 5 minutes.

2 Lift the chicken from the liquid and slice the meat, or shred it with two forks, and set it aside. Strain the liquid and measure 150ml into a bowl or jug. Add half the sweetcorn and purée it in a food processor or with a hand-held mixer. Return the purée to the pan, whisk in the remaining liquid and bring it to the boil.

3 Add the leeks to the pan, then cover and simmer for 6-8 minutes until they are tender.

4 Add the cooked chicken to the chowder with the remaining sweetcorn and simmer for 2-3 minutes to heat both through. Taste and adjust the seasoning then serve hot, with crusty wholemeal bread, if you like.

cheesy leeks

Fresh, full-flavoured leeks make a great alternative to cauliflower, in a comforting cheese dish, served in a delicious creamy sauce, topped with crispy breadcrumbs.

6-8 leeks
Salt and pepper
50g butter
50g flour
125ml single cream
75g grated cheese
Paprika
2 tbsp breadcrumbs

Serves: 4
Cooking time: 40 minutes

Nutrients per serving: Calories 340, Carbohydrate 21g, Protein 11g, Fat 24g (saturated fat 15g)

1 Trim the roots and upper green parts off the leeks, wash thoroughly and cut in half lengthways. Put in a pan with a small amount of boiling, lightly salted water and simmer for about 6 minutes. Drain and set the cooking water aside. Heat the oven to 190°C/gas 5.

2 Melt the butter in a pan and stir in the flour, cook for a few minutes, then gradually add about 150ml of the reserved cooking liquid. Continue stirring until the sauce is smooth and thick, then add cream to give the required consistency. Season to taste and stir in two-thirds of the cheese.

3 Arrange the leeks in a buttered ovenproof dish, spoon the sauce over them and sprinkle with a little paprika. Mix the remaining cheese with the breadcrumbs and sprinkle over the sauce. Dot with a little butter and cook in the oven for about 20 minutes, or until the topping has crisped.

braised leeks [with capers & currants]

Young leeks braised in a peppery dressing, sprinkled with capers and currants, make a tempting side dish.

75ml olive oil
4 tbsp white wine
1 tbsp white wine vinegar
Salt and black pepper
8 slim leeks
1 tbsp capers, rinsed
25g currants
Pinch of cayenne pepper

Serves: 4
Prep time: 10 minutes
Cooking time: 25 minutes

Nutrients per serving: Calories 195, Carbohydrate 10g, Protein 3g, Fat 15g (saturated fat 2g)

1 Mix the oil, wine, vinegar, salt and pepper in a pan wide enough to hold the leeks in one layer. Add the leeks, scattering the capers and currants in among them.

2 Bring to the boil, cover and then simmer for 15 minutes, basting once or twice with cooking liquor. The leeks are done when their centres can be easily pierced with a knife.

3 Uncover the pan, raise the heat and boil for 5 minutes to reduce the liquor, basting the leeks regularly. Transfer the leeks and the dressing to a serving dish and sprinkle with a light dusting of cayenne to serve.

duck breasts with ginger sauce
[on a bed of leeks]

Duck, served on a bed of lightly stir-fried leeks is dressed with sauce made with four different kinds of ginger.

4 boneless duck breasts, about 200g each
20g fresh root ginger
1 piece preserved stem ginger
2 medium leeks
3 tbsp raspberry vinegar
2 tbsp stem ginger syrup
225ml green ginger wine
225ml chicken stock
15g butter
Salt and black pepper

Serves: 4
Cooking time: 30 minutes

Nutrients per serving: Calories 914, Carbohydrate 15g, Protein 27g, Fat 78g (saturated fat 23g)

1 Heat the oven to a low setting to keep the duck warm later. Dry fry the duck breasts, skin sides down, over a moderate heat for about 8 minutes, turn and cook for a further 6 minutes.

2 While the duck is cooking, peel the fresh ginger and cut it into thin strips. Chop the stem ginger and set both aside.

3 Trim the leeks, cut them in half lengthways, rinse them well, then cut them into matchstick-sized strips and set them aside.

4 Transfer the cooked duck to the oven to keep warm. Drain off all but about a tablespoon of the duck fat. Add the vinegar and bring it to the boil, scraping up the brown residue, then add the fresh and stem ginger, ginger syrup, ginger wine and stock. Bring back to the boil, reduce the heat and simmer for 8-10 minutes, until the liquid has reduced by half.

5 Meanwhile, melt the butter in a small frying pan, add the leeks, season with salt and pepper and stir-fry gently for 3-4 minutes until just tender.

6 Return the duck breasts to the ginger sauce, reheat for 2 minutes, then add salt and pepper to taste.

7 Arrange the leeks on a serving dish, lay the duck breasts on top and spoon over the ginger sauce.

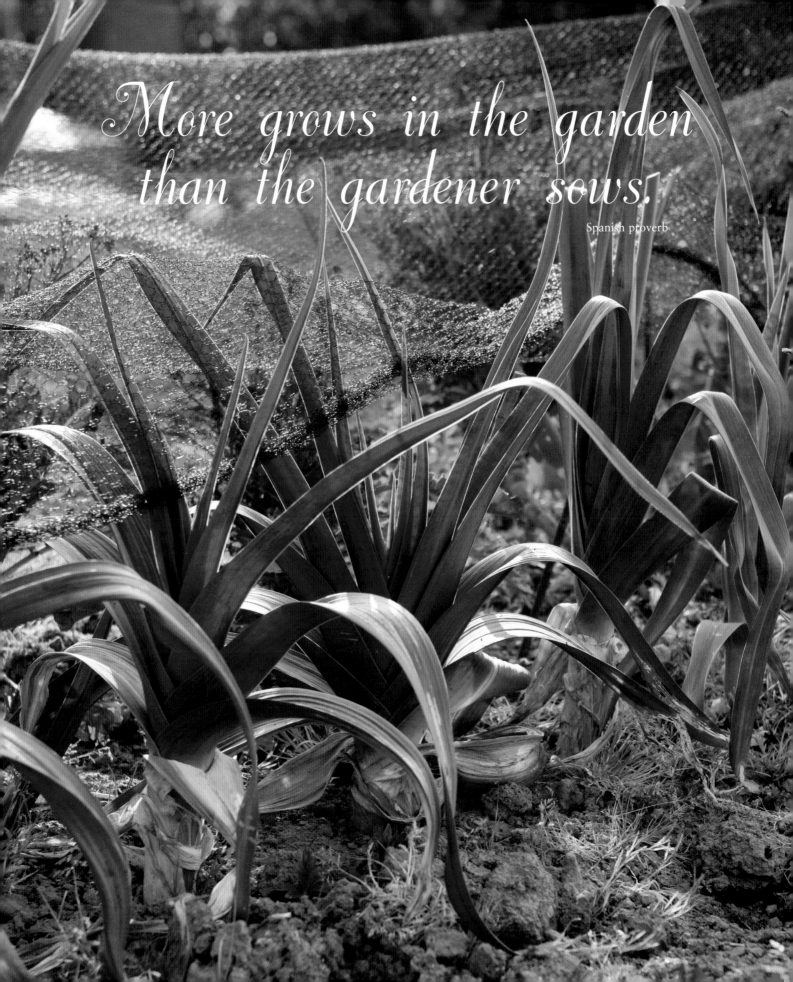

More grows in the garden
than the gardener sows.

Spanish proverb

gammon & leek pie

An excellent casual supper, this variation on shepherd's pie pairs the smoky flavour of gammon with the delicate sweetness of leeks in a mature Cheddar sauce, enhanced by juicy cherry tomatoes.

900g potatoes
Salt and black pepper
500g leeks
70g butter
500g lean gammon steaks
85g mature Cheddar cheese
115g cherry tomatoes
2 tbsp plain flour
1 tsp mixed dried herbs
300ml milk, plus 1-2 tbsp
A few sprigs of parsley to garnish

Serves: 4
Cooking time: 30 minutes

Nutrients per serving: Calories 576, Carbohydrate 42g, Protein 37g, Fat 30g (saturated fat 18g)

1 Put a kettle of water on to boil. Peel and dice the potatoes and put them into a saucepan. Add salt, cover with boiling water and cook, covered, for 8-10 minutes until the potatoes are tender.

2 Meanwhile, slice, rinse and drain the leeks. Melt 25g of butter in a frying pan over a moderate heat and fry for 6-8 minutes, stirring frequently, until softened but not browned. Heat the grill to high.

3 Derind and dice the gammon. Melt 15g of the remaining butter in a flameproof casserole about 25cm wide and 5cm deep, or in a frying pan with a flameproof handle. Fry the diced gammon over a moderate heat for 5 minutes, stirring frequently.

4 Grate the cheese, cut the cherry tomatoes in half and set aside.

5 Stir the flour and herbs into the gammon and cook for 1 minute. Add the milk and stir until it comes to the boil. Add the cheese, stir until it melts then add the leeks, season to taste and reduce the heat to low.

6 Drain and mash the potatoes with black pepper, the remaining butter and 1-2 tablespoons of milk. Place large spoonfuls of mash in a circle around the top of the gammon and leek mixture and lay the cherry tomatoes in the centre.

7 Grill the pie for 2-3 minutes, or until the top of the mash is golden. Rinse and dry the parsley, snip it over the pie and serve.

leek & carrot stir-fry

Two favourite winter vegetables team up with tarragon in this refreshing combination, stir-fried in minutes.

750g leeks
250g carrots
2 tbsp olive oil
1 large sprig fresh tarragon
Salt and black pepper

Serves: 4
Cooking time: 20 minutes

Nutrients per serving: Calories 89, Carbohydrate 7g, Protein 2g, Fat 6g (saturated fat 1g)

1 Discard the tough outer leaves and two-thirds of the green tops from the leeks, then slice thinly, widthways. Place them in a colander and rinse under the cold tap, then drain them well.

2 Peel the carrots and grate them.

3 Heat the oil in a wok or large frying pan over a moderate heat. Rinse and chop the tarragon.

4 Add the leeks to the hot oil and fry for about 2 minutes, or until they just begin to wilt.

5 Stir in the grated carrots and add salt, pepper and the chopped tarragon. Continue to cook for a further 2 minutes, then serve.

turkey likkey pie

'Likkey' – or leek – pie, is an old West Country dish, rich with leeks, bacon, cream and eggs. This healthy adaptation uses lean turkey breast and a reduced-fat suet crust.

400g turkey breast steaks, cut into
    2cm chunks
400g leeks, thinly sliced
150ml semi-skimmed milk
1 large egg, beaten, plus extra to glaze
½ tsp freshly grated nutmeg
Salt and black pepper
150g self-raising flour
75g low-fat vegetable suet

Serves: 4
Prep time: 25 minutes
Cooking time: 35-40 minutes

Nutrients per serving: Calories 400,
Carbohydrate 35g, Protein 30g, Fat 16g
(saturated fat 7g)

1 Heat the oven to 200°C/gas 6. Put the turkey in a saucepan with the leeks and milk. Bring to the boil, cover and simmer for 8-10 minutes, until the leeks are soft.

2 Strain the milk into a jug, then gradually whisk into the beaten egg. Add the nutmeg, with salt and pepper to taste. Spoon the turkey and leeks into a 1l pie dish. Pour the egg mixture on top.

3 Sift the flour with ¼ teaspoon salt into a bowl and stir in the suet. Add 4-5 tablespoons cold water, or enough to mix to a soft dough.

4 Moisten the rim of the dish with water, then roll out the pastry on a lightly floured surface to just bigger than the dish. Cut a strip of pastry and press it round the rim of the dish. Cover with the pastry lid, pressing and crimping the edges together to seal. Use any leftover pastry to make pastry leaves to decorate the top, if desired.

5 Glaze with beaten egg, make a slit in the top with a knife for the steam to escape and place on a baking sheet. Bake for 25-30 minutes, until the pastry is golden. Serve warm with a tomato and watercress salad.

Onions & shallots

Onions are essential to so many recipes that the gardener faces a challenge in trying to keep up with all the demands from the kitchen. Most of these can be met by careful planning and by planting the right varieties of onions at the right time. Apart from onions grown specially for salads and pickling, there are four groups grown from seed: Japanese onions, sown in August for harvesting the following June; larger August-sown varieties which are transferred to a permanent bed in spring and pulled in August; January-sown varieties, germinated under grass, which produce an autumn crop and spring-sown varieties, sown directly into a permanent bed and harvested in September. Onion sets – immature bulbs ripened the previous summer may be planted in April to produce an autumn crop to ripen at the same time as the January sown varieties.

HARVESTING AND STORING

When the outer leaves of the plants begin to turn yellow, bend over the tops to encourage early ripening. Two weeks later, push a fork underneath the bulbs to loosen the roots. After another fortnight, or sooner if the weather is very wet and the onions show signs of splitting, lift the bulbs and spread them out in a greenhouse or shed to ripen fully. Complete the ripening in a cool, dry place. Do not trim off the withered tops at this stage, as they will be needed if you string the onions. To store, secure the onions one above the other to a length of rope and hang them in place. Or hang them in bags of nylon netting.

PREPARATION

To prepare onions for cooking, cut off the upper part with the stalk attached. Trim off the roots, but do not remove the root base entirely as this holds the onion together, making slicing and chopping easier. Peel off the dry outer layers of skin. To slice an onion, lay it on its side and make a series of close cuts, starting at the neck end. Discard the root end when the onion has been sliced. To chop, first cut the onion into halves from neck to root base and then cut each half into thin vertical slices. Finish each cut just short of the root base so the onion does not disintegrate. Place the sliced halves on a chopping board and cut down across the previous cuts.

cream of onion soup

500g onions, roughly chopped
50g butter
2 tbsp flour
1l white stock
Salt and pepper
75ml dry white wine
75ml double cream
1 tbsp chopped chives; 1 tbsp chopped dill
   to garnish

Serves: 4
Cooking time: 50 minutes

Nutrients per serving: Calories 320,
Carbohydrate 17g, Protein 12g, Fat 23g
(saturated fat 12g)

I Melt the butter in a pan and cook the onions for 5-10 minutes or until soft
   and transparent. Stir in the flour and cook through for 2 minutes.
   Gradually stir in the stock, bring to boiling point, then simmer for about
   25 minutes or until the onions are tender.

2 Blend the soup in a liquidiser. Re-heat and season to taste with salt and
   pepper. Stir in the wine and simmer the soup for a further 10 minutes, then
   add the cream and heat through without boiling.

3 Serve garnished with the mixed chives and dill.

glazed onions

500g button or pickling onions
½-1 tsp dried rosemary
25g butter
1 tbsp black treacle
2 tsp Dijon mustard
1 tbsp soy sauce

Serves: 4-6
Cooking time: 30 minutes

Nutrients per serving, when serving 4:
Calories 110, Carbohydrate 14g),
Protein 2g, Fat 6g (saturated fat 3g)

I Put a kettle of water on to boil. Put the onions into a saucepan, cover them
   with boiling water and leave them to cook over a moderate heat for
   5 minutes. Then pour them into a colander and cool them under a cold
   running tap. When they are cool enough to handle, drain them and peel off
   the skins.

2 Crush the rosemary as finely as possible, using a pestle and mortar or the
   end of a rolling pin.

3 Melt the butter gently in a frying pan over a moderate heat. Then add the
   crushed rosemary, black treacle, Dijon mustard and soy sauce and mix them
   together well to make an emulsion.

4 Stir in the onions and cook them gently, stirring and basting them with the
   sauce, for 10-15 minutes, until the glaze has thickened and the onions are
   tender and golden brown. Watch them continuously as it is important not
   to allow the glaze to burn.

onions braised [with raisins and rosemary]

Succulent braised onions, cooked with raisins, fresh rosemary and bay leaves, have a hint of sweet and sour flavour that goes well with roast meat or poultry.

12-18 small onions, peeled
3 tbsp olive oil
3 tbsp red wine vinegar
Salt and black pepper
1 tsp sugar
2 bay leaves
6-8 short sprigs rosemary
2 tbsp raisins
1 tsp balsamic vinegar

Serves: 4-6 as an accompaniment
Prep time: 10 minutes
Cooking time: 40-45 minutes

Nutrients per serving, when serving 6:
Calories 110, Carbohydrate 14g,
Protein 1.5g, Fat 6g (saturated fat 0.5g)

1 Put the onions in a pan in a single layer. Add the oil and fry gently for about 5-8 minutes, shaking them regularly, until patched with brown.

2 Pour in cold water to almost cover the onions and add the vinegar, some salt, the sugar, bay leaves, four sprigs of rosemary and the raisins. Partially cover and simmer for 10 minutes. Then remove the lid, increase the heat and cook just below the boil for 25-35 minutes, shaking the pan regularly to turn the onions. They are done when they look translucent and feel soft when pierced with a knife. The braising liquid will have reduced to a sticky brown sauce.

3 Sprinkle on the balsamic vinegar and pepper to taste. Serve garnished with the remaining rosemary sprigs.

lamb's liver [with bacon & onion]

1 large onion
8 large, fresh sage leaves
2 tbsp olive oil
4 slices lamb's liver, about 85g each
2 tbsp plain flour
Salt and black pepper
300ml lamb stock
4 lean, rindless rashers smoked back
    bacon, about 150g in total
150ml soured cream
Small, fresh sage leaves, to garnish

Serves: 4
Cooking time: 25 minutes

Nutrients per serving: Calories 374,
Carbohydrate 10g, Protein 26g, Fat 26g
(saturated fat 10g)

1 Heat the oven to low to keep the bacon warm later. Halve, peel and slice the onion. Rinse, dry and shred the large sage leaves.

2 Heat 1 tablespoon of olive oil in a frying pan, add the onion and fry it over a moderate heat for 4-5 minutes, until lightly browned.

3 Meanwhile, rinse the liver and pat it dry with kitchen paper. Put the flour onto a plate, season it well with pepper, then coat each slice of liver with the flour.

4 Stir the leftover flour and the shredded sage into the onions and cook, stirring, for 1 minute. Add the stock and bring to the boil, stirring. Reduce the heat; leave to simmer.

5 Heat the remaining olive oil in a frying pan and fry the bacon for 1-2 minutes on each side, then remove it from the pan and keep it warm in the oven. Add the liver to the pan and fry over a moderate-to-high heat for 2 minutes each side, or until lightly browned.

6 Return the bacon to the pan. Add the sauce and stir, scraping up any residue from the bottom. Simmer for 3-4 minutes, or until the liver is cooked but still slightly pink in the centre.

7 Stir the cream into the pan and season to taste, but be cautious with the salt as the bacon may be salty. Simmer for 1-2 minutes to heat the cream.

8 Transfer to a warmed serving dish, garnish with the small sage leaves, if using, and serve.

stuffed chicken breasts

[with red onion marmalade]

The sweetness of a fruit stuffing and the onion marmalade is balanced by a mixed salad of mixed slightly bitter leaves such as red chard, red mustard or rocket.

1 dessert apple, peeled and coarsely grated
75g ready-to-eat stoned prunes, chopped
2 skinned and boned chicken breasts, about 175g each
A pinch of ground mace
Salt and black pepper
For the marmalade:
1 tsp olive oil
250g red onions, thinly sliced
150ml chicken stock
2 tbsp balsamic vinegar

Serves: 4
Prep time: 30 minutes
Cooking time: 1 hour, plus 3-4 hours, or overnight, chilling

Nutrients per serving: Calories 190, Carbohydrate 17g, Protein 26g, Fat 2g (no saturated fat)

1 To make the onion marmalade, heat the oil in a saucepan, add the onions and cook over a medium heat for 2-3 minutes until they start to soften. Add the stock and vinegar, reduce the heat to low, partially cover the pan and simmer for 30-45 minutes, stirring frequently, until the onions are very soft and the stock is reduced to a thick syrup. Remove the pan from the heat and allow the marmalade to cool, then cover and refrigerate until needed.

2 Meanwhile, mix the apple and prunes together in a small bowl and set aside.

3 Place each chicken breast between two large sheets of cling film, then use a meat mallet or a rolling pin to beat each one out to a thin rectangular shape, about 15 x 20cm. Place them on a board with the inner side uppermost. Remove and discard the white sinews and trim each breast into a neat rectangle, reserving the trimmings.

4 Put a kettle on to boil. Finely chop the chicken trimmings and mix them into the apple and prune mixture. Season the stuffing and the chicken breasts well with mace and salt and pepper to taste.

5 Lay a spoonful of the stuffing along the shorter side of each chicken breast, then roll them up.

6 Take a large sheet of cling film and place a chicken breast at one end. Then roll up the breast so that it is enclosed in several layers of film. Tightly twist the ends of the film and gently roll the chicken breast back and forth several times to form a neat, sausage-shaped roll, twisting the ends tightly each time you roll. Tie the ends with string to seal securely. Repeat with the other breast.

7 Put the chicken breasts side by side into a small saucepan and cover with boiling water. Return to the boil, reduce the heat to low, cover the pan and poach the chicken for 10-15 minutes until a skewer inserted into the centre of each roll feels hot on the back of your hand.

8 Transfer the chicken rolls to a plate and allow to cool (do not remove the cling film). Then chill for 3-4 hours, or overnight, to allow the flavours to develop.

9 To serve, unwrap the chicken breasts and slice them thinly. Divide the salad leaves between four serving plates, top with a spoonful of onion marmalade and arrange the chicken slices alongside.

fillet steak [with roasted shallots & garlic]

Slowly roasted in their skins, shallots and garlic have a mellow sweetness that marries beautifully with juicy chargrilled fillet steak.

500g shallots
2 whole heads garlic, roots and tops trimmed off
3 tbsp olive oil
1 tsp balsamic vinegar
2 tbsp chopped fresh flat-leaved parsley
Salt and black pepper
4 lean fillet steaks, about 125g each
1 tsp Worcestershire sauce

Serves: 4
Prep time: 10 minutes
Cooking time: 45-55 minutes

Nutrients per serving: Calories 304, Carbohydrate 9g, Protein 29g, Fat 17g (saturated fat 9g)

1 Heat the oven to 200°C/gas 6. Cut off the roots of the shallots, leaving them in their skins, and place them in a small roasting tin. Add the garlic to the shallots. Drizzle with 1 tablespoon of oil, cover with foil and roast for 40-50 minutes until they are very soft.

2 When the shallots and garlic are cool enough to handle, slip them out of their skins and place them in a small mixing bowl. Dress with 1 tablespoon of olive oil and the balsamic vinegar, stir in the parsley and season to taste.

3 Heat a ridged, iron grill pan over a high heat. Cut any fat off the steaks and rub them with the remaining olive oil and the Worcestershire sauce. Season to taste, then grill them for 2 minutes on each side for medium-rare steaks, or longer to taste. Serve with the garlic and shallot dressing.

onion & feta cheese flan

Sweet onions and the subtle flavour of fresh thyme perfectly complements the sharper taste and thick, creamy texture of the Greek cheese filling.

175g plain flour
1 tsp baking powder
85g butter, at room temperature
150ml soured cream
500g onions
2 sprigs of fresh thyme
3-4 tbsp olive oil
125g button mushrooms
250g Greek feta cheese
Salt and black pepper
A few chives to garnish

Serves: 4
Cooking time: 30 minutes

Nutrients per serving: Calories 674, Carbohydrate 46g, Protein 17g, Fat 48g (saturated fat 26g)

1 Heat the oven to 220°C/gas 7. Sift the flour and baking powder into a bowl, then rub in 50g of butter. Add 5 tablespoons of the soured cream – just under half – and mix to a soft dough.

2 Roll out the dough on a floured surface into a circle about 28cm in diameter, and use it to line a 25cm loose-based flan or sandwich tin. Trim the edge, prick the base, line with greaseproof paper and fill with baking beans or small balls of cooking foil. Bake blind for 10 minutes.

3 Meanwhile, halve, peel and thinly slice the onions, then rinse and dry the thyme, strip the leaves from the stems and chop them finely. Heat the oil in a large frying pan, add the onions and thyme and fry over a moderate heat until the onions are soft and golden.

4 Melt the remaining butter in another frying pan. Clean and halve the mushrooms and fry until lightly browned, then stir in the rest of the soured cream and keep warm.

5 Remove the paper and baking beans or foil from the flan case, then return it to the oven for a few minutes until the pastry is golden.

6 Rinse, dry and snip the chives. Crumble the feta cheese into the onions. Heat for 1 minute then season to taste. Spoon the mixture into the flan case and spoon the mushrooms over the top. Sprinkle with chives and pepper and serve.

shallots in red wine

The classic sauce for sirloin or entrecôte steaks.

Meat juices from cooking steak
4 shallots
1 clove garlic
250ml red wine
1 tbsp chopped parsley

Serves: 4
Cooking time: 10 minutes

Nutrients per tablespoon: Calories 35, Carbohydrate 7g, Protein 0g, Fat 0g (no saturated fat)

1 Peel and slice the shallots, then peel and crush the garlic. Add to the retained meat juices in the pan. Sizzle both in the pan juices for 1-2 minutes then stir in the red wine and chopped parsley.

2 Bring the wine to the boil over a medium heat, stirring and scraping the deposits from the bottom of the pan, until the liquid is reduced to about a third.

3 Season to taste, then spoon over the steaks and sprinkle with more chopped parsley.

A good garden may have some weeds.

Proverb

rich roast onions

4 very large white onions, about 300g each
100ml balsamic vinegar
1 tbsp brown sugar
Salt and black pepper

Serves: 4
Prep time: 5 minutes
Cooking time: 1 hour–1 hour 15 minutes

Nutrients per person: Calories 492,
Carbohydrates 88g, Protein 19g, Fat 8g
(no saturated fat)

I Heat the oven to 200°C/gas 6. Cut the onions in half through the root, leaving the skin on, and place them, cut side down, in a single layer in a roasting tin.

2 Mix the vinegar and sugar with 200ml of water, pour it over the onions and roast for 1 hour to 1 hour 15 minutes until they are soft.

3 Arrange the onions, cut side up, on a platter, season and serve warm.

onion & apple pickle

2kg onions
1kg cooking apples
Spiced vinegar

Nutrients per tablespoon: Calories 30,
Carbohydrate 6g, Protein 0g, Fat 0g
(no saturated fat)

I Peel the onions and cut into thin slices. Peel and core the apples and slice, or cut into cubes. Mix the two ingredients quickly or the apples will turn brown.

2 Pot at once into clean jars, cover with hot vinegar and seal.

3 The pickle can be eaten the following day but it improves with keeping.

pickled onions

3kg pickling onions or small shallots
Coarse salt
1l spiced vinegar

Nutrients per tablespoon: Calories 25,
Carbohydrate 5g, Protein 0g, Fat 0g
(no saturated fat)

I Steep the small, unpeeled onions in a brine solution (125g coarse salt to 1l water) for 12 hours. Drain, peel and soak in fresh brine for 24-36 hours.

2 Rinse and drain well, pack into jars and cover with cold vinegar. Leave for two or three months before using.

Parsnips are the earliest vegetable seeds to be sown in the open – in early March in the south, if the weather is favourable. As they are not harvested until the following winter, this means that the crop occupies ground for almost a year. Despite their long growing time, parsnips require little attention once the seedlings have been thinned. They are harvested when fresh vegetables are scarce and they are very hardy. Parsnips do best in deep, rich, fairly light soil, but can be grown in almost any kind of soil. Choose an open, sunny position and a bed that has been well manured for a previous crop – but not in fresh manure or your parsnips will split up into several forked roots rather than making one clean root.

Parsnips

HARVESTING

Parsnips can be used as soon as the leaves die back in autumn but it is better to wait until a sharp frost improves their flavour. When lifting the roots, take care not to damage them with the fork. Parsnips may be left in the soil until they are needed, but the last of the crop should be dug up during February, or before the roots start to produce new leaves, and put in a cool place and covered with soil.

PREPARATION

Prepare the roots for cooking by cutting off the tops and the tapering roots. Peel the parsnips thinly and cut lengthways into thin slices. Cut large roots into quarters and take out the woody cores. Boil for 20-25 minutes or steam; you could use butter, stock and a little white wine. Parsnips can also be roasted in the same way as potatoes and shallow-fried after par-boiling for 5 minutes.

aromatic parsnip soup

A fragrant, warming winter soup with subtle spicing, yoghurt creaminess and a sweet undertone of apple.

850ml vegetable stock
1 large cooking apple
550g parsnips
1 medium onion
1 tbsp sunflower oil
1 clove garlic
2 tsp ground coriander
1 tsp ground cumin
1 tsp turmeric
Salt
300ml milk
A few sprigs of coriander; 4-6 tbsp natural
   yoghurt to garnish

Serves: 4-6
Cooking time: 30 minutes

Nutrients per serving, when serving 4:
Calories 211, Carbohydrate 30g,
Protein 9g, Fat 8g (saturated fat 2g)

1 Warm the stock over a low heat. Peel the apple and the parsnips. Quarter and core the apple, then chop the apple and parsnips into chunks.

2 Peel and chop the onion. Heat the oil in a large saucepan, add the onion and leave it to soften.

3 Peel and roughly chop the garlic, add it to the pan, then add the three spices and cook for 1 minute.

4 Pour the warmed stock into the pan and add the apple, parsnips and salt. Bring to the boil, then reduce the heat, cover and simmer for 15 minutes.

5 Meanwhile, rinse and dry the coriander and strip off the leaves.

6 Remove the pan from the heat and stir in the milk. Process or blend the soup to a smooth purée, then reheat.

7 Ladle the soup into bowls, garnish it with the coriander and serve. Prepare a dish of yoghurt to hand around separately for people to help themselves.

curried parsnip purée

Sweet-tasting parsnips mingle with hot curry and fresh herbs to make a warmly substantial purée.

650g parsnips
Salt and black pepper
3-4 sprigs of fresh parsley
25g butter
1 tbsp medium or hot curry powder
4 tbsp soured cream

Serves: 4 as an accompaniment
Cooking time: 20 minutes

Nutrients per serving: Calories 162,
Carbohydrate 16g, Protein 3g, Fat 10g
(saturated fat 6g)

1 Put a kettle of water on to boil. Peel the parsnips, cut them into small chunks and put them into a saucepan with a little salt. Cover with boiling water and return to the boil, then reduce the heat and simmer them for 8-10 minutes, or until they are tender.

2 While the parsnips are cooking, rinse, dry and chop the parsley and set it aside.

3 Drain the parsnips thoroughly, then return them to the saucepan and mash them coarsely with a potato masher.

4 Add the butter, curry powder and soured cream to the mashed parsnips, season the mixture well with black pepper, and beat it until it becomes a smooth purée.

5 Transfer the parsnip purée into a heated serving dish, then fluff it up or swirl over the surface with a fork. As a finishing touch, sprinkle the chopped parsley over the top of the purée.

parsnip cakes

In the Middle Ages, parsnips were a staple food for people who could not afford meat and game. These little cakes can be served with meat or as a vegetarian dish.

350g floury potatoes, peeled and cut into evenly sized pieces
675g parsnips, peeled and cut into evenly sized pieces
3 tsp sunflower oil
1 onion, finely chopped
1 clove garlic, crushed
15g butter
4 tbsp buttermilk
Pinch of mace or nutmeg
1 tbsp finely chopped fresh parsley
Salt and black pepper
1 egg, beaten
115g fresh white breadcrumbs

Makes about: 14-16 cakes
Prep time: 20 minutes
Cooking time: 25 minutes

Nutrients per cake: Calories 83, Carbohydrate 13g, Protein 2.5g, Fat 2.5g (saturated fat 0.5g)

1 Cook the potatoes in plenty of boiling, salted water for 10 minutes until soft, adding the parsnips after 2-3 minutes. Drain.

2 Heat 2 teaspoons of the oil in a frying pan, add the onion and garlic and cook for 3-4 minutes until the onion is soft.

3 Put the drained potatoes and parsnips in a bowl with the butter and buttermilk. Mash thoroughly, then add the onion and garlic and beat together with a fork. Add the mace or nutmeg, parsley and salt and pepper. Set aside until cool enough to handle.

4 Put the egg in a shallow bowl with 1 tablespoon water. Put the breadcrumbs in a separate bowl. Shape a tablespoon of mixture into a cake about 7.5cm in diameter. Dip briefly into the egg mixture and then in the breadcrumbs to coat. Repeat with the remaining mixture to make 14-16 cakes.

5 Brush the base of a nonstick frying pan with the remaining oil. When hot, fry the parsnip cakes, a few at a time, turning them when browned underneath. Continue cooking until evenly browned and transfer to a serving plate lined with kitchen paper. Keep them warm while you cook the remaining cakes, adding a little more oil as necessary.

6 Serve either as part of a main meat or vegetarian meal or as a snack with a tasty relish.

fried parsnips

500g parsnips, peeled and cut in half lengthways
Salt and pepper
1 egg, lightly beaten
4 tbsp breadcrumbs
50g butter
Lemon slices to garnish

Serves: 4
Cooking time: 25-30 minutes

Nutrients per serving: Calories 248, Carbohydrate 27g, Protein 6g, Fat 14g (saturated fat 7g). High fibre

1 Put the parsnips in a pan of boiling, lightly salted water and cook for 15 minutes. They should still be firm and not quite tender. Drain thoroughly.

2 Dip the parsnips in the lightly beaten egg and coat with breadcrumbs seasoned with salt and pepper. Melt the butter in a pan and shallow-fry the coated parsnips until they are golden and crisp on both sides, turning once.

3 Garnish the fried parsnips with thin slices of lemon to serve.

parsnip & apple cream

The tart flavour of cooking apple balances the sweetness of parsnips as they are melted into double cream in a luxurious dish, that is perfect with plain roasts or grills.

500g parsnips
2 tbsp olive oil
1 cooking apple
Salt and black pepper
½ lemon
3 sprigs of fresh thyme
75ml double cream

Serves: 4
Cooking time: 20 minutes

Nutrients per serving: Calories 212, Carbohydrate 17g, Protein 2g, Fat 16g (saturated fat 7g)

1 Peel and coarsely grate the parsnips. If they are old, cut them into quarters and remove and discard the woody cores before you begin grating.

2 Heat the olive oil in a large, shallow saucepan, add the grated parsnips and cook them over a moderate heat.

3 Meanwhile, peel and coarsely grate the apple, stopping when you reach the core. Stir it into the pan with the parsnips, season, then squeeze in half a tablespoon of juice from the half lemon.

4 Rinse the thyme, strip the leaves from the stems and add them. Cook for 3-5 minutes more, stirring occasionally, until the parsnips are tender.

5 Pour the cream into the pan and stir while you heat it through. Transfer to a heated dish and serve.

Pears will grow wherever apples do, but they need slightly different conditions and treatment. As their flowers open earlier, when there are fewer flying insects to pollinate them, they should ideally be placed in a less exposed position. Pears also need watering more frequently during dry spells as they are more sensitive to drought than apples. As few pears are self-fertile, when buying trees, you should get two different varieties that will flower at the same time. If space permits, by choosing early, mid-season and late varieties, it is possible to have your own pears from August until the new year.

HARVESTING

Most varieties of pears ripen on the tree. Harvest early varieties by cutting the stalk when the fruit is mature but still hard. Pick mid-season fruits (for eating in October or November) and late varieties (for use from December) when the stalk parts easily from the spur after a gentle twist. Store the pears in a cool room or shed at a temperature of 2-4°C. Do not wrap them but lay them on a tray or shelf in a single layer. Make sure the fruits do not touch each other. Check frequently and when they approach maturity, shown by a slight softening of the flesh close to the stalk, bring them into a place with a temperature of about 16°C for two or three days to finish off the ripening.

Pears

PREPARATION

Prepare pears for cooking by first peeling them with a stainless-steel knife to prevent discoloration. If they are to stand for any length of time before cooking, brush them with lemon juice to prevent browning. Pears may be poached whole, first removing the blossom end by leaving the stalk intact and scraping it clean with a knife. Alternatively, cut the peeled pears into halves and use a pointed teaspoon to scoop out the centre cores and the woody filaments running through the stalk ends.

Stilton rarebit [with pears & walnuts]

A classic combination of nutty and sweet flavours makes a delicious snack for almost any time of day.

4 slices of wholemeal bread
25g unsalted butter
175g Stilton cheese, finely crumbled
1 tbsp milk or beer
1½ tsp wholegrain mustard
Black pepper
1 small egg yolk
2 ripe pears, halved, cored and sliced
3 tbsp finely chopped walnuts

Serves: 4
Prep time: 5 minutes
Cooking time: 10 minutes

Nutrients per serving: Calories 420,
Carbohydrate 21g, Protein 16g, Fat 30g
(saturated fat 15g)

I Heat the grill and toast the bread on both sides. Meanwhile, melt the butter in a small, nonstick saucepan, then stir in the Stilton, milk or beer and mustard, with pepper to taste. Heat gently, stirring, until the cheese has melted, being careful not to overheat it.

2 Remove the pan from the heat and stir in the egg yolk. Spread the cheese mixture on the toast and place under the hot grill for 2-3 minutes, to brown. Reduce the grill to medium and arrange the pear slices on top of the cheese. Sprinkle over the walnuts.

3 Grill for 2-3 minutes to crisp the nuts. Serve at once.

pear & ginger [upside-down pudding]

This dessert has all the rich stickiness of a traditional gingerbread pudding but is surprising low in calories.

Sunflower oil for greasing
1 tbsp dark muscovado sugar
450g firm pears, such as Conference,
    peeled, cored and sliced
For the batter:
125g plain white flour
½ tsp bicarbonate of soda
1 tsp ground cinnamon
2 tsp ground ginger
100ml skimmed milk
125g dark muscovado sugar
3 tbsp black treacle
1 egg
2 tbsp sunflower oil
Low-fat custard or natural yoghurt to serve

Serves: 6
Prep time: 25 minutes
Cooking time: 40-45 minutes

Nutrients per serving: Calories 358,
Carbohydrate 65g, Protein 10g, Fat 8g
(saturated fat 2g)

I Heat the oven to 180°C/gas 4. Brush a 22cm round cake tin with oil. Line the base with baking paper and sprinkle it with sugar. Arrange the pears in the base in a wagon wheel pattern.

2 To make the batter, sift together the flour, bicarbonate of soda, cinnamon and ginger. Heat the milk, sugar and treacle together, stirring until the sugar has dissolved. Beat together the egg and oil, then stir them and the milk mixture into the flour, beating well to give a smooth texture.

3 Tip the mixture over the pears and bake for 35-40 minutes until risen and firm to the touch.

4 Run a knife around the edge of the pudding and turn it out onto a plate. Serve hot, with custard or yoghurt.

pan-fried pear & fig pancakes

300ml skimmed milk

1 egg

100g plain white or plain wholemeal flour,
    or a mixture

1 tbsp caster sugar

Salt

2 tsp sunflower oil

For the filling:

20g butter

700g pears, peeled, cored and chopped

100g ready-to-eat dried figs, chopped

½ tsp ground cinnamon

A pinch of ground cloves

Grated zest of ½ orange

90g soft brown sugar

4 tbsp half-fat crème fraîche or Greek
    yoghurt and 4 tbsp maple syrup to serve

Serves: 4

Prep time: 15-20 minutes, plus 30 minutes
    resting

Cooking time: 35 minutes

Nutrients per serving: Calories 420,
Carbohydrate 76g, Protein 8g, Fat 11g
(saturated fat 5g)

1 To make the pancake batter, place the milk, egg, flour, sugar and a pinch of salt in a food processor and blend for 1 minute to a smooth consistency. Alternatively, place the flour, sugar and a pinch of salt in a bowl, make a well in the centre and pour in the egg and milk. Stir slowly with a wooden spoon to incorporate the flour until a smooth batter forms. Set the batter aside to rest for 30 minutes.

2 Heat the oven to a low setting. Grease an 18cm nonstick frying pan with a little oil and heat the pan until it is very hot. Pour in 1-2 ladles of batter and tilt the pan so that it covers the base. Cook for 30-45 seconds until the underside is golden. Turn the pancake over and cook the other side for 1 minute, or until it is set.

3 Transfer the pancake to a piece of kitchen paper. Repeat the process to make eight pancakes, separating each with a piece of kitchen paper. Wrap the stack of pancakes in foil and place in the oven to keep warm.

4 To make the filling, melt the butter in a small frying pan over a medium heat. Add the pears and figs, reduce the heat and cover, then simmer for about 10 minutes, or until the pears are tender when tested with a knife.

5 Stir the cinnamon, cloves, orange zest and soft brown sugar into the fruit and simmer for a further 5 minutes.

6 Divide the fruit mixture between the warm pancakes. Fold them up and serve two per person, with 1 tablespoon of half-fat crème fraîche or Greek yoghurt, and some maple syrup if desired.

pear & lemon chutney

Lemon, shallots, garlic and stem ginger add plenty of spice and tang to the gentler taste of pears to make a great accompaniment to a variety of meats and cheeses.

1.5kg pears, peeled, cored and diced
5 shallots, peeled and chopped
3 cloves garlic, crushed
1 large lemon, thinly sliced
125g stem ginger, chopped
125g sultanas
125g seedless raisins
500g brown sugar
600ml white wine vinegar
1 tsp each of turmeric, cinnamon, pepper, salt and coriander

Approx yield: 2kg

Nutrients per tablespoon: Calories 23, Carbohydrate 6g, Protein 0g, Fat 0g (no saturated fat)

1 Put all the ingredients into a large pan and simmer gently until they are soft and the chutney has a firm consistency.

2 Pot at once and seal tightly.

Peas are some of the most challenging and yet rewarding of vegetable crops. They need a good deal of attention, are prone to pests and disease and give a comparatively small yield for the space they take up. But the flavour of freshly picked garden peas is much finer than that of either fresh or frozen field grown peas and is one of the great treats of the vegetable gardener's year. There are two main types of peas. Hardy, round seeded peas are sown in late autumn and early spring for picking in late May and June; the wrinkled type which taste sweeter, can be sown only from March to July for harvesting from June onwards. Sugar peas or mangetout are grown in the same way as garden peas but are picked when the seeds have only just begun to develop. They are cooked and eaten whole.

Peas

HARVESTING

When the pods seem to have reached their full length, check daily to feel if the peas are swelling inside. Aim to pick the pods when the seeds are well developed but before they are fully mature. To harvest, pull the pod upwards with one hand while holding the stem with the other. Harvest mangetout when the pods are about 5cm long and the seeds only just beginning to develop inside If there are not enough available at a single picking, keep the first batch in the fridge until more can be gathered.

PREPARATION

Top and tail mangetout peas but do not string. Wash them in cold water and cook for no more than 5 minutes in boiling water. Tiny petit pois, like other garden peas are shelled from their pods. They can be boiled but are delicious if only par-boiled and finished off in butter under cover and sprinkled with chopped mint. Shell full-sized peas and cook in boiling water with a sprig of mint, I teaspoon of sugar and a little lemon juice to preserve the fresh green colour. Boil for 15-20 minutes and serve tossed in butter or sprinkled with mint, parsley, dill or basil.

minted pea soup [with prawns & chives]

Peas in the pod are available in summer, and are best soon after picking, while they still have their natural sweetness.

700g peas in pods
500g cooked shell-on prawns
2 tbsp vegetable oil
5-6 spring onions, trimmed and sliced
1 large clove garlic, roughly chopped
2.5cm piece of fresh ginger, unpeeled and coarsely grated
2 sprigs of mint
1 tsp black peppercorns
1 large floury potato, about 250g, peeled, grated and rinsed
Salt and black pepper
Sugar (optional)
Small bunch of chives, snipped

Serves: 4
Prep & cooking time: 50 minutes

Nutrients per serving: Calories 280, Carbohydrate 17g, Protein 33g, Fat 8g (saturated fat 2g)

1 Pod the peas into a bowl. Reserve and roughly chop the pods. Peel the prawns, reserving their heads, shells and any roe.

2 Heat the oil in a saucepan, add the spring onions and cook over a gentle heat for 1-2 minutes until soft, then add the garlic, pea pods and prawn shells and cook, stirring frequently, for 4-5 minutes until the prawn shells release a powerful aroma.

3 Add the ginger, mint, peppercorns and 1l water and bring to the boil. Skim, reduce the heat and simmer for 15 minutes. Strain the contents of the pan through a large sieve into a deep bowl, pressing down with the back of a spoon to extract as much liquid as possible. Discard the flavourings.

4 Return the liquid to the rinsed saucepan and add the grated potato and half the peas. Bring to the boil, then cook at a low boil for 5 minutes. Purée, using a hand-held blender. Return to the heat, add the remaining peas and simmer for 3-4 minutes until tender.

5 Add salt, pepper to taste and sugar, if needed, and transfer the soup to warmed soup plates or bowls. Add the shelled prawns, top with chives and serve.

pea & asparagus soup

600ml chicken or vegetable stock
8-9 spring onions
450g frozen peas
150g small asparagus spears
Salt and black pepper
3 rashers rindless streaky bacon
1-2 tbsp vegetable oil
2 slices day-old white bread
3 tbsp crème fraîche

Serves: 4
Cooking time: 30 minutes

Nutrients per serving: Calories 330, Carbohydrate 24g, Protein 13g, Fat 21g (saturated fat 9g)

1 Put the stock on to heat, then rinse the spring onions, trim and chop them roughly, add them to the stock with the frozen peas and bring to the boil.

2 Rinse the asparagus spears, remove the tips and set them aside. Roughly chop the stems and add them to the saucepan with a pinch of salt. Reduce the heat, cover and simmer for 10-15 minutes, or until the asparagus is tender.

3 Meanwhile, snip the bacon rashers directly into a frying pan and fry until crisp and golden. Transfer to a plate and set aside.

4 If there is not enough bacon fat left in the pan for frying, add 1-2 tablespoons of oil and heat. Cut the bread into small dice and fry for 2-3 minutes over a high heat, turning frequently, until golden, then drain on kitchen paper.

5 When the peas and asparagus are done, blend or process the soup to a purée.

6 Add the reserved asparagus tips to the pea soup and simmer for 5 minutes, or until tender.

7 Pour the soup into warmed serving bowls. Swirl a little crème fraîche into each and sprinkle with the crispy bacon pieces, croutons and some freshly ground black pepper to serve.

He who sows peas on the highway does not get all the pods into his barn.

Danish proverb

pea & Puy lentil salad [in mint dressing]

Redcurrants enliven the green peas, spring onions and Puy lentils while mint and ground cumin add an exotic flavour.

350g Puy lentils
2 bay leaves
700g unshelled peas
1 tsp sugar
Salt and black pepper
1 tsp ground cumin
4-6 spring onions
3-4 springs mint
2-3 sprays redcurrants
Dressing:
90ml olive oil
1 tbsp sherry vinegar
1 tsp raspberry vinegar

Serves: 6-8
Prep time: 15 minutes
Cooking time: 30-35 minutes

Nutrients per serving when serving 8:
Calories 281, Carbohydrate 32g,
Protein 17g, Fat 10g (saturated fat 1.5g)

I Put the lentils into a pan with the bay leaves and cover them well with cold water. Bring to the boil, skim, then turn down the head and simmer for about 30-35 minutes or until tender. Drain, rinse and leave to drain further in a colander.

2 Shell the peas and put them in a small pan. Add the sugar and enough water to cover. Simmer the peas for 7-10 minutes, or until they are soft and sweet.

3 While the peas are cooking, put the ingredients for the dressing into a small screw-top jar and shake well.

4 When the peas and lentils are done, mix them together in a bowl. Season with the salt, black pepper and ground cumin and toss in the salad dressing. This can be done a few hours in advance if you like.

5 Shortly before serving, wash, trim and shred the spring onions, then shred the mint and toss them both into the pea and lentil salad. Garnish with the redcurrants if you like or add an extra sprig of mint to decorate.

buttered mangetout

500g mangetout, topped, tailed and
    destrung
Salt
50g butter
1 dsp mixed parsley and mint

Serves: 4
Cooking time: 10 minutes

Nutrients per serving: Calories 133,
Carbohydrate 5g, Protein 4.5g, Fat 11g
(saturated fat 6g)

I Put the mangetout in a pan with a small amount of boiling, lightly salted water and cook for 4-5 minutes. Drain thoroughly in a colander.

2 Melt the butter in a pan without letting it brown, add the pods and cover with a lid. Cook over a gentle heat for 5 minutes, shaking the pan frequently to prevent sticking and to ensure that the peas are evenly coated with butter. Stir in the mixed, finely chopped herbs.

3 Spoon the pods and cooking liquid into a dish and serve. For a variation, add small, finely chopped onions to the butter before adding the mangetout.

pea orzotto

Parmesan cheese and white wine or sherry add body to this versatile pea and barley dish which makes a lovely base for simply grilled meat or fish.

850ml vegetable stock
2 tsp olive oil
50g onions, finely chopped
125g pearl barley
50ml white wine or sherry
150g frozen peas, defrosted
2 tbsp freshly grated Parmesan cheese
Salt and black pepper

Serves: 4
Prep time: 10 minutes
Cooking time: 1 hour

Nutrients per serving: Calories 193, Carbohydrate 32g, Protein 7g, Fat 5g (saturated fat 1g)

1 Put a kettle on to boil. Heat the stock to simmering point in a small saucepan. Meanwhile, in a larger saucepan, heat the olive oil then add the onions and fry them over a medium heat for 5 minutes, stirring frequently, until tender.

2 Add the pearl barley to the pan and stir continuously for 1-2 minutes until the grains are evenly coated with the oil and onion mixture. Increase the heat, add the wine or sherry to the pan and simmer for 1-2 minutes until the barley has absorbed the liquid.

3 Add a ladle of the hot stock to the barley, stirring continuously until it has been absorbed. Continue to add the stock a ladle at a time, stirring, and add half the peas before the last few ladles of stock. Continue stirring frequently until all the stock has been absorbed and the barley is *al dente*. This takes 35-45 minutes.

4 Meanwhile, place the remaining peas in a bowl and pour 100ml of boiling water over them, or just enough to cover them. Leave them to stand for 1-2 minutes, then purée them with their liquid using a food processor or a hand-held mixer.

5 Just before serving, stir the puréed peas and Parmesan into the orzotto and quickly heat them through. Season with salt and pepper to taste.

roast monkfish [with pea purée]

A creamy, colourful pool of sweet-tasting pea purée complements the earthy flavour of Indian spices, roasted to form a golden brown crust around the monkfish.

1 monkfish tail, skinned, weighing at
   least 400g
1 clove garlic
½-1 fresh red chilli
1 tbsp olive oil
1 tsp ground cumin
1 tsp ground coriander
½ tsp sugar
½ lemon
For the pea purée:
140g frozen peas
350ml vegetable stock
1 clove garlic
1 tbsp single cream
Salt and black pepper

Serves: 2
Cooking time: 30 minutes

Nutrients per serving: Calories 259,
Carbohydrate 10g, Protein 37g, Fat 10g
(saturated fat 2g)

1 Heat the oven to 200°C/gas 6. Trim the tail of any fins and tough outer membrane and place on a rack in a baking tray.

2 Peel and crush the garlic. Rinse, deseed and finely chop the chilli and place them in a small bowl with the olive oil, cumin, coriander and sugar. Add 1 teaspoon of juice from the lemon and stir to make a thick paste.

3 Spread the paste evenly over the monkfish tail, then roast it in the oven for 20 minutes or until cooked.

4 Meanwhile, make the pea purée. Put the peas into a pan with the stock and bring it to the boil. Peel the garlic, crush it into the peas and simmer, uncovered, for 5 minutes, skimming off any scum.

5 When the peas are tender, drain the stock into a measuring jug. Blend the peas with the cream and 150ml of the stock to make a textured purée. Season to taste and keep warm.

6 When the fish is cooked, cut the fillets carefully from both sides of the central bone. Divide the pea purée between two plates; serve the monkfish on top.

Plums
& gages

The home gardener with only a small plot must plan carefully where to plant and what variety of plums to grow. A bush or half-standard tree may have a spread of 4.5m or more and many varieties also need a nearby tree of a different variety for cross-pollination. A pyramid that can be restricted by pruning to 2.7m, with a spread of 2.5-3m, or a fan-shaped tree is the answer for a smaller space. Dessert plums will grow best against a sunny wall. If there is space for only one tree, choose a variety that is self-fertile and does not require the presence of another tree.

HARVESTING

Pick plums for cooking, bottling or freezing before they are quite ripe. If plums are intended for eating, leave them on the tree as long as possible so that they ripen. Go over the tree a number of times, choosing only the plums that are ready at each picking. In wet weather, pick gages before they are quite ripe or their skins are likely to split. Pick plums and gages so that the stalk comes away with the fruit.

PREPARATION

Wash plums and greengages and wipe them dry before serving. Serve them whole as dessert fruits but remove the stones before cooking. Cut along the indentations in the flesh, twist the halves apart and remove the stones with the tip of a knife.

braised turkey crown [with apples & plums]

Turkey breast, gently braised to keep it moist and tender and served with plums and apples makes a special Sunday lunch, or a small Christmas dinner.

1½ tbsp olive oil
1.8kg turkey breast crown joint
400g onions, cut into quarters
4 dessert apples such as Cox's or Russets, cut into quarters and cored
1 tbsp caster sugar
400g plums, halved and stoned
Salt and black pepper
225ml dry white wine
225ml concentrated turkey or chicken stock

For the garnish:
1 tbsp caster sugar
3 plums, halved, stoned and thickly sliced
2 dessert apples, cored, quartered and thickly sliced

Serves: 6
Prep time: 25 minutes
Cooking time: 1 hour 50 minutes

Nutrients per serving: Calories 410, Carbohydrate 30g, Protein 47g, Fat 10g (saturated fat 2g)

I Heat the oven to 220°C/gas 7. Warm the oil in a large, lidded flameproof casserole over a medium heat. Add the turkey crown and lightly brown it all over, taking care not to let the oil burn. Transfer the turkey crown to a plate and set aside.

2 Add the onions and the apples to the oil remaining in the casserole, sprinkle them with the sugar and cook for 3-4 minutes until lightly browned, stirring occasionally. Then mix in the plums and season with salt and a generous grinding of pepper.

3 Place the turkey, flesh side up, on top of the fruit and onion mixture and pour in the wine. Bring to the boil, then remove the casserole from the heat, cover with a tight-fitting lid and transfer it to the oven.

4 After 15 minutes, baste the turkey well with the wine, then replace the lid and return the casserole to the oven. Reduce the temperature to 190°C/gas 5) and cook for a further 15 minutes. Baste the turkey again, then cook it for 45 minutes to 1 hour, basting every 15 minutes, until the turkey juices run clear when the breast is pierced at its thickest point with a knife.

5 Meanwhile, to prepare the garnish, pour 225ml of water into a frying pan, add the sugar, stir to dissolve and bring to the boil. Then add the plum and apple slices. Reduce the heat to low and simmer for 2-3 minutes, until the fruit is just tender. Lift the fruit onto a plate. Boil the cooking juices until they become slightly syrupy, then return the fruit to the pan. Remove the pan from the heat and set aside.

6 When the turkey is cooked through, lift it onto a serving dish, cover and set aside in a warm place while you complete the sauce.

7 Purée the onion, fruit and cooking juices from the casserole dish in a food processor, or with a hand-held mixer, then pass the purée through a fine sieve into a saucepan. Stir in the stock and bring to the boil. Taste and adjust the seasoning, then pour the sauce into a serving jug.

8 Reheat the fruit garnish, spoon it around the turkey crown, and serve with the sauce.

chargrilled duck [with plum & chilli salsa]

A spicy sauce made with sweet and sour plums is a
wonderful companion for tender duck breasts.

2 Barbary duck breasts, about 350g each,
  or 4 ordinary duck breasts about
  175g each
Oil for greasing
A pinch of Chinese 5-spice powder
For the salsa:
1 tbsp olive or sunflower oil
150g onions, finely chopped
2 large cloves garlic, crushed
2 green chillies, deseeded and finely
  chopped
8 red plums, stoned and diced
1 small yellow or red pepper, finely
  chopped
2 tbsp coarsely chopped fresh
  coriander leaves
Juice of 2 limes
Salt and black pepper, or Chinese Sichuan
  peppercorns, ground
A few sprigs of fresh coriander to garnish

Serves: 4
Prep time: 25 minutes, plus 30 minutes,
  or overnight, marinating
Cooking time: 10-15 minutes

Nutrients per serving: Calories 269,
Carbohydrate 15g, Protein 26g, Fat 12g
(saturated fat 3g)

1 First make the salsa: heat the oil in a small frying pan, add the onions and
  garlic and cook over a high heat for 1-2 minutes until lightly browned.
  Remove and leave to cool.

2 Mix together the chillies, plums, pepper and coriander with the lime juice,
  add salt and pepper to taste, then stir in the onions and garlic. Set aside for
  at least 30 minutes, or overnight, to allow the flavours to develop.

3 Cut the skin and fat from the duck breasts and slash them several times.

4 Lightly brush a ridged, iron grill pan or heavy nonstick frying pan with oil
  and heat it until you feel a steady heat rising. Fry the breasts for at least
  3 minutes on each side, or until they feel springy when pressed with the
  back of a fork. Larger breasts will need longer cooking, and the length of
  time depends on how pink you like to serve your meat.

5 Sprinkle the breasts lightly with salt, pepper and 5-spice powder, then leave
  them to stand for 5 minutes.

6 Spoon the salsa in mounds onto four dinner plates. Slice the duck breasts
  diagonally and arrange them on top of the salsa. Garnish with sprigs of
  coriander.

deep custard tart [with caramelised plums]

Plums add sharp-sweet flavour and attractive colour to a traditional custard tart, popular since the Middle Ages.

85g plain flour
55g plain wholemeal flour
60g butter, diced
2 eggs, plus 2 egg yolks
4 tbsp caster sugar
1 tsp vanilla extract
500ml semi-skimmed milk
Grated nutmeg
For the caramelised plums:
6 large plums, stoned and quartered
2 tbsp sugar

Serves: 6
Prep time: 20 minutes, plus
    30 minutes chilling
Cooking time: 1½ hours

Nutrients per serving: Calories 320, Carbohydrate 42g, Protein 9g, Fat 14g (saturated fat 7g), Fibre 2g

1 Put both flours in a bowl and rub in the butter until the mixture resembles fine breadcrumbs. Mix in 2-3 tablespoons of cold water, until the mixture comes together.

2 Roll out the pastry on a lightly floured surface, then use to line a 24 x 18cm pie dish. Trim off excess pastry and pinch round the edge to decorate. Prick the base and chill for 30 minutes.

3 Heat the oven to 200°C/gas 6. Line the pastry case with greaseproof paper and baking beans and bake for 20 minutes. Remove the paper and beans and bake for a further 5 minutes until dry and part-cooked. Reduce the oven to 160°C/gas 3.

4 Beat the whole eggs and yolks with the sugar and vanilla until well mixed. Gradually beat in the milk. Pour into the pastry case and sprinkle with a little grated nutmeg. Bake for about 50 minutes, until the custard is lightly set but still slightly wobbly. Set aside while you cook the plums.

5 Heat the grill on the hottest setting. Place the plums, cut side up, in a shallow flameproof dish just big enough to hold them. Sprinkle with the sugar and grill for about 5 minutes until juicy and well browned in places.

6 Serve slices of the warm custard tart with the hot plums, or serve both cold.

oaty plum crumble

Sweet poached fresh plums are given a buttery, golden topping of crunchy oats, nuts, mixed spices and brown sugar, and baked to make a comforting, homely pudding.

900g ripe but firm plums
115g caster sugar
60g unsalted butter
1 tsp mixed spice
115g jumbo rolled oats
60g demerara sugar
60g mixed chopped nuts
Whipped cream or ice cream to serve

Serves: 4
Cooking time: 30 minutes

Nutrients per serving: Calories 679, Carbohydrate 87g, Protein 9g, Fat 35g (saturated fat 17g)

1 Heat the oven to 230°C/gas 8. Rinse, dry and halve the plums and remove the stones. If the plums are large, cut them into quarters.

2 Put the plums into a flameproof casserole, about 20cm in diameter and 5cm deep. Add 2-3 tablespoons of water and the caster sugar. Cover, and poach over a moderate heat for 8-10 minutes, until the plums begin to soften, stirring occasionally.

3 Meanwhile, melt the butter in a frying pan, then stir in the mixed spice, rolled oats, demerara sugar and chopped nuts.

4 Spoon the oat crumble mixture evenly over the top of the plums. Put the casserole into the oven and bake for 12-15 minutes, checking from time to time, until the oats are golden brown. Serve with whipped cream or ice cream.

plum & apple meringue tart

Serve this fruity tart, with its soft, gooey topping, soon after it is baked so that the juices do not make the crust soggy.

100g plain white flour
1 tsp caster sugar
50g 70 per cent fat spread, diced
1 egg white
For the filling:
600g Bramley apples
90g caster sugar
Finely grated zest of 1 lemon
Juice of ½ lemon
500g sweet, purple dessert plums,
  such as Victoria
For the meringue:
2 egg whites
80g caster sugar

Serves: 4-6
Prep time: 30 minutes, plus at least
  30 minutes chilling
Cooking time: 1 hour 10 minutes

Nutrients per serving, when serving 4:
Calories 431, Carbohydrate 87g,
Protein 6g, Fat 9g (saturated fat 2g)

1 Sift the flour and sugar into a bowl and rub in the fat spread until the mixture resembles breadcrumbs. Stir in the egg white to make a slightly soft, but not sticky, pastry.

2 Put the pastry onto a lightly floured surface and knead for a few seconds until it is smooth. Roll out thinly into a 23cm round. Use the pastry to line a 20cm round tart tin with a removable base, pressing down firmly. Trim the edges, then lightly prick the base with a fork. Put the pastry case into the refrigerator to chill for at least 30 minutes.

3 Meanwhile, make the filling. Peel and cut the apples into quarters, then core and cut them into 1cm slices. Put the apples into a nonstick saucepan, stir in 50g of the sugar, the lemon zest and juice and 1 tablespoon of water. Cover and simmer over a medium-low heat for 10-15 minutes, stirring occasionally, until the apples are just soft and fluffy, but still retain some texture.

4 Halve and stone the plums. Pour 150ml of water into a large frying pan over a high heat, stir in the remaining sugar and bring to the boil, stirring continuously. Reduce the heat to medium, place the plums in a single layer in the syrup and poach for 15 minutes, turning them over halfway through, until they are soft when pricked with a knife.

5 Spoon the apples into a sieve and leave them to drain. Using a slotted spoon, transfer the plums to a plate. Bring the plum liquid to the boil and continue boiling until it has reduced to a thick syrup. Pour the syrup over the plums and set aside to cool.

6 Meanwhile, heat the oven to 220°C/gas 7 and place a baking sheet in the centre to warm.

7 Line the chilled pastry case with foil, weigh down with baking beans, place it on the hot baking sheet and bake for 15 minutes. Remove the foil and bake the pastry for a further 5-10 minutes until it is golden brown and cooked through.

8 Spoon the apples into the pastry case, spreading them out evenly, then arrange the plums on top. Set aside.

9 To make the meringue, put the egg whites into a clean bowl and whisk until they form soft peaks. Add the caster sugar a tablespoon at a time, whisking well between each addition, until the meringue is stiff and shiny.

10 Spoon the meringue on top of the pie and spread it evenly over the plums, then make large peaks in it with a palette knife.

11 Bake the tart for 4-5 minutes until the meringue is golden brown. Leave it to set for 1-2 minutes, then remove it from the tin. Serve the tart warm or at room temperature.

plum jam

3kg plums
850ml-1l water
3kg sugar

Nutrients per teaspoon: Calories 13,
Carbohydrate 4g, Protein 0g, Fat 0g
(no saturated fat)

1 Wash and dry the plums; cut in half and remove the stones. Crack 12-24 stones, extract the kernels and blanch them. Put the plums, kernels and water in a pan and simmer until reduced by half.

2 Add the sugar, stirring until dissolved, then increase the heat and boil rapidly until setting point is reached. Test for setting point by dropping a teaspoon of jam onto a cold saucer. If it is not ready, continue boiling and testing every 10 minutes until it is.

3 Remove from the heat and use a jug to pour the jam into clean, warmed jars. Cover and seal immediately, then label and date each jar. Store in a cool, dark place for up to a year.

plum wine

2.25kg Victoria plums
525g raisins
1.3kg sugar
½ tsp grape tannin
1 tsp citric acid
1 tsp pectin-destroying enzyme
1 Campden tablet
3.5l water
Sherry yeast and nutrient

Nutrients per serving: Calories 115,
Carbohydrate 7g, Protein 0g, Fat 0g
(no saturated fat)

1 Pour the water into a bin and add the tannin, the citric acid, pectin-destroying enzyme and a crushed Campden tablet.

2 Wash and crush the plums and drop them into the bin. Cover the bin and leave it in a warm place for 24 hours.

3 Activate the yeast in a starter bottle. Add the raisins, nutrient and yeast to the mash, re-cover the bin and place it in the warm for 4-5 days.

4 Press and strain the pulp and add the sugar, dissolving this first in warm water. Since this is a high-alcohol wine, add the sugar in small doses each time fermentation slows down.

5 Best results are obtained by using a hydrometer, but there is also a good rule-of-thumb method. Put in half the total amount of sugar at first, half the remainder about ten days later and the residue about eight days after that.

6 When adding the extra sugar, extract a little of the wine and dissolve the sugar in it. Pour the solution back gently.

7 Pour the strained mixture into a fermentation jar, top up with cold water and fit an airlock to the jar. Tie on a label describing the contents and store the jar at room temperature until fermentation is complete.

A native of South America, most probably brought to England in the wake of raiding expeditions by Sir Francis Drake in the 1580s, it was not until the 18th century that the British regarded the potato as anything more than a novelty or cattle food. Since then it has grown in popularity to become one of Britain's most important food crops. Unless space is at an absolute premium, it is a good idea to grow at least a few potatoes – preferably of an early variety. Potatoes grow best in an open position and the best results are obtained from soil that has been well manured. Dig the ground in autumn or winter, working in compost or well-rotted mature at the rate of a bucketful to the square metre.

Potatoes

HARVESTING

As a rough guide, you should be able to gather a few new potatoes about 12-14 weeks after planting though this may vary considerably. Maincrop potatoes take at least 20 weeks to come to full maturity and be ready for storing. To gather a few early potatoes, brush away a little soil from the side of a ridge and remove any potatoes that have grown to the size of an egg. Replace the soil over the smaller tubers and leave them to grow. They should at least double in size over the next two or three weeks, after which the crop can be lifted as required.

When lifting potatoes, insert the fork at least 15cm away from the stems to avoid impaling the tubers. Push it well into the sides of the ridge so that the plant can be lifted and thrown between the rows in a single action. Before lifting the whole crop of maincrop potatoes, test the potatoes by rubbing the skin with your thumb. If it does not rub off the crop is ready for storing. Store in a dry, cool, frost-free place. Place them in light proof but ventilated containers such as boxes or hessian, or pile on a dry floor and cover with straw.

PREPARATION

New potatoes should be scrubbed or scraped but never peeled or boiled in their skins. Maincrop potatoes should be scrubbed free of dirt, peeled and any eyes removed, then cut into even sized pieces. Place in cold water and boil for 20 minutes. Baked potatoes in their jackets need at least an hour in a hot oven.

potato soup

750g potatoes, peeled and roughly
   chopped
1 large onion, finely chopped
2 leeks, cut crossways into narrow slices
2 carrots, peeled and chopped
50g butter
1l white stock
1 bouquet garni
Salt and pepper
50g cooked ham
Chopped chives to garnish

Serves: 4
Cooking time: 40 minutes

Nutrients per serving: Calories 335,
Carbohydrate 41g, Protein 18g, Fat 14g
(saturated fat 6g)

1 Melt the butter in a pan, add the onion and cook gently for about
   5 minutes, until soft but not coloured. Add the potatoes, leeks and
   carrots and cook until all the vegetables are coated.

2 Add the stock and bouquet garni. Season with salt and pepper, cover and
   simmer for about 30 minutes or until the vegetables are tender and the
   potatoes are breaking up. Remove the bouquet garni. Put the soup in a
   liquidiser briefly.

3 Reheat the soup, adding milk to give the required consistency. Dice the
   ham, stir it into the soup and correct the seasoning.

4 Serve sprinkled with chopped chives.

Cajun potato salad

Green pepper, celery and onion, known as the 'holy trinity'
of Cajun cooking, are the basis of many dishes, including
this salad, which is ideal for picnics and barbecues.

500g waxy salad potatoes
Salt and black pepper
1 small green pepper
2 sticks celery
1 small red onion
For the dressing:
150ml mayonnaise
2 tsp Dijon mustard
A few dashes of Tabasco sauce

Serves: 4
Cooking time: 30 minutes

Nutrients per serving: Calories 346,
Carbohydrate 19g, Protein 3g, Fat 29g
(saturated fat 4g)

1 Put a kettle of water on to boil. Scrape the potatoes and put them into a
   pan with the boiling water and some salt. Return to the boil and simmer for
   15-20 minutes or until the potatoes are tender.

2 Rinse, dry, halve and deseed the pepper, slice it into strips and put it into a
   salad bowl. Rinse, dry, destring and finely slice the celery; reserve the leaves
   for a garnish and add the rest to the pepper. Peel the onion, halve it
   lengthways and slice it lengthways again into crescents. Add it to the bowl.

3 To make the dressing, mix the mayonnaise and mustard in a small bowl
   and add Tabasco to taste.

4 Drain the potatoes, cool under running water, drain again and
   add to the salad. Add the dressing, grind pepper over the salad and mix.
   Garnish with celery leaves.

cheese potato puffs

Crispy little puffs of mashed potato are given extra taste with nutmeg and spring onion and a generous helping of strong Cheddar cheese.

450g mashed potatoes
4 spring onions, finely shredded
50g mature Cheddar cheese, finely grated
3 tbsp milk
25g butter
Salt and black pepper
Grated nutmeg to taste
2 eggs, separated

Serves: 4-6
Prep time: 20 minutes
Cooking time: 15 minutes

Nutrients per serving when serving 6:
Calories 180, Carbohydrate 12g,
Protein 6g, Fat 12g (saturated fat 7g)

1 Heat the oven to 220°C/gas 7 and generously butter a nonstick bun tin, also greasing the sections between the pans.

2 Mix the mashed potatoes, spring onions and cheese in a bowl.

3 Warm the milk and butter with salt, pepper and nutmeg, swirling the saucepan to help to melt the butter. Heat to just below boiling point, then beat the milk into the potato mixture and beat in the egg yolks.

4 Whisk the egg whites to form soft peaks, mix a spoonful or two into the potato mixture to loosen it, then fold in the rest as lightly as possible.

5 Spoon the mixture into the bun tins and bake for about 15 minutes until golden brown and well risen.

light haddock pie [with pesto mash]

Firm textured haddock makes an excellent pie filling, especially when teamed with potatoes, cider and prawns.

300g white haddock fillet

300g undyed smoked haddock fillet

1 large bay leaf

500ml skimmed milk

Salt and black pepper

800g floury potatoes, such as
   King Edwards

40g low-fat spread

1-2 tbsp pesto

200g leeks, thinly sliced, or 1 small onion,
   thinly sliced

150ml dry cider

25g plain white flour

125g cooked, peeled prawns,
   defrosted if frozen

2 tbsp half-fat crème fraîche

2 tbsp dried breadcrumbs

3-4 tomatoes, thinly sliced

Serves: 4-6
Prep time: 20 minutes
Cooking time: 30-35 minutes

Nutrients per serving, when serving 4:
Calories 526, Carbohydrate 52g,
Protein 49g, Fat 14g (saturated fat 3g)

1 Place all the haddock in a single layer in a roasting tin or a large frying pan, add the bay leaf, milk and pepper to taste and poach over a medium heat for 6-8 minutes until the flesh turns opaque and flakes easily when tested with a knife.

2 Meanwhile, peel the potatoes and cut them into chunks.

3 Put a large saucepan of lightly salted water on to boil. Remove the fish from the tin, and skin and flake the flesh, checking for any bones. Strain the milk into a measuring jug, discard the bay leaf and set the milk aside.

4 Add the potatoes to the saucepan, bring the water back to the boil and cook the potatoes for 10-15 minutes until they are tender.

5 Drain the potatoes well, reserving a little of the water, and return them to the pan over a medium heat to dry. Mash well, then beat in 1 tablespoon of the spread, check the seasoning and stir in the pesto to taste. (If the potatoes are a little dry, beat in 1-2 tablespoons of the reserved cooking water.) Set the mash aside. Heat the grill to high.

6 Melt the remaining spread in a saucepan, add the leeks or onion and cook for 7 minutes, or until softened. Pour in the cider, increase the heat to high and boil until the cider is reduced by half.

7 Stir in the flour and continue boiling for about 1 minute, then gradually stir in the reserved poaching milk, stirring briskly until the sauce thickens and becomes smooth. Reduce the heat, season to taste and simmer for 3 minutes, stirring occasionally.

8 Stir in the prawns, crème fraîche and flaked fish and reheat for 2 minutes. Be careful not to let the mixture boil or to break up the fish.

9 Spoon the fish mixture into a shallow 20 x 30cm flameproof serving dish. Spread the pesto mash over the top and smooth the surface. Sprinkle on the breadcrumbs and arrange the tomato slices on top.

10 Reduce the grill heat to medium and grill the pie until it is crisp, but not burnt, then serve.

roasted mediterranean lamb [& potatoes]

This one-dish meal is an easy Greek-style roast bursting with the fresh flavours of lemon and herbs.

550g lean lamb leg steak

300g onions, cut into quarters, or shallots, peeled but left whole

500g small new potatoes, scrubbed

1 large lemon, cut into 8 wedges

1 tbsp olive oil

12 cloves garlic, peeled

6 sprigs each of fresh rosemary and thyme

Salt and black pepper

180g cherry or baby plum tomatoes, cut in half

1 tbsp mint sauce, or 2 tbsp mint jelly, melted

Serves: 4
Prep time: 15-20 minutes
Cooking time: 1 hour-1 hour 5 minutes

Nutrients per serving: Calories 346, Carbohydrate 27g, Protein 29g, Fat 14g (saturated fat 5g)

1 Heat the oven to 200°C/gas 6. Trim any fat off the lamb, cut the meat into 2.5cm cubes and arrange them in a large roasting tin with the onions or shallots and potatoes, cut in half if large.

2 Squeeze the juice from four of the lemon wedges, whisk it into the oil and drizzle it over the meat and vegetables. Tuck all eight lemon wedges, the garlic and half of the herbs into the dish and season to taste. Cover the tin tightly with foil and cook for 45 minutes.

3 Remove the foil and the herbs and discard them, then increase the oven heat to 220°C/gas 7. Add the tomatoes and remaining herbs and baste the meat and vegetables with the mint sauce or melted jelly. Roast for a further 15-20 minutes, uncovered, until the meat and vegetables are browned and tender.

4 Divide the lamb and vegetables between four plates, spoon on any roasting juices and serve.

venison sausages [with Stilton mash]

An old favourite is given a distinctive new flavour: game bangers and a designer mash of celeriac, potatoes and blue cheese excellent with a bottle of hearty red wine.

700g floury potatoes, such as Desirée or King Edwards

400g celeriac

Salt and black pepper

2 tbsp olive oil

8 fat venison sausages, about 75g each

3 tbsp milk

50g butter

50g Stilton cheese

A pinch of ground mace

Mustards, chutneys and pickles to serve

Serves: 4
Cooking time: 30 minutes

Nutrients per serving: Calories 531, Carbohydrate 41g, Protein 29g, Fat 60g (saturated fat 27g)

1 Put a kettle of water on to boil; heat the oven to a low setting. Peel the potatoes and the celeriac, cut them into small chunks and put them into separate saucepans. Cover both with boiling water, add salt and cook gently for 15 minutes, or until soft.

2 Meanwhile, heat the oil in a pan over a moderate heat and fry the sausages for 10 minutes, turning frequently to brown them well all over, then transfer to the oven to keep warm.

3 Drain the celeriac and purée it with the milk in a blender, or by hand. Drain the potatoes, add the butter and mash them by hand. Combine the celeriac and potato purées, then crumble in the Stilton cheese, season with salt, pepper and mace, and mash again.

4 Pile the purée onto a warm dish and arrange the sausages round or on top. Serve with a selection of mustards, chutneys and pickles.

The more help a man has
in his garden, the less it
belongs to him.

William M. Davies

new potatoes [in watercress & walnut vinaigrette]

50g walnut kernels
1 bunch watercress
4 spring onions
400g small waxy potatoes
3 tbsp olive oil
2 tbsp walnut oil
1 tbsp red wine vinegar
Salt and black pepper

Serves: 4
Prep time: 10 minutes
Cooking time: 20-30 minutes

Nutrients per serving: Calories 293,
Carbohydrate 18g, Protein 5g, Fat 23g
(saturated fat 3g)

I Crush half the walnut kernels in a mortar or food processor. Trim and chop the watercress and finely shred the spring onions.

2 Wash the potatoes but do not scrape them. Leave the smallest ones whole but cut larger ones to the same size as the smallest ones. Cook in salted water until tender.

3 Put the crushed walnuts in a jar with the oils, vinegar, salt and pepper and shake it well to combine.

4 Drain the cooked potatoes. Shake the dressing again and toss it gently through the potatoes. Leave to cool.

5 Scatter the watercress and spring onions over the salad, toss again and then serve the salad scattered with the uncrushed walnut kernels.

new potato & spinach fritatta

This chunky omelette makes a perfect light lunch, and is an ideal way of using up leftover new potatoes.

1 tbsp olive oil
150g red onions, finely chopped
1 large red pepper, chopped
150g baby spinach leaves
1 clove garlic, crushed
6 spring onions, chopped
500g cooked new potatoes, sliced
3 eggs
4 tbsp skimmed milk
1 tbsp chopped fresh basil
2 tsp finely chopped fresh chives
1 tbsp chopped fresh flat-leaved
  parsley
Salt and black pepper
25g Parmesan cheese, finely grated
25g half-fat mature Cheddar cheese,
  finely grated

Serves: 4
Prep time: 20 minutes
Cooking time: 20-30 minutes

Nutrients per serving: Calories 261,
Carbohydrate 26g, Protein 15g, Fat 12g
(saturated fat 4g)

I Heat the oil in a large frying pan with a flameproof handle and sauté the onions and pepper for 5 minutes, or until they have softened.

2 Add the spinach, garlic and spring onions and continue frying for 2 minutes, or until the spinach has wilted. Then stir in the potatoes.

3 Beat the eggs in a large bowl with the milk, basil, chives and parsley, and add salt and pepper to taste. Pour the mixture over the vegetables, reduce the heat and cook for 10-20 minutes until the egg begins to set.

4 Meanwhile, heat the grill to medium. Sprinkle the cheeses over the fritatta, then place the pan under the grill for 2 minutes, or until the cheese has melted and turned golden. Cut the fritatta into wedges and serve.

potato & horseradish rösti

Tasty horseradish brings unusual piquancy to these golden brown potato cakes.

400g floury potatoes, such as
   King Edwards, peeled and grated
1 egg, beaten
1 tbsp creamed horseradish
6 spring onions, finely chopped
Salt and black pepper
1 tbsp sunflower oil
Chopped fresh parsley to garnish
4 tbsp half-fat crème fraîche to serve

Serves: 4
Prep time: 10 minutes
Cooking time: 8-12 minutes

Nutrients per serving: Calories 144,
Carbohydrate 15g, Protein 4g, Fat 8g
(saturated fat 3g)

1 Squeeze out any moisture from the grated potatoes with your hands, then place them in a bowl. Add the egg, horseradish, spring onions and salt and pepper, and mix thoroughly.

2 Heat the oil in a large, nonstick frying pan over a medium heat. Drop eight mounds of the mixture into the pan and press down with the back of the spoon to make 5mm thick potato cakes.

3 Fry the rösti for 2-3 minutes on each side until they are firm and golden. You may need to cook the rösti in two batches to prevent them sticking together.

4 Drain them well on kitchen paper. Serve hot, topped with the crème fraîche and garnished with parsley.

potato pancakes [with smoked salmon]

The humble potato makes a sophisticated starter when it is sharpened with onion, made into crisp pancakes and topped with soured cream and strips of smoked salmon.

500g floury potatoes, such as
   King Edwards
1 medium onion
1 large egg
2 tbsp wholemeal flour
Salt and black pepper
Sunflower oil for frying
200g smoked salmon
150ml thick, soured cream
Sprigs of fresh dill or flat-leaved parsley
   to garnish

Serves: 4-6 (makes 12 pancakes)
Cooking time: 30 minutes

Nutrients per serving, when serving 4:
Calories 342, Carbohydrate 28g,
Protein 20g, Fat 18g (saturated fat 6g)

1 Heat the oven to low. Peel and grate the potatoes and finely chop the onions; put them both in a sieve. Press with a spoon to squeeze out as much starchy liquid as possible.

2 Transfer to a bowl, add the egg, flour, salt and pepper and mix well.

3 Pour the oil into a frying pan to a depth of about 8mm and heat it until it shows a haze.

4 Put a tablespoon of the potato mixture into the oil, flattening it to a small pancake about 5cm in diameter. Keep adding more tablespoons of the mixture to the pan, cooking four to six at a time. Fry them for about 1 minute or until they are golden on the bottom, then turn them over and cook the other side until they are crisp and golden but still soft in the centre.

5 Remove the pancakes from the pan, drain them on kitchen paper and keep them warm in the oven while you cook the remainder.

6 Cut the salmon into small strips. Rinse and dry the dill or parsley. Serve each pancake topped with a spoonful of soured cream and a few strips of salmon, and garnished with the dill or parsley.

roast new potatoes [with rosemary]

Tiny, tender new potatoes, delicately scented with lemon and flavoured with fresh rosemary, are roasted to glowing, golden perfection in this quick, simple, tasty dish.

600g even-sized baby new potatoes
2 tbsp olive oil
1 lemon
2 -3 large sprigs of fresh rosemary
Salt and black pepper

Serves: 4
Cooking time: 30 minutes

Nutrients per serving: Calories 158, Carbohydrate 25g, Protein 3g, Fat 6g (saturated fat 1g)

1 Heat the oven to 230°C/gas 8 and put a kettle of water on to boil.

2 Scrub the potatoes and put them into a large saucepan. Cover with boiling water, bring back to the boil and boil gently for 5 minutes.

3 Meanwhile, pour the olive oil into a large, shallow roasting tin and put it into the oven to heat.

4 Wash any wax off the lemon and finely grate the rind or remove with a zester. Rinse and strip the rosemary leaves from the stems.

5 Drain the potatoes well. Put them into the hot oil and stir well to coat evenly. Sprinkle the lemon rind, rosemary leaves and some salt and black pepper over them. Make sure the oil is really hot before you begin roasting – the potatoes should start to sizzle as soon as you put them into the tin.

6 Roast the potatoes on the top shelf of the oven for 20 minutes, until golden.

roast potatoes [with a sesame seed crust]

1kg floury maincrop potatoes, peeled
Salt
3 tbsp sesame seeds
100g vegetable fat, dripping or meat fat (eg from a roast joint)

Serves: 6
Prep time: 20 minutes
Cooking time: about 1½ hours

Nutrients per serving: Calories 320, Carbohydrate 28g, Protein 5g, Fat 21g (saturated fat 7g)

1 Heat the oven to 200°C/gas 6. Cut the potatoes into evenly sized pieces then bring them to the boil in a large pan of salted water and keep at a low rolling boil for 5 minutes. Drain and leave until cool enough to handle.

2 Pull the tines of a fork over the surface of each potato to score it. Roll each potato in sesame seeds.

3 Melt the fat in a large roasting tin in the hot oven. Turn the potatoes in the fat a few times then roast them for about 1½ hours, turning the potatoes again every 20 minutes or so until they are brown and crispy.

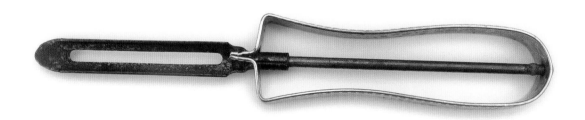

To forget how to dig
the earth and to tend the soil
is to forget ourselves.

Mahatma Gandhi

Pumpkins & squashes

Pumpkins, squashes and edible gourds are found in one form or another in most tropical regions. There are two types of plants, bushes and trailers, both of which occupy a great deal of space so they may not be suitable if you have limited land. Pumpkins thrive in full sun in rich, well-drained soil; the top of a compost heap is ideal. They mature in early autumn and the hollowed out pumpkin, lit with a night light, is indelibly associated with the grinning jack o' lanterns of halloween.

HARVESTING

Cut small-fruited varieties as they mature in summer. Leave large-fruited types on the plants until late autumn. Store for winter use in a frost-free shed.

PREPARATION

Pumpkins and squashes belong to the same family as marrows and courgettes. The smaller squashes, which often have crooked necks, may be cooked like courgettes after the thin skin has been removed. Young, ripe squashes are also suitable for steaming, baking, mashing and soups. Two classic pumpkin dishes are pumpkin pie and pumpkin soup but they can also be roasted and mashed – or boiled for a more unusual accompanying dish.

spiced pumpkin [& bacon soup]

Aromatic cumin enlivens a hearty cold-weather soup of colourful pumpkin and bacon.

1 tbsp olive oil
200g onions, sliced
1.3kg pumpkin, peeled, deseeded and cut into chunks
125g extra-trimmed smoked back bacon, diced
1 tbsp ground cumin
750ml vegetable stock
Salt and black pepper
Sprigs of fresh coriander to garnish
Crusty bread rolls, to serve

Serves: 4
Prep time: 15 minutes
Cooking time: 40 minutes

Nutrients per serving: Calories 90, Carbohydrate 29g, Protein 13g, Fat 7g (saturated fat 1g)

I Heat the oil in a saucepan and add the onions. Stir to coat them with oil, then cover and cook them over a low heat for 5-10 minutes until they start to soften, stirring occasionally.

2 Add the pumpkin, bacon and cumin to the pan. Stir, then cover and simmer for 10 minutes, stirring occasionally.

3 Add the stock, raise the heat and bring to the boil. Lower the heat and simmer, uncovered, for 20 minutes, or until the pumpkin is tender.

4 Purée the soup with a hand-held mixer or in a food processor. Season to taste, garnish with coriander and black pepper and serve, accompanied by a crusty bread roll, if you like.

spiced butternut [& millet soup]

Chillies add bite to a warming winter squash soup.

1kg butternut squash or other winter
   squash or pumpkin
3 tbsp cooking oil
1 large onion, finely chopped
2-3 cloves garlic, finely chopped
5cm piece of ginger, grated
2 dried red chillies, crumbled
2 bay leaves
1 tsp mustard seeds
1 tsp cumin seeds
50g millet
Salt and black pepper
3 tbsp tomato ketchup
Juice of ½ lemon
2 tsp garam masala
1 bunch chopped watercress to garnish

Serves: 6
Prep time: 20-25 minutes
Cooking time: 30-35 minutes

1 Cut the squash in half, remove and discard the seeds and fibre, chop the flesh into chunks and peel them.

2 Heat the cooking oil in a deep pan and fry the onion, garlic, ginger and chillies over a low heat for 5 minutes.

3 Add 1.7 litres of water to the pan. Grate in the squash and add the bay leaves. Bring to the boil and simmer for about 10 minutes until the squash is soft, then mash it well.

4 Dry-fry the mustard, cumin and millet over a moderate heat until the millet looks mildly toasted and the mustard seeds have mostly popped.

5 Tip the spiced millet into the soup, sprinkle on some salt and simmer for about 15 minutes until the millet is soft. Remove from the heat and leave to stand for at least 10 minutes.

6 When you are ready to serve the soup, remove the bay leaves and stir in the ketchup, lemon juice, garam masala and a generous sprinkling of pepper. Reheat, stir in the watercress and serve with hot bread.

Nutrients per serving: Calories 155,
Carbohydrate 24, Protein 3g, Fat 6g
(saturated fat 1g)

butternut, blue cheese [& walnut salad]

An autumnal salad to make the most of the squash season. Dorset Blue Vinney cheese adds good, sharp flavour.

400g butternut squash
1 small frisée lettuce, washed
40g lamb's lettuce, washed
85g Blue Vinney cheese, rind removed
55g walnuts, roughly chopped
Salt and black pepper
2 tbsp extra virgin olive oil
2 tbsp walnut oil
1 tbsp sherry vinegar

Serves: 4
Prep time: 15 minutes
Cooking time: 1 minute

Nutrients per serving: Calories 324,
Carbohydrate 10g, Protein 8g, Fat 28g
(saturated fat 7g)

1 Halve the squash lengthways and scoop out the pith and seeds. Peel each half, then cut into 3mm slices. Transfer the slices to a saucepan and add plenty of boiling water. Bring to the boil for 30 seconds, drain in a colander, then run cold tap water over to cool. Set aside to drain.

2 Tear the frisée into a salad bowl. Add the lamb's lettuce and mix briefly.

3 Crumble the cheese over the salad, then sprinkle with the walnuts and drained squash. Add salt and pepper to taste.

4 Put both oils and the vinegar into a small screw-top jar, cover and shake vigorously to emulsify. Trickle over the salad, toss gently to coat, then serve with granary bread.

Native American trinity

Tuck into a filling vegetarian stew of squash, tomatoes, corn and beans, spiced up with green chillies and herbs.

200g dried haricot beans, soaked in boiling water for 30 minutes
3 tbsp olive oil
2 onions, finely chopped
1 tsp dried oregano
1 large butternut squash, about 800g
2 green chillies, deseeded and finely chopped
500g tomatoes, peeled and chopped
2 cobs of corn
Salt and black pepper
3 tbsp chopped parsley

Serves: 6
Prep time: 25-30 minutes plus 30 minutes soaking for beans
Cooking time: about 2 hours

Nutrients per serving: Calories 375, Carbohydrate 56g, Protein 16g, Fat 11g (saturated fat 1.5g). High in fibre.

1 Drain the soaked beans, put them into a pan of fresh water, bring to the boil and cook fast for 10 minutes. Drain and put the beans into fresh water, bring to the boil then simmer for a further 1 hour 20 minutes or until tender. Drain and set aside.

2 Heat the oil in a large saucepan, add the onions and oregano and cook over a low heat for about 10 minutes, stirring them regularly.

3 Cut the squash into quarters and cut away and discard the central seeds and fibre. Peel the flesh and cut it into 2.5cm cubes.

4 Add the cut-up squash, chillies and 125ml of water to the onions in the pan. Cover and leave to simmer for 10 minutes.

5 Add the tomatoes and simmer, covered, for a further 20-25 minutes, until the squash is very soft and the tomatoes have reduced to a sauce.

6 Pull away the husks and silk from the corn cobs. Strip off the kernels with a strong, sharp knife, holding the cobs upright on a board and cutting downwards.

7 Add the corn and drained beans to the stew and simmer gently for a further 5 minutes. Season, sprinkle with chopped parsley and serve.

pumpkin pie

The classic American autumn dessert.

500g pumpkin purée
250g shortcrust pastry
300ml single cream
3 eggs
1 tbsp grated lemon peel
150g caster sugar
½ tsp salt
1 tsp ground ginger
½ tsp each of ground cinnamon and ground cloves

Serves: 6
Cooking time: 1¼ hours

Nutrients per serving: Calories 437, Carbohydrate 49g, Protein 8g, Fat 25g (saturated fat 11g)

1 Make the purée by cutting the pumpkin into chunks, removing the skin and seeds and boiling in lightly salted water until tender. Drain, rub through a sieve, then set aside to cool.

2 Roll out the pastry and line a 23-25cm flan ring set on a baking sheet. Bake blind in the oven at a temperature of 200°C/gas 6, until brown.

3 Beat the cream lightly with the eggs, lemon peel and sugar. Stir this mixture into the pumpkin purée and add the salt, ginger, cinnamon and ground cloves. Combine thoroughly, then spoon the filling into the pie shell and bake until set and brown.

4 Serve cold with whipped cream to accompany.

summer squash [with polenta]

This colourful and adaptable stew on a base of polenta is an excellent way to deal with a glut of ripe summer vegetables.

175g instant polenta
3 tbsp olive oil
1 small onion
1 clove garlic
500g mixed yellow and green patty pan squashes and/or young green and yellow courgettes
4 sprigs of fresh thyme
Salt and black pepper
175g Cheshire cheese
25g butter
2 beef tomatoes
1 lemon
A few sprigs of parsley

Serves: 4
Cooking time: 30 minutes

Nutrients per serving: Calories 485, Carbohydrate 39g, Protein 18g, Fat 29g (saturated fat 14g)

1 Put the polenta into a saucepan with 700ml of water. Bring to the boil, reduce the heat and simmer for 8 minutes. Stir occasionally to remove any lumps.

2 Slowly heat the olive oil in a shallow pan over a moderate heat. Halve, peel and finely chop the onion, peel and crush the garlic and cook for 5-8 minutes, until soft.

3 Meanwhile, rinse, top and tail the squashes and/or the courgettes. Cut the squashes into quarters, the courgettes into rounds, and add them to the onion. Rinse and add the thyme, add salt and pepper, and cook for 10 minutes.

4 When the polenta comes away cleanly from the sides of the pan, remove it from the heat. Grate the cheese and beat it into the polenta with the butter, then season to taste, cover and leave in a warm place.

5 Rinse and dice the tomatoes and add them to the squash stew.

6 Wash any wax from the lemon, then finely grate the rind. Rinse, dry and finely chop the parsley. Add both to the vegetables. Remove and discard the thyme, then serve the stew with the polenta.

pumpkin chutney

A spicy chutney that goes well with both meat and cheese.

1.25kg pumpkin (prepared weight), cut into small chunks
500g red tomatoes, skinned and sliced
250g onions, peeled and sliced
50g sultanas
750g soft brown sugar
2 cloves garlic, crushed
2 tsp each of ground ginger, black pepper and ground allspice
2½ tbsp salt
600ml tarragon vinegar

Approx yield: 2kg

Nutrients per tablespoon: Calories 25, Carbohydrate 6g, Protein 0g, Fat 0g (no saturated fat)

1 Put the pumpkin, tomatoes and onions in a pan with the sultanas, sugar, garlic, spices, salt and vinegar.

2 Bring to the boil and simmer gently until soft and the chutney is of the consistency of jam.

3 Pot at once.

Raspberries

Among the most delicious of summer fruits, raspberries are grown throughout the cooler parts of Europe. A site in full sun will produce the best crops, but the canes will also thrive in partial shade and will yield well even during a cool, damp summer. For the space they occupy, raspberries give a higher yield than any fruit other than strawberries. There are two kinds of raspberries: summer fruiting varieties that produce fruit on the previous season's shoots during July and August, and the lighter cropping autumn varieties that fruit on current season's growth from mid September onwards.

HARVESTING

Pick raspberries when they are well-coloured all over. At this stage they will come away easily from the stalk, leaving the core behind.

PREPARATION

Use raspberries as soon as possible after picking. They bruise easily so if washing is needed, place in single layers in a colander and immerse in cold water. Drain thoroughly before erving.
The berries should be hulled by removing the flower calyces.

berry jellies

Traditional homemade jellies taste quite different from packet versions and are full of vitamins and flavour.

450g raspberries, defrosted if frozen,
  plus extra for layering
Grated zest and juice of 1 unwaxed lemon
55g caster sugar
2 sachets of gelatine, 11.7g each

Serves: 4
Prep time: 10 minutes, plus 3 hours
  chilling and setting
Cooking time: 15 minutes

1 Put the raspberries, lemon zest, sugar and 800ml cold water in a large saucepan. Bring to the boil, then simmer for about 10 minutes, until the raspberries are soft but not mushy.

2 Line a nonmetallic sieve with a double layer of muslin and strain the raspberry liquid into a large bowl, allowing it to drip through slowly.

3 Put the gelatine with 3 tbsp cold water in a small bowl. Leave for 10 minutes to swell, then set the bowl over a saucepan of boiling water and heat until the gelatine dissolves.

4 Add 2 tbsp of the raspberry liquid to the gelatine and stir to mix, then tip the gelatine mixture into the remaining raspberry liquid and stir. Leave to cool slightly.

5 Divide half the mixture between four glasses, then chill until slightly set. Add a layer of fresh raspberries, then top with the remaining raspberry mixture. Chill again to set.

6 Decorate each jelly with extra raspberries or strawberries and serve with long spoons.

Nutrients per serving: Calories 82,
Carbohydrate 20g, Protein 1.5g, Fat 0g
(no saturated fat)

pancakes [with raspberry cream]

Luxurious pancakes with a sumptuous fruity filling.

300ml pancake batter (see pages 6-7)
375g raspberries, sieved to a purée
150ml double cream
250g cream cheese
Sugar
2 tbsp Kirsch (optional)

Makes: 8 pancakes
Cooking time: 20 minutes plus
  2 hours chilling

Nutrients per pancake: Calories 337,
Carbohydrate 21g, Protein 5g, Fat 27g
(saturated fat 16g)

1 Stir the cream cheese smooth with a little of the cream, fold in the raspberry purée and sweeten to taste with sugar. Add the Kirsch if used.

2 Whisk the cream fairly stiff and fold it into the raspberry mixture. Chill for about 2 hours.

3 Make eight pancakes from the batter, sprinkle with sugar and keep warm in the oven.

4 Serve the pancakes hot, each rolled round a filling of the chilled raspberry cream.

raspberry flan

A gorgeous summer dessert with a dash of Cointreau.

375g raspberries, hulled and drained
3 tbsp sugar
1 miniature bottle of Cointreau
50g gooseberry jam (see page 108)
1 flan case 25cm diameter
300g double cream

Serves: 6
Chilling time: 30 minutes

Nutrients per serving: Calories 500,
Carbohydrate 35g, Protein 4g, Fat 37g
(saturated fat 20g)

1 Put the raspberries in a shallow dish, sprinkle with sugar and Cointreau and leave in a cool place for a couple of hours while the sugar dissolves.

2 Heat the gooseberry jam until runny, then spread it over the base of the flan case. Set aside to cool.

3 Drain the raspberries. Whisk the cream with the raspberry juice until thick, then spread two-thirds of the mixture over the gooseberry jam. Arrange the raspberries on top and chill in the fridge for 30 minutes.

4 Serve with the remaining cream.

raspberry ice cream

Forget shop-bought raspberry ripple – this is the real thing.

250g raspberries, hulled, rinsed and
    drained
Juice of ½ lime or 1 tsp lime juice
75g icing sugar
150ml single cream
150ml double cream

Serves: 4
Freezing time: 8 hours

Nutrients per serving: Calories 350,
Carbohydrate 24g, Protein 3g, Fat 27g
(saturated fat 17g)

1 Put the berries and the lime juice in the liquidiser and blend to a fine purée. Rub this through a fine sieve to get rid of the pips.

2 Sweeten the purée to taste with the sifted icing sugar. Mix the two creams and whisk them until thick but not stiff. Fold in the raspberry purée.

3 Spoon the mixture into a plastic freezing container, cover with a lid and leave to freeze overnight, or for about 8 hours.

4 Remove the ice cream from the freezer 2 hours before serving and put it in the fridge to thaw. Scoop into glasses and serve. Add a topping of grated dark chocolate if liked.

raspberry pavlova [with red berry sauce]

A dash of raspberry vinegar makes a slightly tart base for sweet summer fruit.

6 egg whites
350g caster sugar
1 tbsp raspberry vinegar
A pinch of cream of tartar
300-400g raspberries and other mixed fruit, such as blueberries, red and white currants or strawberries, halved if necessary

For the sauce:
125g fresh raspberries or other red berries such as loganberries or tayberries, defrosted if frozen
300g low-fat fromage frais
2 tbsp icing sugar, or to taste
Fresh mint leaves to garnish

Serves: 6-8
Prep time: 25 minutes, plus 2 hours, or overnight, cooling
Cooking time: 1½-2 hours

Nutrients per serving (when serving 6)
Calories 313, Carbohydrate 71g,
Protein 7g, Fat 2g (saturated fat 1g)

1 Heat the oven to 120°C/gas ½. Line a large baking sheet with greaseproof paper or baking paper.

2 Whisk the egg whites in a very large bowl until soft peaks form, then gradually whisk in the sugar to make a stiff meringue. Whisk in the raspberry vinegar and cream of tartar.

3 Pile the meringue into a round measuring about 30cm across, on the lined baking sheet. Bake for 1½-2 hours until it is crisp on the outside and only very slightly coloured.

4 Leave the meringue to cool on the baking sheet for at least 2 hours, or overnight, then transfer it to a serving platter.

5 Meanwhile, make the sauce. Purée the berries and strain them through a fine sieve to remove the seeds. Stir in the fromage frais. Add sugar to taste, cover and chill.

6 Pick over, rinse and dry the mixed soft fruits as necessary. Serve the pavlova cut into wedges, partly covered with chilled sauce and soft fruit, and garnished with mint, if you like.

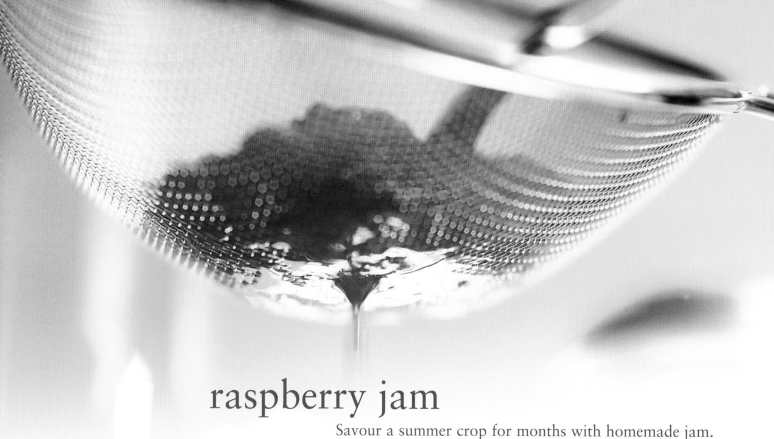

raspberry jam

Savour a summer crop for months with homemade jam.

3kg raspberries
3kg sugar

Nutrients per tablespoon: Calories 13,
Carbohydrate 4g, Protein 0g, Fat 0g
(no saturated fat)

1 Put the cleaned berries in a pan and cook gently until the juice begins to run, then simmer until soft.

2 Stir in the sugar and boil rapidly to setting point. Test for setting point by dropping a teaspoon of jam onto a cold saucer. If it is not ready, continue boiling and testing every 10 minutes until it is.

raspberry wine

1kg raspberries
525g sultanas
1kg sugar
1 tsp pectin-destroying enzyme
1 Campden tablet
3½l water
Port yeast and nutrient
Saccharin

Nutrients per small glass: Calories 118,
Carbohydrate 7g, Protein 0g, Fat 0g
(no saturated fat)

1 Pour the water into a bin and add the pectin-destroying enzyme and a crushed Campden tablet

2 Wash the raspberries, crush them into a mash or cut them up and drop them into the bin. Cover the bin and leave it in a warm place for 24 hours.

3 Activate the yeast in a starter bottle. Add the sultanas, nutrient and yeast to the mash, re-cover the bin and place it in a warm place for 4-5 days.

4 Press and strain the pulp. Dissolve the sugar in warm water and add it to the pulp.

5 Pour the strained mixture into a fermentation jar, top up with cold water and fit an airlock to the jar. Tie on a label describing the contents and store the jar at room temperature until fermentation is complete.

6 When fermentation is complete add saccharin to taste.

Rhubarb gives gardeners an early foretaste of the fruit season to come. Its pale pink stems can be used as a dessert as early as January, nearly five months before any other fruit is ready. By various methods of forcing and cultivation, it can be encouraged to yield heavily throughout spring and early summer. Once established, a rhubarb bed needs little attention for some years except for a good mulching each year with well-rotted manure or compost.

HARVESTING

Do not pull any of the stems in the first year. In the second and third years pick only a few stems. In following years, pull fully grown stems as needed. To pull rhubarb, place your thumb inside the stem as far down as possible and, with a twisting motion, pull it from the crown. Cut off the leaves, which are poisonous, and put them to rot on the compost heap.

Rhubarb

PREPARATION

The tender, pink rhubarb forced for use in late winter and early spring has a more delicate, less acid flavour than the thicker and coarser maincrop stalks. Prepare young, forced rhubarb simply by trimming off the leafy tops and the pale pink root slivers at the base of the stalks. Wash and dry carefully. Older rhubarb often develops a stringy covering which must be peeled off, together with any bruised or damaged parts, as the stems are being cut into pieces.

rhubarb & strawberry [compote]

Tart rhubarb and sweet strawberries, simmered in orange juice, make a refreshing way to use a glut of summer fruit.

650g rhubarb
60g caster sugar
100ml fresh orange juice
250g strawberries
200ml cream or crème fraîche to serve

Serves: 4
Prep time: 20 minutes

Nutrients per serving: Calories 317, Carbohydrate 24g, Protein 3g, Fat 24g (saturated fat 15g)

1 Trim and rinse the rhubarb, cut it into 2.5cm lengths and put it into a large saucepan with the sugar and the orange juice. Cover the pan, bring the mixture to the boil, reduce the heat and simmer gently, uncovered, for 5-6 minutes, stirring occasionally.

2 While the rhubarb is cooking, hull and rinse the strawberries, and halve or quarter any large ones. Add the strawberries to the rhubarb and simmer them for 4-5 minutes, or until they are slightly softened but maintain their shape, and still have some bite.

3 Taste and add a little more sugar if necessary. Transfer the compote to a serving dish and serve warm with the cream or crème fraîche.

rhubarb pie

Rhubarb's tartness makes a great alternative to apple pie.

750g young rhubarb, trimmed and
    cut into 1cm pieces
100-125g sugar
Rind and juice of ½ orange
250g sweet shortcrust pastry

Serves: 6
Cooking time: 35-40 minutes

Nutrients per serving: Calories 260, Carbohydrate 40g, Protein 3g, Fat 11g (saturated fat 3g)

1 Heat the oven to 200°C/gas 6. Mix the rhubarb with the sugar and the finely grated rind from the orange. Put a pie funnel in a deep pie dish and arrange the rhubarb around it.

2 Roll out the pastry to fit the pie dish. Make a slit in the pastry for the steam to escape, brush the pastry with orange juice and sprinkle with sugar.

3 Bake in the oven for 35-40 minutes, or until golden. If the pastry browns too quickly, cover it with a double layer of moistened greaseproof paper.

4 Serve warm, with a jug of cream or custard.

rhubarb gingerbread puddings

Based on an old recipe these puddings combine tangy rhubarb with sweet ginger.

450g tender rhubarb, sliced
125g plain flour
½ tsp bicarbonate of soda
½ tsp ground ginger
½ tsp ground cinnamon
70g golden syrup
40g butter
40g light muscovado sugar
2 tbsp semi-skimmed milk
1 egg
½ tsp icing sugar for dusting
For the sauce:
15g butter
1 tsp cornflour
150ml ruby port wine
4 tbsp redcurrant jelly

Serves: 4
Prep time: 25 minutes,
    plus 20 minutes cooling
Cooking time: 30 minutes

Nutrients per serving: Calories 430,
Carbohydrate 650g, Protein 6g, Fat 13g
(saturated fat 8g)

1 Heat the oven to 180°C/gas 4. Divide half the rhubarb between four individual 200ml soufflé dishes, reserving the rest.

2 Sift the flour, bicarbonate of soda, ginger and cinnamon into a bowl. Heat the syrup, butter, sugar and milk in a saucepan, stirring, until the butter has melted. Pour into the dry ingredients and mix well. Beat in the egg.

3 Divide the mixture between the dishes, spreading it evenly over the rhubarb. Stand the dishes on a baking sheet and bake for about 25 minutes, until well risen, firm and cracked across the top. Set aside to cool slightly.

4 While the puddings are cooking, make the sauce: put the remaining rhubarb, butter and 2 tbsp water in a small saucepan. Cover and cook over a medium heat for about 10 minutes until soft. Press the rhubarb through a sieve, discarding the fibres that remain.

5 Return the purée to a clean saucepan. Mix the cornflour to a smooth paste with the port wine. Add the redcurrant jelly to the purée and stir in the port mixture. Heat, stirring, until the mixture boils and thickens. Continue cooking, still stirring, until the jelly has melted. Remove from the heat and leave to cool slightly.

6 Dust the warm puddings with a little icing sugar and serve with the warm port wine sauce, or with ginger syllabub.

rhubarb & banana fool

An unusual combination of flavours in a creamy pudding.

500g young rhubarb, cut into small pieces
Juice of ½ lemon
4 bananas, 3 peeled and sliced
100-125g sugar
150ml whipping cream
50g small macaroons

Serves: 4
Cooking time: 15 minutes, 1 hour to chill

Nutrients per serving: Calories 150,
Carbohydrate 21g, Protein 7g, Fat 5g
(saturated fat 1.5g)

1 Put the rhubarb in a pan with the lemon juice and simmer over a gentle heat for about 15 minutes, until the rhubarb is quite tender and pulpy.

2 Rub the rhubarb through a sieve or liquidise, and if necessary, thicken the purée by boiling it to evaporate some of the liquid.

3 Mash the peeled bananas with a fork. Mix the rhubarb purée and mashed bananas and sweeten the mixture to taste.

4 Whisk the cream lightly until it just holds its shape. Crush the macaroons with a rolling pin and fold them into the cream. Blend the cream into the rhubarb mixture, spoon it into glasses and chill for 1 hour.

5 If liked, peel and slice the remaining banana just before serving and arrange on top of the rhubarb fool.

Nothing is more the child of art than a garden.

Sir Walter Scott

rhubarb & ginger jam

Try this with toast as an alternative to marmalade.

1.5kg rhubarb cut into small chunks
1.5kg sugar
Juice of 3 lemons
25g root ginger, bruised

Nutrients per tablespoon: Calories 15,
Carbohydrate 4.5g, Protein 0g, Fat 0g
(no saturated fat)

1 Place the rhubarb in alternate layers with the sugar in a deep bowl, add the lemon juice and leave for about 8 hours.

2 Put the contents of the bowl into a pan, with the bruised ginger tied in a muslin bag. Bring to boiling point and boil rapidly before setting point is reached. Test for setting point by dropping a teaspoon of jam onto a cold saucer. If it is not ready, continue boiling and testing every 10 minutes until it is.

rhubarb wine

2.25kg rhubarb
Thinly pared rind of 1 lemon
250g sultanas
1.25kg sugar
1 Campden tablet
1 tsp pectin-destroying enzyme
3½l water
Graves yeast and nutrient

Nutrients per small glass: Calories 120,
Carbohydrate 9g, Protein 0g, Fat 0g
(no saturated fat)

1 Pour the water into a bin and add the pectin-destroying enzyme and a crushed Campden tablet.

2 Wash the rhubarb, wipe and chop the stems and drop them into the bin with the lemon rind. Cover the bin and leave it in a warm place for 24 hours.

3 Activate the yeast in a starter bottle. Add the sultanas, nutrient and yeast to the mash, re-cover the bin and place it in a warm place for 4-5 days.

4 Press and strain the pulp and add the sugar, dissolving this first in warm water.

5 Pour the strained must into a fermentation jar, top up with cold water and fit an airlock to the jar. Tie on a label describing the contents and store the jar at room temperature until fermentation is complete.

6 When fermentation is complete add saccharin to taste.

rhubarb chutney

An excellent accompaniment for cold meats.

2.5kg rhubarb, cut into small chunks
1kg onions, peeled and minced
1l white vinegar
1kg granulated sugar
½ tsp salt
2 tbsp ground ginger
3 tsp mixed spice

Approx yield: 3 kg

Nutrients per serving: Calories 30,
Carbohydrate 7g, Protein 0g, Fat 0g
(no saturated fat)

1 Place the rhubarb and onion in a pan with a third of the vinegar, the sugar, salt, ginger and spice, and simmer gently until the rhubarb is soft.

2 Add the remaining vinegar and simmer to the required consistency, stirring frequently.

3 For a hot chutney, use 3 tsp of curry powder instead of the mixed spice. Pot at once.

If you want really fresh summer salads it is worth growing your own. A wide range of lettuces are now available was well as the traditional butterhead: crisphead, Batavian, loose-leaf and cos. Other delicious salad leaves include peppery rocket, endive, multicoloured chard and raddichio. You can now buy premixed mesclun (salad leaves) blends of mild, spicy and bitter greens or try mixing your own. Most salad crops will thrive in a fairly rich soil and do need frequent watering in summer, especially in hot weather. Most salad crops will be available from mid spring but sow frequently throughout summer to extend the season into late summer and autumn.

HARVESTING

Harvest as required. With some varieties of salad leaves such as rocket, the young leaves will be ready to harvest with a few weeks of sowing. Baby lettuce leaves can be harvested two weeks after planting transplants. Pick leaves from the outside and the plants will contine producing new leaves from the centre. When harvesting whole heads cut heads 2.5cm above ground level and the plants may resprout and produce another head.

Salad leaves

PREPARATION AND STORAGE

Most salad leaves should be used immediately. Wash carefully and dry in a spinner or between kitchen towels. If you need to store them, keep loosely packed in a plastic bag in the fridge for between two days – and up to three weeks for radiccio.

lettuce soup

1 large lettuce, washed and separated
Salt and pepper
600ml vegetable stock
Nutmeg and sugar
50g butter
1 small onion, finely chopped
25g flour
600ml milk
Grated cheese to garnish

Serves: 4
Cooking time: 25 minutes

1 Blanch the lettuce for 5 minutes in boiling water, then drain and refresh in cold water.

2 Shred the leaves and put them in a pan, together with the stock. Bring to the boil and simmer for 5 minutes. Season to taste with salt and pepper, grated nutmeg and sugar.

3 Blend the soup in a liquidiser. Melt the butter in a pan and cook the onion for about 5 minutes or until soft but not browned.

4 Stir in the flour and let it cook for a few minutes before gradually adding the milk. Blend in the lettuce purée and heat the soup; season and serve.

Nutrients per serving: Calories 270, Carbohydrate 16g, Protein 14g, Fat 18g (saturated fat 10g)

Florida salad

1 lettuce or equivalent mix of salad leaves, washed and separated into single leaves
2 sweet oranges
1 grapefruit
2 tomatoes
4 tbsp olive oil
1 tbsp sugar
1 tbsp hot water
Salt and pepper
Chopped chives to garnish

Serves: 4
Prep time: 10 minutes

1 Arrange the salad leaves in a bowl.

2 Peel the oranges and the grapefruit, removing all the white pith, and divide the fruit into segments. Cut the tomatoes into quarters, and add the orange and grapefruit segments and tomato quarters to the lettuce.

3 Put the oil in a small bowl. Melt the sugar in the water and blend this into the oil, seasoning to taste with salt and pepper.

4 Pour the dressing over the salad and sprinkle with finely chopped chives.

Nutrients per serving: Calories 165, Carbohydrate 15g, Protein 2g, Fat 11g (saturated fat 1.5g)

Greek mixed salad

1 lettuce or equivalent mix of salad leaves, washed and shredded
2 sticks of celery, chopped
1 small cucumber, diced
3 tomatoes, each cut into eight pieces
½ green pepper, deseeded and diced
50g anchovy fillets, drained
75g feta cheese, drained
8-12 black olives, stoned
6 tbsp olive oil
2 tbsp white wine vinegar or lemon juice
1 tsp chopped marjoram
Salt and pepper

Serves: 4
Prep time: 10 minutes

1 Mix the lettuce, celery, cucumber, tomatoes and peppers together and arrange on a flat dish. Cut the anchovy fillets and feta cheese into bite-sized pieces and sprinkle them over the salad, together with the olives.

2 Make a dressing from the oil, vinegar, finely chopped marjoram, and season with salt and pepper.

3 Pour the dressing over the salad and serve at once as a first course, accompanied with coarse wholemeal bread and butter.

Nutrients per serving: Calories 260, Carbohydrate 5g, Protein 8g, Fat 23g (saturated fat 5g)

lettuce [with soured cream dressing]

1-2 lettuces, reserve a few leaves, shred the
  remainder
1 green pepper, deseeded and thinly sliced
1 red pepper, deseeded and thinly sliced
2 hard-boiled eggs
1 clove garlic, crushed
4 tbsp olive oil
1 tbsp white wine vinegar
2 tbsp soured cream
Salt and pepper

Nutrients per serving: Calories 190,
Carbohydrate 6g, Protein 5g, Fat 16g
(saturated fat 3.5g)

1 Use a few lettuce leaves to line the bowl. Mix the shredded lettuce with the
  pepper and place in the bowl.

2 Separate the yolks from the hard-boiled egg whites and mash with a fork.
  Blend in the garlic and gradually stir in the oil, vinegar and soured cream.
  Stir until quite smooth and season to taste with salt and pepper.

3 Pour the soured cream dressing over the salad and sprinkle with the
  chopped egg whites. Serve as a light salad dish on its own.

Waldorf salad

Salad leaves separated into single leaves
500g red dessert apples, one cut into thin
  slices, the remainder diced
2 tbsp lemon juice
1 tsp caster sugar
150ml mayonnaise
½ head celery, roughly chopped
50g shelled walnuts, chopped

Nutrients per serving: Calories 410,
Carbohydrate 12g, Protein 3g, Fat 39g
(saturated fat 5g)

1 Mix the lemon juice with the sugar and 1 tbsp of the mayonnaise and brush
  over the apple slices to prevent them going brown. Blend the diced apples
  into the remainder of this dressing.

2 Mix the celery and walnuts thoroughly with the diced apples, adding the
  rest of the mayonnaise.

3 Line a bowl with the salad leaves and pile diced apple mixture into
  the centre.

4 Arrange the apple slices in an overlapping pattern between the lettuce leaves
  and the centre filling.

warm potted shrimps [on shredded lettuce]

1 egg
A pinch of dried mustard
1-2 tbsp lemon juice
300ml olive oil
4 x 55g pots of potted shrimps
4 heads Little Gem lettuce, washed, dried
  and finely sliced
Petals from 2 marigold flowers (optional)

Serves: 4
Prep time: 20 minutes

Nutrients per serving: Calories 220,
Carbohydrate 1g, Protein 12g, Fat 18g
(saturated fat 5g)

1 Put the egg in a blender, then add the mustard and lemon juice and blend
  for a few seconds. With the motor running, start adding the oil through the
  hole in the lid, drop-by-drop at first, then in a thin stream, until the mixture
  is thick.

2 About 15 minutes before serving, stand the shrimp pots in an enamel dish
  or tin. Pour hot water into the dish or tin to about half way up the pots,
  but not deep enough to float them.

3 Divide the lettuce between four plates. Invert a pot of shrimps on to each
  serving, allowing the buttery sauce to run into the lettuce. Top with
  marigold petals, if desired. Serve with a tablespoonful of the mayonnaise
  and wholemeal bread.

A garden gives the body
the dignity of working in
its own support.
It is a way of rejoining
the human race.

Wendell Berry

There are two types of true spinach, the round-seeded, which is generally harvested in summer, and the hardier, prickly seeded variety that is grown for use in winter and spring. There are also three other vegetables that resemble spinach and are cooked in exactly the same way. New Zealand spinach is a branching, mat-forming plant that withstands drought and does well on poor dry soils where other spinachs fail. Spinach beet or perpetual spinach produces a succession of fresh leaves over a long period. It is perhaps the easiest of all the spinach-type crops to grow although it does tend to run to seed during the spring of its second year. The leaves of seakale beet or Swiss chard are eaten like spinach although the midribs are cooked like seakale. By planting at least some of these crops, you can enjoy fresh spinach or an indistinguishable substitute throughout most of the year.

Spinach

HARVESTING

With all types of spinach, pick the leaves when they are ready. Even when not required in the kitchen, the leaves of spinach beet, New Zealand spinach and Swiss chard should be picked regularly to encourage further growth. When picking New Zealand spinach, gather the young shoot leaves, each with two or three leaves.

PREPARATION

Spinach deteriorates quickly after picking and should be used as quickly as possible, while still crisp. Pick the spinach just before cooking, strip the leaves from the stalks, and if the midribs are coarse, remove these as well. Immerse the leaves in a large bowl of cold water, lift them out and repeat with fresh water, once or twice more, until the water is quite clear of sand and grit. As spinach has a high water content, it does not need additional water for cooking. It is sufficient to put the leaves in a large pan with only the water that adheres to the leaves from the last rinsing.

chilled spinach [& yoghurt soup]

Dried mint gives an authentic Middle Eastern flavour to this refreshing soup.

250g frozen leaf spinach, defrosted
1 clove garlic, finely crushed
500g low-fat natural yoghurt
Salt and black pepper
3 tsp dried mint
Fresh mint leaves and grated
 nutmeg, to garnish

Serves: 4
Prep time: 15 minutes

Nutrients per serving: Calories 84, Carbohydrate 10g, Protein 8g, Fat 1g (saturated fat 1g)

1 Add some ice cubes to 300ml of cold water and chill it in the fridge. Squeeze the water from the spinach, then chop the spinach finely and place in a large bowl.

2 Mix in the garlic and yoghurt, season and stir in the dried mint. If the spinach was not chopped finely enough, briefly process the mixture in a food processor or with a hand-held mixer.

3 Add the iced water gradually, stirring continuously, until you achieve the desired consistency. Check seasoning, cover and chill until ready to serve.

4 Decorate with fresh mint leaves, and a little grated nutmeg if you like, and serve at once.

lamb noisettes [with spinach]

Stir-fried spinach studded with the Middle Eastern flavours of raisins and pine kernels is a great partner to lamb noisettes, flavoured with mustard, then roasted until tender.

2 tbsp olive oil
2 tbsp mustard (honey or herb-flavoured)
8-12 lamb noisettes, about 800g in total
2 large sprigs rosemary, optional
Salt and black pepper
½ red onion, peeled and thinly sliced
3 cloves garlic, peeled and thinly sliced
50g pine kernels
40g seedless raisins
1 medium tomato, chopped
500g young spinach, trimmed and rinsed
Crusty bread to serve

Serves: 4
Prep time: 30 minutes

Nutrients per serving: Calories 705, Carbohydrate 48g, Protein 54g, Fat 34g (saturated fat 9g)

1 Heat the oven to 220°C/gas 7. Use a little of the oil to grease a small baking tray.

2 Using half the mustard, spread some on top of each noisette. Rinse and dry the rosemary, if using, and snip some over the noisettes. Season with salt and pepper and set aside until the oven is hot enough.

3 Roast the noisettes on the top shelf of the oven for 10 minutes, then turn them over, spread with the remaining mustard, scatter with more rosemary, if using, and season. Roast for another 5-8 minutes, until cooked but still slightly pink. If you prefer them well done, cook a few minutes longer.

4 While the lamb is cooking, heat the remaining oil in a large pan. Add the onion and garlic, cover and cook over a low heat for 5 minutes, or until the onion is soft but not coloured. Add the pine kernels and raisins and fry for 3 minutes.

5 Add the tomato to the pan and cook for 1 minute. Then add the spinach and a pinch of salt and stir for 3-4 minutes, until the spinach wilts and is only just cooked. If there is too much spinach to stir easily, cover the pan for a minute until the spinach wilts slightly, then uncover and stir-fry.

6 Divide the mixture among individual serving plates and arrange the lamb on top. Serve with crusty bread to mop up the juices.

spicy chicken [with tomatoes & spinach]

Chicken thighs are tastier than breast meat, and here their flavour is boosted with mild spices and vegetables.

500g skinned, boned chicken thighs
150g onions, finely chopped
4 green cardamom pods, split open
    at the top
¼ tsp cayenne pepper
5cm cinnamon stick, broken in half
2 tsp garlic purée, or crushed garlic
2 tsp ginger purée, or grated ginger
¼ tsp turmeric
50g low-fat natural yoghurt
Salt
250g spinach, defrosted if frozen
225g canned chopped tomatoes
50g low-fat fromage frais
A pinch of garam masala

Serves: 4
Prep time: 15 minutes
Cooking time: 30-35 minutes

Nutrients per serving: Calories 220, Carbohydrate 8g, Protein 28g, Fat 9g (saturated fat 3g)

1 Trim any fat off the chicken thighs, then cut each in half. Put them into a large saucepan with the onions, cardamom, cayenne pepper, cinnamon, garlic, ginger, turmeric, yoghurt and salt to taste.

2 Place the pan over a medium-high heat and stir until the chicken starts sizzling. Continue to cook, stirring frequently, until the chicken begins to release its juices, then reduce the heat to low, cover the pan and simmer for 12 minutes, stirring occasionally.

3 Meanwhile, chop the spinach, discarding any thick stems. If using defrosted leaf spinach, place it between two plates and squeeze out the excess liquid before chopping.

4 Uncover the saucepan and increase the heat to medium-high. Continue cooking for 5-6 minutes until most of the liquid has evaporated and the sauce has thickened, stirring frequently to prevent it sticking to the bottom of the pan.

5 Stir the tomatoes into the chicken mixture and continue to cook, uncovered, for 1-2 minutes until they are well blended into the sauce.

6 Add the spinach in batches, stirring well. As soon as the first batch begins to wilt, add the next and keep stirring. Reduce the heat to low and cook, uncovered, for 5 minutes, or until the chicken juices run clear when the pieces are pierced.

7 Add the fromage frais and garam masala, stirring until well blended. Remove the cinnamon stick and serve.

[Spinach, cheese & egg] filo pie

Filo pastry is a good, healthy alternative to its buttery cousins. This delicious pie includes spinach, which is high in vitamin C, zinc and potassium.

1 Heat the oven to 200°C/gas 6. Lightly brush each sheet of filo with oil and put in a layer, oiled side down, to cover the base and sides of a 20cm loose-bottomed, deep flan tin, letting the excess hang over the edges. Brush the pastry all over with a little oil.

2 Put the spinach in a large saucepan. Cover and cook over a medium heat for 3-4 minutes, stirring occasionally, until wilted. Drain well, pressing as much liquid from the leaves as possible with the back of a spoon. Roughly chop and add salt, pepper and nutmeg to taste. Mix in the parsley.

3 Place half the spinach in an even layer in the pastry case. Add the cheeses and make four hollows with a spoon. Break an egg into each. Top with the remaining spinach and carefully fold over the edges of the filo to cover the spinach and egg. Drizzle with the remaining oil and sprinkle over the sesame seeds.

4 Transfer to the oven and cook for 20-25 minutes until golden. Serve hot or warm with a tomato salad or spring onion and crisp green salad.

125g filo pastry, about eight sheets
4 tbsp olive oil
500g fresh spinach leaves, washed
Salt and black pepper
Freshly grated nutmeg
2 tbsp chopped fresh parsley
175g Wensleydale and Lancashire cheese, crumbled
4 eggs
1 tbsp sesame seeds

Serves: 4
Prep time: 30 minutes
Cooking time: 35 minutes

Nutrients per serving: Calories 516, Carbohydrate 21g, Protein 25g, Fat 36g (saturated fat 13g)

[plain, chilli or] spinach chapattis

High in fibre and easy to make, chapatti breads are a classic accompaniment to Indian meals.

425g chapatti flour, plus extra for dusting
1 tsp salt
2 tbsp sunflower oil
For chilli chapattis
1 green chilli, deseeded and finely chopped
1 fresh red chilli, deseeded and finely chopped
A pinch of cayenne pepper
3 cloves garlic, crushed
For spinach chapattis
1 green chilli, deseeded and finely chopped
2 tsp garlic purée, or crushed garlic
1 tsp finely grated ginger
250g spinach leaves, rinsed and finely chopped
¼ tsp cayenne pepper

Makes: 16 chapattis
Prep time: 20 minutes, plus 30 minutes resting
Cooking time: 30 minutes

Nutrients per chapatti, [for all three types], Calories 101-108, Carbohydrate 21g, Protein 3g, Fat 2g (no saturated fat)

1 To make plain chapattis, sift the flour and salt into a large bowl. Add the oil and work it into the flour, then gradually stir in 250ml of lukewarm water, mixing until a soft dough forms.

2 Transfer the dough to a lightly floured surface and knead it for 4-5 minutes until any excess moisture has been absorbed. Add a little more flour if the dough is too sticky to handle. Cover with a damp cloth and leave it to rest for 30 minutes.

3 Meanwhile, line a large piece of foil with kitchen paper to keep the chapattis hot when they are cooked.

4 Cut the dough in half and divide each half into eight equal balls. Cover them with a clean cloth to prevent them from drying out.

5 Heat a nonstick frying pan over a medium heat. Meanwhile, flatten out one ball of dough between your palms, lightly dust it with flour, then roll it out into a 15cm round.

6 Place the dough on the hot pan and cook for 30 seconds, then turn it over and continue cooking until bubbles begin to appear on the surface. Turn it over again, pressing the edges down gently to encourage the chapatti to puff up, and continue cooking until brown patches appear on the underside. Wrap the cooked chapatti in the foil and continue making chapattis in the same way. For a cool contrast, serve them with yoghurt raita.
To make chilli chapattis: add the chillies, cayenne pepper and garlic to the flour mixture in Step 1 before adding the oil and water.
To make spinach chapattis: heat a large wok or frying pan over a low heat and add the oil. When it is hot, add the chilli, garlic and ginger, and stir-fry for 1 minute. Then add the spinach, cayenne pepper and the salt, and stir-fry for 5-6 minutes until all the moisture from the spinach has evaporated. Transfer the mixture to a large bowl. Add the flour and 150ml of water (you do not need any more oil) and mix until a soft dough forms. Then continue with the basic recipe from Step 2.

Strawberries

Strawberries are an essential part of the British summer and are not hard to grow. They also give a quicker return than any other fruit, because plants set out in late summer will provide a crop the following June. In a large garden, strawberries can be picked from May to October if a number of selected varieties are planted, and cloches are used to extend the growing season. There are two types: those that carry a single crop in June and July and 'perpetual' varieties that begin to crop slowly in June, reaching a peak in August, but then continue until October.

HARVESTING
Pick strawberries by the stalk to avoid bruising. Eat them as soon as possible after picking.

PREPARATION
Serve fresh strawberries whole unless they are very large, in which case cut them in half. The green flower calyx is attractive and may be left on the berry but usually strawberries are hulled by removing this and the soft centre stalk. Rinse the strawberries carefully in a colander in cold water and drain thoroughly before serving.

strawberry yoghurt ice

Creamy Greek yoghurt and fresh strawberries blend well in this honey-sweetened dessert.

450g strawberries, hulled
4 tbsp clear honey
1 tsp lemon juice
A few drops vanilla essence
500g low-fat Greek yoghurt
4 strawberries to garnish

Serves: 4
Prep time: 5-10 minutes, plus 4-6 hours
   freezing

Nutrients per serving: Calories 198,
Carbohydrate 29g, Protein 8g, Fat 6g
(saturated fat 4g)

1 Place the strawberries in a liquidiser or food processor with the honey, lemon juice and vanilla essence. Purée until the mixture is smooth, then beat in the yoghurt.

2 Transfer the mixture to a shallow, freezerproof plastic container, cover and freeze for 4-6 hours, beating it with a hand-held whisk after 2 hours and then at hourly intervals until it is frozen. Alternatively, freeze in an ice-cream maker according to the manufacturer's instructions.

3 Spoon into four dessert bowls and garnish each with a fresh strawberry.

rose-strawberry yoghurt ice

This healthy strawberry ice, made with yoghurt, is light but still creamy, and flavoured with delicate rosewater.

400g strawberries, hulled and chilled, plus extra to decorate
100g icing sugar
3 tbsp rosewater
450g Greek yoghurt

Serves: 6
Prep time: 15 minutes, plus 8 hours freezing

Nutrients per serving: Calories 170, Carbohydrate 23g, Protein 5g, Fat 7g (saturated fat 4g)

1 Turn the freezer to the fast-freeze setting about 1 hour before starting. Coarsely purée the strawberries in a blender or food processor, then transfer the mixture to a bowl.

2 Stir in the icing sugar, rosewater and yoghurt. Pour the mixture into a large freezer container and freeze for 3 hours, or until part frozen.

3 Transfer the mixture to a blender or food processor and purée until smooth, then return it to the freezer. Purée the mixture again once or twice more over the next 2-3 hours. Leave to freeze until firm. (Remember to turn the freezer back to the normal setting.)

4 Remove the yoghurt-ice from the freezer 30 minutes before serving. Scoop into glasses or bowls and serve decorated with strawberries.

strawberry ice cream

500g strawberries
125g icing sugar
2 tsp lemon juice
Double cream

Serves: 6
Prep time: 15 minutes and 8 hours freezing

Nutrients per serving: Calories 339, Carbohydrate 27g, Protein 1g, Fat 25g (saturated fat 16g)

1 Liquidise the strawberries and measure the purée. Stir in the icing sugar and lemon juice.

2 Whisk an even quantity of double cream until floppy, and fold into the strawberry purée.

3 Freeze, stirring occasionally during the first 2 hours. Serve in glasses or bowls, decorated with strawberries

strawberry mousse

175-250g strawberries, cut into thick slices
3 tbsp sugar
3-4 tbsp rum
4 eggs
50g caster sugar
20g powdered gelatine
300ml double cream

Serves: 6
Prep time: 15 minutes and 2 hours chilling

Nutrients per serving: Calories 396, Carbohydrate 19g, Protein .5g, Fat 31g (saturated fat 18g)

1 Put the strawberries in a bowl, sprinkling with sugar and rum. Set aside in a cool place until the sugar has dissolved.

2 Beat the eggs with the caster sugar until they are creamy, fluffy and pale yellow. Dissolve the gelatine in 3 tbsp water and stir it quickly into the egg mixture. Whip the cream lightly and fold most of it, together with the liquid drained from the strawberries, into the eggs when these begin to set.

3 Spoon the mixture into a serving dish and put in the fridge to chill. Just before serving, arrange the sliced strawberries on the mousse. Serve with the remaining cream.

The fruit derived from labour is the sweetest of pleasures.

Luc de Clapier de Vauvanargues

strawberry trifle

500g strawberries, hulled, rinsed and
   drained
100-125g macaroons
2 tbsp sherry
1 tsp caster sugar
3 egg yolks
50g sugar
½ vanilla pod
300ml single cream
1 tsp cornflour

Serves: 6
Prep time: 20 minutes

Nutrients per serving: Calories 267,
Carbohydrate 27g, Protein 5g, Fat 15g
(saturated fat 7g)

1 Break up the macaroons roughly and put them over the base of a glass dish. Pour the sherry over them and leave to soak.

2 Set 8-10 strawberries aside, cut the rest into pieces and mash to a rough purée. Stir in the sugar and spoon over the macaroons.

3 Beat the egg yolks and the sugar. Bring the cream, with the vanilla pod, to the boil, cover, and leave for 10 minutes.

4 Remove the vanilla pod and gradually whisk the cream into the egg yolks. Strain back into the pan and bring back to just under boiling point, whisking constantly to prevent the custard curdling. Remove from the heat and stir in the cornflour, first blending it with a little cold milk.

5 Leave the custard to cool, sprinkling the top with sugar to prevent a skin forming, then pour it over the strawberries.

6 Decorate with the reserved strawberries.

strawberry jam

Delicious with cream on scones, bread, in tarts or in
sponge cakes, homemade strawberry jam tastes better than
any bought from a shop.

3.2kg strawberries, small and
   firm if possible
Juice of 2 lemons
2.7kg preserving or granulated sugar

Makes: about 4.5kg
Prep time: 20 minutes
Cooking time: 20-30 minutes

Nutrients per tablespoon: Calories 40,
Carbohydrate 10g, Protein 0g, Fat 0g,

1 Put two saucers in the refrigerator or freezer, to chill. Do not wash the strawberries. Remove any stems and lightly brush off any grit or dirt. Put in a large pan with the lemon juice.

2 Heat gently until the juices start to run, then use a potato masher to break up the fruit to the required texture, leaving whole berries if desired. Continue cooking and stirring until reduced to a thick slush.

3 Warm the sugar and add to the pan. Increase the heat and stir continuously until the sugar dissolves. Bring to a steady boil and cook for 8-10 minutes, stirring frequently. Test for setting point by dropping a teaspoon of jam onto a cold saucer. If it is not ready, continue boiling and testing every 10 minutes until it is.

4 Remove from the heat and use a jug to pour the jam into clean, warmed jars. Cover and seal immediately, then label and date each jar. Store in a cool, dark place for up to a year.

A fairly open plot is needed to grow swedes successfully as they are essentially a field crop and seem to do best where fences or walls do not restrict the flow of air. If conditions are right, the mild, turnip-flavoured roots, which are extremely hardy, can be left in the ground for using as required during the winter. Swedes will grow well in any fertile soil except one that is acid.

Swede

HARVESTING

Lift the roots as required from autumn until spring. A few may be lifted as a reserve and kept in a cool, airy place such as a garage or shed, for use when the soil is frozen.

PREPARATION

Prepare swedes by cutting a thick slice off the top and trimming the root end until the yellow flesh is revealed. Cut off the tough peel in a thick layer. Wash peeled roots in cold water, cut them into quarters or large cubes and boil for 30-40 minutes or until soft. Alternatively, par-boil quartered swedes for about 10 minutes, drain them and add to a roasting joint for the last 30 minutes, as for parsnips.

fish supper [with swede patties]

Rich in antioxidants, high in fibre and vitamin C, swedes are an unexpected and tasty accompaniment to fish.

650g swede, peeled and cut into chunks
100g medium oatmeal
Salt and black pepper
2½ tbsp olive oil
100g mushrooms, sliced
100g tomatoes, cut in wedges
1 spring onion, finely chopped
225g halibut, plaice or sole fillets, skinned
Creamed horseradish or vegetable chutney
   to serve

Serves: 2
Prep time: 10 minutes
Cooking time: 25 minutes

Nutrients per serving: Calories 500, Carbohydrate 54g, Protein 30g, Fat 19g (saturated fat 2g)

1 Cook the swede in boiling, salted water for about 12 minutes until tender, then drain. Mash well and add three-quarters of the oatmeal. Mix, adding salt and pepper to taste and more of the oatmeal as necessary to give a stiff mixture. Shape into four patties and set aside.

2 Heat ½ tbsp of the olive oil in a small saucepan and add the mushrooms. Sauté over a moderate heat until they release their juices, 3-5 minutes. Add the tomatoes and spring onion and cook for a further 2-3 minutes until the tomatoes are softened and heated through. Season and set aside in a warm place.

3 Meanwhile, heat the remaining olive oil in a large, heavy frying pan. Add the fish fillets and swede patties and cook for 5-8 minutes over a moderate heat, turning once, until nicely browned on each side.

4 Reheat the mushroom mixture if necessary and serve on warmed plates with the swede patties, fish and horseradish or chutney.

swedes [with bacon]

50g swede, cut into small chunks
Salt and pepper
50g butter
Milk
100-125g bacon, diced

Serves: 4
Cooking time: 40 minutes

Nutrients per serving: Calories 166, Carbohydrate 2g, Protein 5g, Fat 15g (saturated fat 8g)

1 Put the swede in a pan of boiling, lightly salted water, cover with a lid and simmer for 35 minutes or until quite tender.

2 Drain through a colander, then mash well with a potato masher. Return to the pan and cream the mashed swede with half the butter and a little milk. Season to taste with salt and pepper.

3 Fry the bacon in the remaining butter until crisp.

4 Serve the swede topped with the remaining butter and bacon.

mashed swede & carrot [with allspice]

A favourite vegetable purée, the flavours of swede and carrot blend beautifully to make a terrific accompaniment to roast meat, especially beef.

500g swede, cut into chunks
400g large carrots, cut into chunks
75g butter
4 tbsp double or whipping cream
150g mashed potatoes
1 tsp ground allspice
Salt and black pepper

Serves: 6
Preparation time: 25 minutes
Cooking time: 20 minutes

Nutrients per serving: Calories 318, Carbohydrate 20g, Protein 2.5g, Fat 26g (saturated fat 15g)

1 Put the swede into a large pan of water, bring to the boil and simmer for 10-15 minutes until soft.

2 Cook and drain the carrots, then put them into a food processor with the butter and cream.

3 Drain the swede, then return it to the dry pan, and shake over a low heat to encourage evaporation.

4 Add the chunks of swede to the carrots in the food processor and purée them together.

5 In a large bowl, stir the mashed potato and the purée of swede and carrot together by hand. Season with allspice, salt and black pepper.

6 Spread the purée in an oven dish and serve immediately or reheat in the oven when required.

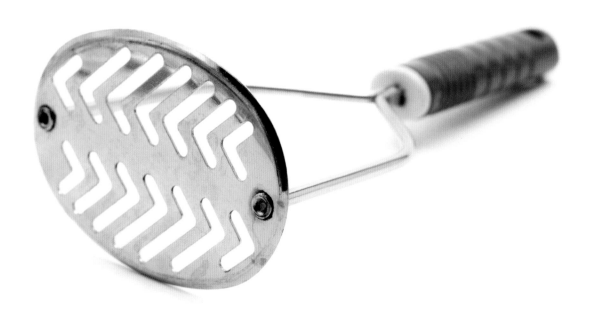

Also known as maize, corn on the cob and Indian Corn, sweetcorn is believed to have been introduced to Europe from America by Christopher Columbus at the end of the 15th century. There are plenty of varieties suited to the British climate that will produce reasonable crops, even in poor summers. Sweetcorn needs a sunny, sheltered position. It will grow in any soil but for good-quality crops enrich the bed with well-rotted compost or manure, during the winter before planting. It also does best when grown in a block, which provides the best chance for the light, airborne pollen to fall from the male flowers at the top of the plants on to the silky female flower tassels which hang from the tops of the immature cobs.

Sweetcorn

HARVESTING

Cobs are ready for picking about six weeks after the silky tassels have appeared at their tops. These will shrivel and turn brown as the seeds develop. Test by pulling back part of the cob's sheath and pressing one of the seeds with your thumbnail. If it exudes a creamy liquid, the cobs should be picked and used. If the liquid is watery, the cob is not yet ready. If there is no liquid, the cob is well past its prime. Colour is also a useful guide. The cob is ready to use when the seeds start to turn pale yellow. Twist the cobs from the plants or snap them outwards, just before they are needed, as they become dry and lose their flavour if they are stored.

PREPARATION

Corn on the cob is most succulent when the cobs are picked just before the kernels become fully mature, woody and deep yellow. Strip the outer husks from the cobs in a downward direction, trim the stalk close to the cob and pull off the silky tassels from the top. Cook for up to 8 minutes in boiling water and do not add salt until the kernels are half-cooked or they will become tough. Test the tenderness of the cobs by inserting the prongs of a fork in the corn. When they are ready, drain the cobs thoroughly and serve with a liberal quantity of butter. The kernels of cooked corn may also be stripped off the cobs with the aid of a fork, or the kernels may be cut from the fresh cobs.

sweetcorn & leek soup

500g corn cobs
2 leeks, finely chopped
75g butter
4 tbsp flour
600ml water
600ml dry white wine or milk
Salt, pepper and nutmeg
150ml cream
Croutons to garnish

Serves: 4
Cooking time: 40 minutes

1 Boil the corn cobs for 6-7 minutes, drain and strip off the kernels.

2 Melt the butter in a pan, add the leeks and cook over a gentle heat for 5 minutes or until soft. Stir in the flour and cook through before gradually blending in the water and wine or milk. Add the corn kernels and bring to the boil. Season to taste and simmer for 15 minutes.

3 Blend the soup in a liquidiser. Return to the pan and re-heat, checking the seasoning if necessary. Blend a little of the hot soup with the cream, stir back into the pan and heat through without boiling.

Nutrients per serving: Calories 466, Carbohydrate 35g, Protein 9g, Fat 28g (saturated fat 15g)

devilled turkey [& sweetcorn skewers]

1 tbsp English mustard powder
2 tbsp tomato purée
1 tbsp dark muscovado sugar
1 tbsp grated fresh ginger
2 cloves garlic, crushed
1 tbsp red wine vinegar
1 tbsp Worcestershire sauce
550g boneless turkey breast, cut into
    2.5cm cubes
2 sweetcorn cobs, husks removed, cut into
    2.5cm slices

Serves: 4
Prep time: 10 minutes, plus 1-2 hours
    marinating
Cooking time: 20 minutes

1 Put the mustard powder, tomato purée, sugar, ginger, garlic, vinegar and Worcestershire sauce in a large bowl. Mix, then add the turkey and mix again to coat. Cover and leave to marinate in the fridge for 1-2 hours.

2 Thread the corn slices and turkey in alternating pieces onto four metal skewers.

3 Cook the skewers under a hot grill or on a barbecue, turning often, for 15-20 minutes or until the turkey is cooked through and the corn is tender and golden. Serve with crusty bread and a fresh spinach salad.

Nutrients per serving: Calories 200, Carbohydrate 7g, Protein 33g, Fat 4g (saturated fat 1g)

creamed sweetcorn

750g corn cobs, stripped and cleaned
25g butter
25g flour
150ml milk
150ml single cream
1 egg yolk
Crumbled bacon to garnish
Salt and pepper

Serves: 4
Cooking time: 30 minutes

Nutrients per serving: Calories 321, Carbohydrate 26g, Protein 11g, Fat 20g (saturated fat 10g)

1 Put the corn cobs into a pan of boiling water. Bring back to the boil and cook for 7-8 minutes or until the kernels are tender. Add a teaspoon of salt halfway through cooking. Drain the cobs.

2 Strip the kernels from the cobs, using a fork and working from the stalk end towards the tip.

3 Melt the butter, stir in the flour and let it cook through. Gradually add the milk and cream, stirring all the time until the sauce is smooth.

4 Fold in the corn kernels and simmer for 10 minutes. Beat the egg yolk lightly, mix it with a little of the sauce and return it to the pan. Heat through to thicken slightly and season to taste with salt and pepper.

5 Serve sprinkled with crumbled, crisp-fried bacon.

hot corn cakes [with salad]

Crispy sweetcorn pancakes spiced with Tabasco sauce are accompanied by a salad of cool lettuce, sweet pepper and rich avocado, with a soured cream dressing on the side.

200g canned or frozen sweetcorn
90ml milk
Salt and black pepper
A few drops of Tabasco sauce
1 medium iceberg lettuce
2 avocados
1 yellow pepper
4 tbsp olive oil
1 tbsp wine vinegar
100g self-raising flour
2 large eggs
2-3 tbsp vegetable oil
For the dressing:
3 spring onions
4-5 sprigs of dill
150ml soured cream
Salt and black pepper

Serves: 4
Cooking time: 30 minutes

Nutrients per serving: Calories 667, Carbohydrate 40g, Protein 13g, Fat 52g (saturated fat 13g)

1 Drain canned sweetcorn, set aside and mix the milk, salt, pepper and Tabasco in a bowl. Put frozen sweetcorn into a pan with the milk, salt, pepper and Tabasco and shake over a low heat for 1 minute. Then turn off the heat and leave to thaw.

2 To make the dressing, rinse, trim and finely slice the spring onions, rinse and chop the dill, reserving one sprig for a garnish, mix them into the soured cream and season to taste.

3 Rinse and dry the lettuce leaves and put them into a salad bowl. Peel and slice the avocados, rinse, deseed and slice the pepper and add both to the bowl. Mix the olive oil and vinegar together, season and toss gently into the salad.

4 Put the flour into a bowl, make a well in the centre and break in the eggs. Add the seasoned milk, or strain in the milk from the defrosted corn, beat until smooth, then stir in the corn.

5 Take two frying pans and heat 1-1½ tbsp of vegetable oil in each. Drop 6 tbsp of batter into each pan. Fry gently for 4-5 minutes until golden underneath and set at the edges. Turn and fry for another 1-2 minutes.

6 Divide the salad among four plates. Drain the corn cakes and arrange three with each salad. Garnish with fronds of dill and serve the dressing separately.

Tomatoes, grown under glass or in the open, are the gardener's most consistent money-saver. In an unheated greenhouse, ripe tomatoes can be picked from the end of June until autumn, provided the plants are fed correctly, tended daily and protected against pests and diseases. In the open, good crops ripen in August and September in warm summers, but even in cooler years plants produce a worthwhile crop of ripe tomatoes. Any remaining green fruits can be ripened indoors or made into chutney. Tomatoes can also be grown successfully in pots and containers, or in bags of specially prepared compost, in sunny, sheltered spots, such as on a patio or balcony. Bush tomatoes will produce large numbers of relatively small fruits and can be grown under cloches to produce an early crop of good-quality fruits.

Tomatoes

HARVESTING AND RIPENING

Tomatoes can be left to ripen fully on the plant, which tends to increase their flavour, or removed when they stat to change colour. Hold the tomato in your hand and press the stalk with your thumb to break it neatly at the joint just above the fruit. At the end of September or early October, ripening of fruits that are already turning colour can be completed under cloches. Place straw along the row, lay the stems horizontally and cover with the cloches. Remove green fruits, wrap them separately in newspaper and place in a drawer or boxes indoors. Remove the tomatoes as they become ripe.

tomato & red lentil soup

An unusual green-and-white garnish of cream cheese speckled with fresh basil adds a festive touch to this intensely flavoured, richly coloured soup of tomatoes, garlic and lentils.

600ml chicken or vegetable stock
2 tbsp olive oil
3 shallots
2-3 cloves garlic
A few sprigs of fresh basil
115g split red lentils
400g skinned and chopped tomatoes
100g soft cream cheese
Salt and black pepper

Serves: 4
Cooking time: 30 minutes

Nutrients per serving: Calories 280, Carbohydrate 20g, Protein 10g, Fat 18g (saturated fat 8g)

1 Put the stock on to heat. Heat the oil in a large saucepan. Peel and chop the shallots and garlic and fry gently for 5 minutes, or until soft.

2 Rinse and dry the basil, reserve a few leaves for a garnish, then shred enough to produce 1 tbsp.

3 Rinse and drain the lentils, and add them to the pan with the stock and the tomatoes. Bring to the boil, cover and simmer for about 15 minutes, adding half the shredded basil after 10 minutes.

4 Beat the cream cheese in a small bowl until softened. Stir in the remaining shredded basil.

5 Blend or process the soup to a purée and season to taste with salt and pepper. Serve with spoons of the cream cheese mixture; garnish with basil leaves.

creamed tomato soup

750g tomatoes, skinned and roughly chopped
1 onion, finely chopped
1 clove garlic, peeled and finely chopped
50g butter
300-600ml beef stock
Bicarbonate of soda
Salt, pepper and sugar
150ml double cream
2 tbsp chopped basil to garnish

Serves: 4
Cooking time: 25-30 minutes

Nutrients per serving: Calories 331, Carbohydrate 10g, Protein 3g, Fat 31g (saturated fat 18g)

1 Melt the butter in a pan and fry the onion and garlic for 5 minutes or until soft. Add 300ml of stock, a pinch of bicarbonate of soda and the tomatoes.

2 Bring the soup to the boil, then cover with a lid and simmer for 15 minutes. Blend the soup in a liquidiser and strain through a sieve back into the pan.

3 Re-heat the soup, adding more stock to give the desired consistency. Season to taste with salt, pepper and sugar. Bring the cream almost to boiling point in a separate pan, stir it into the soup and remove from the heat.

4 Serve sprinkled with basil.

fattoush

Tomatoes and pitta bread are the base of Arabic fattoush, a fresh, chunky purée of salad vegetables.

250g firm, ripe tomatoes, skinned and roughly chopped
4 spring onions, roughly chopped
1 small green pepper, deseeded and roughly chopped
½ cucumber, roughly chopped
1 clove garlic, peeled and chopped
3 tbsp chopped fresh parsley
1 tbsp finely shredded fresh mint
Juice of ½ lemon
3 tbsp olive oil
Salt and black pepper
1 pitta bread
Black olives and roughly torn parsley and mint leaves to garnish

Serves: 4 as a starter
Prep time: 15 minutes

1 Put all the ingredients except the salt, pepper and pitta bread into a food processor and process to a chunky purée. Season to taste.

2 Lightly toast the pitta bread, break it up in a shallow bowl and spread the purée on top. The mixture can be served immediately but can also be covered and set aside or chilled for an hour or two during which time the flavours will develop.

3 Just before serving stir the salad gently and garnish with the black olives, parsley and mint leaves. Serve with lemon slices and hot pitta bread.

Nutrients per serving: Calories 150, Carbohydrate 15g, Protein 3g, Fat 9g (saturated fat 1g)

Italian spirals [with burst tomatoes]

Cherry tomatoes are cooked to bursting on a bed of chilli, oregano and garlic and served with spicy Italian sausage.

500g length of thin Italian sausage (salsiccia), peppered or spiced
2 tbsp olive oil
2 cloves garlic
1 tsp dried oregano
½ tsp dried chilli flakes
700g cherry tomatoes
Salt and black pepper
Fresh basil leaves to garnish

Serves: 4
Cooking time: 30 minutes

Nutrients per serving: Calories 472, Carbohydrate 6.5g, Protein 30g, Fat 36g (saturated fat 15g)

1 Preheat the grill to high. Cut the sausage into quarters and wind up each length into a coil. Pass a thin metal skewer horizontally through each coil to hold it in place, then arrange all four on the rack of the grill pan.

2 Heat the oil in a large frying pan. Peel the garlic and crush it into the oil. Then add the oregano and the chilli flakes and fry them gently for about 30 seconds, without allowing the crushed garlic to change colour.

3 Spread the tomatoes in a single layer on top of the garlic and chilli, cover and cook over a low heat for about 10-12 minutes, or until most of the tomatoes have burst and are half-submerged in the juices.

4 Meanwhile, grill the sausage coils for 5-6 minutes on each side, turning them about to ensure that they become evenly crusty and brown on all sides.

5 Uncover the tomatoes, raise the heat to moderate and cook for a further 5 minutes, or until the juices have reduced and thickened. Press lightly now and then with the back of a spoon to ensure that all the tomatoes have burst.

6 Season the tomato sauce to taste with salt and pepper, then pour it onto four warmed serving plates and put a sausage coil in the centre of each. Rinse and dry the basil leaves, strip them from their stems and scatter them over the top.

How fair is a garden among the passions and toils of existence.

Benjamin Disraeli

monkfish & prawn kebabs

[with tomato salsa]

Tomato salsa gives a Mexican flavour boost to fishy kebabs marinaded in garlic and ginger.

1 medium-size monkfish tail, about 700g
4 raw tiger prawns or 8-12 smaller ones, about 100g altogether
1 clove garlic, crushed
1 tsp ginger purée, or grated ginger
1 green chilli, deseeded and finely chopped
1 tbsp sunflower or groundnut oil
Salt and black pepper
For the salsa:
500g plum tomatoes
2 tsp coriander seeds
1 green chilli, deseeded and finely chopped
1 clove garlic, crushed
1 stalk lemongrass, outer leaves removed, very finely sliced
Juice of 1 lime
Wedges of lime to serve

Serves: 4
Prep time: 40 minutes, plus 1 hour marinating
Cooking time: 6-8 minutes

Nutrients per serving: Calories 167, Carbohydrate 4g, Protein 29g, Fat 4g (saturated fat 1g)

I Rinse the fish with cold water, pat it dry with kitchen paper, and remove any grey membrane. Cut the flesh from the cartilage backbone in two long pieces. Cut each piece into 8-12 equal-size chunks.

2 Peel the prawns, removing the legs and heads but leaving the tails on if possible. Run a sharp knife along the back of each prawn and pull away the dark digestive thread. Rinse and pat dry with kitchen paper.

3 Mix the garlic, ginger and chilli with the oil in a large bowl. Add the monkfish and the prawns and mix well. Cover with cling film and chill for 1 hour. If you are using wooden skewers, soak them in cold water for at least 30 minutes before using.

4 Meanwhile, make the salsa. Put a kettle on to boil. Cover the tomatoes with boiling water and leave for 1 minute. Then skin and deseed them and chop the flesh into a chunky purée. This must be done by hand, not in a food processor.

5 Dry-fry the coriander seeds in a heavy-based frying pan over a high heat for a few seconds until they release their aroma. Then crush them in a spice mill or with a pestle and mortar and add them to the tomato. Mix in the chilli, garlic, lemongrass and lime juice and season well. Cover and chill for 30 minutes or more.

6 When you are ready to cook, heat the grill to medium-high. Thread the monkfish and prawns onto four skewers and grill for 3-4 minutes on each side until the prawns are firm and pink but not overcooked. Season the kebabs to taste, garnish with the lime wedges and serve with the salsa on the side.

tiger prawn, tomato [& basil tagliatelle]

Juicy tomato and basil dressing and mouth-watering quick-fried large prawns are tossed into fresh pasta.

750g tomatoes
1 tbsp finely chopped fresh basil
1½ tbsp champagne vinegar or
    other white wine vinegar
2 tbsp olive oil
Salt and black pepper
500g headless raw tiger prawns,
    defrosted if frozen
250g fresh tagliatelle
3 cloves garlic, crushed
Fresh basil leaves to garnish

Serves: 4
Prep time: 40 minutes
Cooking time: 10 minutes

Nutrients per serving: Calories 352, Carbohydrate 40g, Protein 30g, Fat 8g (saturated fat 1g)

1 Put a kettle on to boil. Cut a cross in the base of the tomatoes, cover them with boiling water, leave them for 1-2 minutes then peel off the skins. Cut them into quarters and scrape the seeds into a nylon sieve set over a large mixing bowl. Strain as much of the juice as possible into the bowl and discard the seeds.

2 Dice the tomato flesh and add it to the juice in the bowl, then stir in the basil, vinegar and 1 tbsp of oil. Season to taste and set aside. Put a pan of water on to boil for the pasta.

3 Peel the prawns then run a small sharp knife along the length of each back and pull away the dark digestive thread. Rinse the prawns and pat them dry with kitchen paper.

4 Put the pasta in the boiling water and cook it according to the instructions on the packet.

5 Meanwhile, heat 1 tbsp of oil in a large nonstick frying pan over a high heat. When it is really hot, season the prawns and stir-fry them for 2 minutes. Add the garlic and continue stir-frying for a further 2-3 minutes until the prawns turn completely pink.

6 Drain the pasta and toss it into the tomato vinaigrette. Stir in the cooked prawns and the garlic-flavoured oil, garnish with basil and serve.

stuffed beef tomatoes

8 large beef tomatoes
4 tbsp olive oil
1 onion, chopped
1 tsp dried marjoram
2 cloves garlic, chopped
225g minced beef
1 tbsp thick tomato purée
75g long-grain rice
Salt and black pepper
½ tsp ground allspice
3 tbsp chopped fresh parsley

Serves: 4
Prep time: 20 minutes
Cooking time: 1½ hours

Nutrients per serving: Calories 340,
Carbohydrate 29g, Protein 17g, Fat 18g
(saturated fat 4g)

1 Slice the tops off the tomatoes and set them aside. Scoop the tomato pulp and seeds into a bowl, rub a bit of salt round the inside of the shell and leave upside down on a plate to drain. Chop the tomato pulp finely.

2 Fry the onion and marjoram in half the oil over a low heat for 8-10 minutes until the onion is soft and golden, adding the garlic for the last 2 minutes.

3 Add the minced beef and stir, mashing with a fork. When the meat is browned, stir in half the tomato purée and half the pulp from the tomatoes, cover and simmer over a very low heat for 20 minutes.

4 Rinse the rice, drain and add to the meat. Stir in 75ml of cold water. Season with salt, pepper and allspice, stir well and simmer for a further 10 minutes.

5 Heat the oven to 190°C/gas 5. In a small mixing bowl, blend the remaining tomato purée with 4 tbsp cold water, then add the remaining tomato pulp and the juices that have run off from the upturned tomatoes. Season the mixture to taste and spread it in a baking dish large enough to hold all the tomatoes tightly in a single layer.

6 Stir the parsley into the meat and rice mixture and adjust the seasoning to taste. Spoon the semi-liquid stuffing into the tomatoes, filling them about three-quarters full only to allow for swelling as the rice completes its cooking. Any surplus can be stirred into the sauce at the bottom of the dish.

7 Arrange the stuffed tomatoes in the dish, put their tops back on and trickle the remaining olive oil over them. Bake for 45 minutes or until the tomatoes are very soft and the stuffing has expanded to fill them. Check the sauce halfway through the cooking time and stir in a few tablespoons of water if it threatens to dry out. Serve immediately, giving two tomatoes to each diner.

A garden is the best alternative therapy.

Germaine Greer

tomato chutney

3kg ripe tomatoes, skinned and chopped
500g onion, finely chopped
300ml spiced vinegar
25g salt
Large pinch of cayenne
350g sugar

Nutrients per tablespoon: Calories 24,
Carbohydrate 6g, Protein 0g, Fat 0g
(no saturated fat)

1 Put the tomatoes and onions in a pan and simmer until reduced to a thick pulp. Pour in half the vinegar, the salt and the cayenne and continue cooking until thick.

2 Dissolve the sugar in the remaining vinegar and add it to the mixture.

3 Cook until the chutney has attained the required consistency then pot and cover.

tomato jelly

1.5kg ripe tomatoes
1.5kg sugar
200ml white vinegar
600ml water
6 cloves
½ stick cinnamon

Nutrients per tablespoon: Calories 30,
Carbohydrate 7g, Protein 0g, Fat 0g
(no saturated fat)

1 Places the spices, enclosed in a muslin bag, in the water. Stew gently with the tomatoes, until soft. Remove the spice bag and rub the pulp through a sieve.

2 Return to the pan, adding the vinegar and sugar, stir until the sugar has dissolved, then boil rapidly until setting point is reached.

tomato ketchup

2kg ripe tomatoes, peeled and sliced
1 large onion, chopped
2 large apples peeled and chopped
2 tsp pickling spices
450ml vinegar
Large pinch of cayenne or paprika
175g sugar
Salt

Nutrients per tablespoon: Calories 17,
Carbohydrate 5g, Protein 0g, Fat 0g
(no saturated fat)

1 Boil the pickling spices in the vinegar for 10 minutes and strain.

2 Cook the apples, onion and tomatoes to a thick pulp, stirring frequently. Sieve the pulp and simmer gently with the vinegar, cayenne or paprika and sugar until thick and creamy. Add salt to taste. Pot at once in hot bottles and seal.

Although the turnip has been a favourite since Roman times, its popularity has little to do with its nutritional value. Turnips are about 90 per cent water, with some sugar and pectin – a jelly-like substance that helps jam to set. Nevertheless they adds a fresh flavour to a dish of vegetables, particularly when accompanied by the season's first peas and carrots. Turnips grow best on a light, fertile loam, but they will succeed on most garden soils in an open, sunny position. Do not sow on freshly manured ground, or the roots may split into a number of 'fangs'.

HARVESTING

Pick the turnips regularly, never allowing them to become larger than a tennis ball. Turnips larger than this may be stringy and will have a less pleasant flavour. Summer-harvested turnips may be frozen. Pull winter turnips when needed, or lift a few and store in a shed for use during spells when the soil is frozen.

PREPARATION

Prepare turnips by cutting off a slice from the leafy top and trimming off the fibrous roots. Peel young turnips thinly, maincrop turnips thickly, and on the latter also cut out any woody parts. Wash them well, leaving small turnips whole but cutting winter turnips into rough chunks. Cook young, whole turnips in boiling water for 20-30 minutes. Cook maincrop turnips for 30-40 minutes in boiling water or stock to improve the flavour.

Turnips

herb-buttered turnips

8-12 tiny young turnips with leaves
reserved and shredded (leaves optional)
50g butter
A spring of rosemary
Salt and black pepper
1 tbsp snipped chives
1 tbsp shredded mint
2 tbsp chopped parsley

Serves: 4
Prep time: 5 minutes
Cooking time: 12-15 minutes

Nutrients per serving: Calories 110,
Carbohydrate 3.5g, Protein 1g, Fat 11g
(saturated fat 6g)

1 Wash the turnips gently and cut off the leaves, leaving 1cm green stalk attached. Put the turnips in a pan of salted water and bring them to the boil. Cook them for about 10 minutes until they are just tender, then drain thoroughly.

2 Heat the butter with the rosemary in a wide frying pan and turn the turnips in it for 2-3 minutes until they are shiny and just beginning to show patches of colour.

3 Scoop out the rosemary, add the salt and pepper and then scatter on the chives, mint, parsley and turnip leaves, if using. Shake the pan to coat the turnips evenly then serve them in a warmed dish.

duck [with glazed turnips]

Baby turnips and shallots in a caramelised juice are a delightful accompaniment to tender, pan-fried duck. Serve with steamed potatoes and spinach.

4 duck breasts
8 shallots, peeled and quartered
12 baby turnips, halved
1 clove garlic, crushed
200ml dry white wine
Thinly pared strip of lemon zest and juice
of 1 unwaxed lemon
3 tbsp runny honey
2 tbsp fresh chopped sage
Salt and black pepper

Serves: 4
Prep time: 10 minutes
Cooking time: 30 minutes

Nutrients per serving: Calories 445,
Carbohydrate 18g, Protein 27g, Fat 26g
(saturated fat 7g)

1 Slash the skin of the duck in a diamond pattern, using a sharp knife. Heat a heavy frying pan until very hot, add the duck, skin side down, and cook over a high heat for 8-10 minutes, turning once, until browned and cooked but slightly pink inside.

2 Remove the duck from the pan to a warm place. Drain off the fat from the pan, leaving a thin coating. Add the shallots and turnips and stir over a moderate heat, for 2-3 minutes, until golden, then add the garlic.

3 Add the wine and lemon zest and simmer for about 1 minute, then cover and simmer, stirring occasionally, for 10-12 minutes or until the turnips and shallots are almost tender. Stir in the lemon juice, honey and sage and cook for a further 4-5 minutes, until caramelised and tender.

4 Add the duck breasts, with skin removed if desired, and cook for 1-2 minutes, spooning the juices over the duck. Add salt and pepper to taste. Remove to warmed plates, spoon the vegetables around.

What will I do when I can no longer dig?

Knute Hamsen

index

CONVERSION CHART All food in the UK is now sold in metric units so it makes sense to cook using these measurements. If you feel happier using imperial measurements, you can use the chart below. Remember to use either metric or imperial and don't mix the two.

WEIGHT

Metric	Imperial (approx)	Metric	Imperial (approx)
5g	⅛oz	55g	2oz
10g	¼oz	60g	2¼oz
15g	½oz	70g	2½oz
20g	¾oz	75g	2¾oz
25g	1oz	85g	3oz
35g	1¼oz	90g	3¼oz
40g	1½oz	100g	3½oz
50g	1¾oz	1kg	2lb 4oz

VOLUME

Metric	Imperial (approx)	Metric	Imperial (approx)
30ml	1fl oz	90ml	3¼fl oz
50ml	2fl oz	100ml	3½fl oz
75ml	2½fl oz	1 litre	1¾ pints
85ml	3fl oz		

THE ALLOTMENT GARDENER'S COOKBOOK was published by the Reader's Digest Association Limited, London from material first published in the Reader's Digest books: *Thirty Minute Cookbook*, *Low Fat, No Fat*, *Great British Dishes the Healthy Way*, *Food from Your Garden* and *Your Cookery Questions Answered*.

First edition copyright © 2007
The Reader's Digest Association Limited
11 Westferry Circus, Canary Wharf, London E14 4HE
www.readersdigest.co.uk

We are committed to both the quality of our products and the service we provide to our customers. We value your comments so please feel free to contact us on 08705 113366 or via our website at
www.readersdigest.co.uk

If you have any comments or suggestions about the content of our books you can contact us at
gbeditorial@readersdigest.co.uk

Editor **Lisa Thomas**
Designer **Jane McKenna**
Nutritionist **Fiona Hunter**
Proofreader **Barry Gage**
Indexer **Marie Lorimer**

Allotment photographs specially taken by **Mark Winwood**

READER'S DIGEST GENERAL BOOKS
Editorial Director **Julian Browne**
Art Director **Anne-Marie Bulat**
Head of Book Development **Sarah Bloxham**
Managing Editor **Alastair Holmes**
Picture Resource Manager **Sarah Stewart-Richardson**
Pre-press Account Manager **Penelope Grose**
Product Production Manager **Claudette Bramble**
Senior Production Controller **Deborah Trott**

Origination Colour Systems Ltd
Printed in China

Book code: 400-357 UP0000-1
ISBN: 978 0 287 44304 6
Oracle code: 250011350H.00.24